SHIRLEY BA.
THE KING OF TONGA

NOEL RUTHERFORD, Ph.D. was Senior Lecturer in the Department of History at the University of Newcastle until his retirement in 1994. The first edition of his book *Shirley Baker and the King of Tonga* was published in 1971. He also edited *Friendly Islands: A history of Tonga*.

'ESETA FUSITU'A is Deputy Chief Secretary to the Tongan Cabinet and is Secretary of the Tonga Traditions Committee. Her Masters thesis was on Tupou II, the second king of Tonga.

The Pasifika Library

NOEL RUTHERFORD

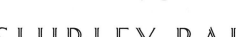

SHIRLEY BAKER
and the
KING *of* TONGA

UNIVERSITY OF HAWAI'I PRESS
HONOLULU

This edition: © Noel Rutherford & Pasifika Press 1996
Introduction: © 'Eseta Fusitu'a 1996

This edition published by:
University of Hawai'i Press
Honolulu, Hawai'i 96822

Production: Robert Holding and Pasifika Press

First edition published in 1971

ISBN 0 8248 1856 3

Published with the assistance
of the Australian South Pacific Cultures Fund

Photographs supplied by the Alexander Turnbull Library,
Wellington, New Zealand; Mitchell Library, Sydney, Australia
and Auckland City Libraries, New Zealand.

Cover design: Christine Hansen
Editing & layout: Tony Murrow
Printed in Hong Kong by Acorn Press

CONTENTS

Introduction by 'Eseta Fusitu'a   *vii*

Maps of Tonga   *x*

Preface   1

Glossary of Tongan Words   7

CHAPTER I
A Missionary to the Heathen   9

CHAPTER II
The King's Advisor   23

CHAPTER III
The Efficient Collector   39

CHAPTER IV
The Champion of an Independent Church   55

CHAPTER V
The Champion of an Independent State   67

CHAPTER VI
The End of a Missionary Career   85

CHAPTER VII
The King's First Minister   125

CHAPTER VIII
    The Affair of the Mu'a Parliament   143

CHAPTER IX
    The Tongan Reformation   164

CHAPTER X
    An Assassination Attempt   181

CHAPTER XI
    The High Commissioner's *Coup d'État*   201

CHAPTER XII
    An Rather Feeble Little Gentleman in Black   220

    Epilogue   227

    Postscript   230

    Notes   248

    Bibliography   262

    Index   274

INTRODUCTION

'Eseta Fusitu'a

REVEREND SHIRLEY WALDEMAR BAKER arrived in Tonga as a Methodist missionary, and became well known for his controversial scuffles with British government officials, expatriate settlers, the local population, and even some of his colleagues. However, his real place in history is at the cornerstone of the modernisation of Tonga and the subsequent protection of her independence. These activities separate Shirley Baker's story from those of other mid-nineteenth century Western missionaries to the South Pacific.

At this time King George Tupou I, already champion of the unification and Christianisation of Tonga, was determined to advance the total welfare of Tonga and to maintain her precious independence from the encroachment of Western imperialism. Tupou I was convinced that modernisation was the key to success. Political modernisation would secure Western recognition of Tonga's sovereignty, itself tantamount to a guarantee of her independence.

Because modernisation meant the adoption of Western concepts, systems and procedures, it was essential that Tupou had Western advice and assistance. He needed advisers who were equally committed to Tonga's independence, and who would not be easily cowed either by the cynicism of the European settlers and their opposition to 'native' governments, or by similarly subversive actions from Western government officials. If his advisers could also show strength and enterprise while being well informed and sympathetic to the Tongan concepts of government and social organisation, then Tupou could rest assured that his aspirations lay in capable hands.

Reverend Baker proved eminently suited to these demanding roles. Perhaps influenced by his mixed background of distinguished descent and material poverty, his vocation as a missionary and a desire to recapture his 'proper' status in life in Tonga, he regarded the Government of Tonga with due seriousness, and was totally committed to its improvement and modernisation. Like Tupou I, he was also vehemently determined to retain Tonga's independence. An unorthodox, strong-willed, hard-working and resourceful man, Reverend Baker was well able to assist Tupou I in realising his vision for Tonga.

The promulgation of Tonga's Constitution and laws, and the establishment of her modern system of government on 4 November 1875 – the cornerstones of modern Tonga – were largely the product of the highly fruitful and mutually beneficial partnership between King George Tupou I and the Reverend Shirley Baker.

Not surprisingly Tupou I's monumental achievements for Tonga – the peaceful passage from a traditional to a Western model of government, the inspired mixing of Tongan and European concepts in the State's transformation, and the confirmation of Tonga's independence by 'most favoured nation' treaties with some of the most influential colonial powers of the time – were achieved in the 1870s during his close partnership with the Reverend Shirley Baker. Not surprisingly also, Baker rose to be the only expatriate Prime Minister of Tonga, an achievement of substantial significance for an ex-missionary – and in a country so jealous of its independence!

Thus, Professor Noel Rutherford's biography of the Reverend Shirley Baker forms a major contribution to the history of the Kingdom of Tonga, and is all the more impressive because its story is unique to both the local and colonial histories of the Pacific. Indeed, the most remarkable testimony to the achievements of this inspired partnership, is the fact that the constitution that Tupou I and Reverend Shirley Baker gave to Tonga has continued to function, and has now held the nation together peacefully and profitably for one hundred and twenty years.

'Eseta Fusiti'a
Nuku'alofa
The Kingdom of Tonga
December 1995

THE KINGDOM
OF TONGA

50 km   100 km   150 km

Approximate scale

Niuafo'ou

Tafahi

Niuatoputapu

N

VAVA'U GROUP

Vava'u

Lifuka   Foa

HA'APAI GROUP

TONGATAPU GROUP

Tongatapu

'Eua

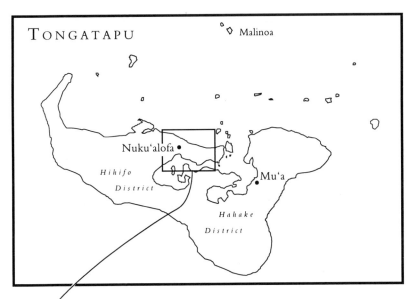

TONGATAPU

Malinoa

Nuku'alofa

Mu'a

Hihifo District

Hahake District

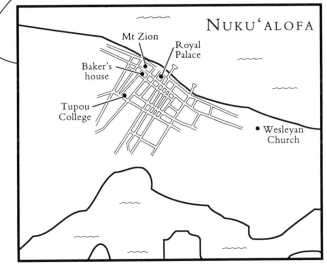

NUKU'ALOFA

Mt Zion

Royal Palace

Baker's house

Tupou College

Wesleyan Church

PREFACE

F OR THE PEOPLES of the Pacific Islands the nineteenth
century was a period of bewildering and demoralizing change.
The islands had received occasional visits from mariners and
explorers before the beginning of the century, but while these visits
excited the cupidity and wonder of the islanders they had little
effect on their lives. From about 1800, however, expanding Western
civilisation forced itself upon the island world, and successive waves
of Europeans began rapidly eroding traditional societies. First came
the beachcombers bringing new technologies. They were followed
by whalers bringing alcohol and new diseases, by missionaries with
their new beliefs, by traders introducing new patterns of economic
activity and by planters insisting on new attitudes to property.
Native societies underwent revolutionary changes within a short
space of time in an attempt to adjust to the demands being made
upon them, but in almost every case their responses were inadequate. Unable to come to terms with the new dispensation, one
by one the island polities succumbed and were absorbed into one
or other of the colonial empires.

All except one. Alone among the island groups of the Pacific,
Tonga emerged from the nineteenth century as a sovereign, independent state. Admittedly its sovereignty was compromised in 1901
when it became a British 'Protected State', but even then it was not
a colony, nor even the usual form of protectorate. Its exact status
within the British Empire was analogous to that of Sarawak. Britain
exercised control over its foreign relations and had the right to advise

on financial matters, but in all other matters there was complete local autonomy. Tonga had its own king, cabinet and legislature. It had its own enlightened constitution, and a code of laws administered by its own judges. In economic terms the country was viable, and the land itself was exclusively and inalienably Tongan. Even in ecclesiastical matters the majority of Tongans were free from outside control, for most Tongans belonged to the Tongan Free Church, a Wesleyan body controlled by an independent Tongan conference.

Tonga made its remarkably successful adjustment to the modern world under King George Tupou I, during the latter half of the nineteenth century. The process began, it is true, a little earlier with the unification of the country, the conversion of the people to Christianity and the promulgation of a written code of laws to which all Tongans were amenable. These preliminary steps had been accomplished by 1850. But the period of most rapid westernisation began in 1862 with the emancipation of the people from the control of the chiefs, and continued with gathering momentum until the late 1880s. During this period the dominant figure in Tonga was the missionary-politician Shirley Waldemar Baker, the friend and adviser of Tupou, and later his Prime Minister.

It is Shirley Baker, his relationship with the ageing Tongan monarch, and his role in Tongan history that forms the subject of this work. During his lifetime Baker was a controversial figure, but since his death writers who have dealt with the history of Tonga have reached a consensus of opinion about him. Unfortunately conformity has been achieved by relying on the unsupported testimony of one man, Basil Thomson, whose skill as a raconteur has given his opinions an authority which they do not really deserve. Thomson was a British government official who was sent to Tonga to fill the gap left by Baker's sudden dismissal and deportation in 1890. For about a year he occupied the position of Deputy Premier in Tonga, and after his retirement he wrote an amusing account of the modernisation of Tonga in his book *The Diversions of a Prime Minister*.[1] This work was later supplemented by another, *Savage Island*,[2] and a third, *The Scene Changes*,[3] as well as several articles in *Blackwood's*

Magazine.[4] In all these works Thomson portrayed Baker as the ignorant, venal, tyrannical and hypocritical parson who manipulated Tongan politics for his own aggrandisement. Thomson, however, was a biased witness. In the first place, he was opposed in Tonga by Baker's supporters, while his allies and associates were Baker's political enemies. This alone would tend to distort his view. Secondly, one of Thomson's primary functions in Tonga was to pave the way for increasing British influence there, and he could not be expected to give praise to one whose political life had been devoted to keeping British influence out. It was Thomson incidentally, who eventually extracted a Treaty of Protection from a very reluctant Tongan king and parliament. Thirdly, Thomson was building himself a career, and enhanced his own reputation as a legislator and administrator by the time-honoured method of belittling the achievements of his predecessor. And fourthly, Thomson was a gentleman, the son of a bishop, with little sympathy for upstarts like Baker who exercised power but wore no old school tie.

For these reasons Thomson's opinions are liable to be untrustworthy, yet his account has been accepted without question by most writers. Wright and Frý used Baker as a dramatic example to support the general theory that the influence of missionaries in the Pacific was pernicious, which they formulated in their book *Puritans in the South Seas.*[5] Their material on Baker was taken verbatim from Thomson's *The Diversions of a Prime Minister.* Koskinen, in his work *Missionary Influence as a Political Factor in the Pacific Islands,*[6] characterised Baker as a 'petty tyrant', citing Thomson as his authority. Martin, in his work *Missionaries and Annexations in the Pacific,* wrote of Baker 'His career does not imply an unlimited condemnation of mission work, but it does suggest that power without real responsibility is inevitably bad'.[7] Again the source is Thomson. A similar appraisal based on the same evidence was made by Oliver in his general history, *The Pacific Islands.*[8] The only attempt to form an independent judgement based on primary sources has been Morrell's *Britain in the Pacific Islands,*[9] but even this account relied heavily on British documents from the Foreign Office and Colonial Office archives, which served only to reinforce the traditional account as formulated by Thomson. The Australian Methodist Church had in its archives material to challenge this view, but the issues involved were so controversial that it preferred to let sleeping dogs lie. In its official mission history, *A Century in the Pacific*, the opportunity was passed over with the simple admission, 'We would fain draw a veil over the history of this regrettable period'.[10]

There has been one attempt to present an entirely different view of Baker. This was the *Memoirs of the Reverend Dr Shirley Waldemar Baker*, a collection of extracts from Baker's letters and journals, compiled by his daughters Lillian and Beatrice.[11] This little work, however, had few literary pretensions, and was so biased that it has generally been ignored. Morrell used it, but specifically warned his readers that it was 'a naive work which must be used with caution'.[12] No one, on the other hand, has suggested that Thomson's account needed to be approached with equal caution.

It therefore seemed important to re-examine the career of Shirley Baker, to recount the events which occurred in Tonga between 1860 and 1890, and to re-evaluate Baker's contribution to developments in Tonga during that period. There existed sufficient primary source material to attempt this without relying either on the Misses Baker or Basil Thomson except to corroborate other testimony. The resulting study is essentially a biographical sketch, but it is hoped that it may also make some small contribution to the understanding of the problems which faced Tonga in the late nineteenth century, and beyond that of the more general problem of acculturation.

Much of the research for this work was done while the author held a research scholarship in the Department of Pacific History at the Australian National University and to the members of that department, in particular, J. W. Davidson, H. E. Maude and the late Sione Lātūkefu, he is deeply indebted. He also wishes to express his gratitude to His Majesty, Tāufaʻāhau Tupou IV, for making it possible for him to work in Tonga and for doing much to smooth his path there. Among others in Tonga who gave assistance special mention must be made of the Hon. Veʻehala, Michael Challons, the Reverend G. Harris, Tupou

Posesi Fanua, Tongilava, Feʻiloakitau Kaho, Siolaʻa Soakai and Tangataʻolakepa Niumeitolu. From librarians and their staffs in Fiji, New Zealand and Australia, the author met nothing but the most generous assistance, for which he now expresses his sincere thanks. To no one, however, is he more indebted than to his wife, whose patience and understanding made the whole thing possible.

Newcastle,
New South Wales,
February 1970

PREFACE TO THE REVISED EDITION

The manuscript which was to appear as *Shirley Baker and the King of Tonga* was written between 1963 and 1968, and when it was completed I believed that I had seen, noted and pondered upon every scrap of evidence that was available on the subject. Since that time, however, some new materials have come to light which, while they do not affect the overall scheme of things, nevertheless alter some details and provide the basis for some reappraisals and new interpretations. Minor corrections have been incorporated in the text of this revised edition, more substantive ones are included in the postscript.

When the original version was published I neglected to thank two people whose assistance was invaluable. The first of these was Mr Ian Diamond, then archivist for the Fiji Government, who allowed me to ravish his archives with a portable photocopying machine, and use his staff lunch room to develop and fix copies – a technology long since consigned to deserved oblivion. As a callow youth I took all of this for granted and saw nothing out-of-the-way in it. Three decades later, and with a much wider experience of government officials, I realise just how extraordinary were the demands I made, and how singular was his forbearance. For his bemused tolerance I now offer him, wherever he may be, my belated thanks. The other person whom I should have thanked was my old friend, Joan Winder, who meticulously typed the original manuscript without reward or recognition. For that labour of love I now express my gratitude.

As far as this revised edition is concerned, I would like to record my appreciation of help given by Mrs Julie Wein, who provided the trail of string to lead me through the labyrinth of word processing.

Noel Rutherford
Newcastle,
New South Wales
September 1995

GLOSSARY OF TONGAN WORDS

'api	household
'api kolo	village allotment
'api 'uta	bush allotment
boobooi(po 'opo 'oi)	a Tongan pudding with many ingredients (the title of Baker's newspaper)
'eiki	chief
fa'ahinga	extended family
fahu	*i)* the systematic kinship superiority of the sororal descent line over the fraternal descent line; *ii)* within such a system, that person who is superior to another
faikava	a party to drink kava
fakamisinale	the missionary meeting, i.e. the annual collection
fakaongo	dependent
fakapapālangi	the European manner
fakataha	a meeting of chiefs
fakatonga	the Tongan manner
fatongia	the right of a chief to the labour and goods of his people
feifekau (or faifekau)	missionary
fei'umu	a basket of baked food
fono	a compulsory meeting
foto tehina	plural of *tehina*
ha'a	lineage
hou'eiki	plural of *'eiki*
kāinga	tribe

7

kau matāpule	plural of *matāpule*
kau 'ulumotu'a	plural of *'ulumotu'a*
laka-laka	war dance
lali	drum
lotu	religion
mala'e	village green
matāpule	spokesman for a chief
Motu'a Mohetō	an old 'night creeper' or rapist (one of Baker's nicknames)
Niu Vakai	look-out coconut palm (the name of Hanslip's newspaper)
ngaahi fa'ahinga	plural of *fa'ahinga*
ngaahi fono	plural of *fono*
ngaahi kāinga	plural of *kāinga*
ngaahi 'ulu	plural of *'ulu*
papālangi	i) European, ii) the homeland of Europeans
siasi	church
sivi	sifting, a collecting technique used by Baker
Ta'emangoi	the irrepressible (one of Baker's nicknames)
tapa	bark cloth
tau'atāina	independent
Taimi o Toga	*Tonga Times* (a Government newspaper)
tehina	minor chief
tofi'a	inheritance, the lands of a chief
tukuofo	ritual presentation to the dead
Tu'i Ha'atakalaua	one of the three great chiefly titles of Tonga
Tu'i Kanokupolu	one of the three great chiefly titles of Tonga
Tu'i Tonga	the paramount chiefly title of Tonga
'ulu	a head of a household
'ulumotu'a	a head of an extended family

CHAPTER I

A MISSIONARY TO THE HEATHEN

S HIRLEY WALDEMAR BAKER was born in London in 1836, the son of the Reverend George Baker, a Church of England clergyman and headmaster of the Oxford Home Grammar School. His mother, Jane Gray Baker, was the daughter of a Methodist minister, the Reverend Samuel Woolmer of Gloucestershire and the sister of Dr Woolmer, a medical practitioner to the Queen's household at Buckingham Palace. Naturally enough, considering his background, Baker was intended for the Church, but, being himself more inclined towards the law, he disappointed his parents by entering the firm of a prominent solicitor. Within a short time, however, he grew tired of working among musty documents and, not knowing where his true vocation lay, he decided to postpone making a decision about his future and to think about it while on a trip to Australia to visit his Uncle Parker, who was Crown Protector of Aborigines in the Colony of Victoria. Thus he arrived in Melbourne in 1852, a young gentleman of good family, with a good education and every prospect of a genteel and useful life before him.

This, at least, is the authorised version of Baker's background, as outlined in the memoir published by his daughters. But there have been dissenting voices. Baker's obituary in *The Times* on 30 December 1903, which was probably written by the British colonial administrator and writer, Basil Thomson, dismissed the official account with the comment: 'of his early career nothing is known but what he chose to tell, and he would have found it difficult to remember which of the many variants of his own story was true'. That comment was rather misleading for Baker had sketched in the outlines of his story at least as early as 1861 when the veteran missionary, the Reverend James Calvert, met him in Tonga and noted in his diary, 'Mr Baker ... is the son of a clergy who formerly resided in London'[1] and he kept to the same story throughout his life. Nevertheless, there are grounds for doubting the truth of the story and for suspecting that Baker's origins were more humble than he claimed.

In the first place it seems that Baker neither wrote nor spoke like the son of a Church of England cleric, possessing the advantages of a gentle upbringing and a good education. His letters contained many errors in spelling, syntax and grammar and some detractors have suggested that even his carefully composed laws and edicts were written in what Thomson described as 'English that would have disgraced a housemaid'.[2] Several people who met him noted his educational deficiencies. Sir Arthur Gordon, the Governor of Fiji, who met him in 1880 described him as 'a narrow minded, selfish and ignorant man';[3] even the more kindly disposed J. B. Thurston, a successor of Gordon's, but a self-made man, described him as 'illiterate'.[4] Speech is perhaps a more reliable indication of social origins than the written word, and Baker's accent was even more incompatible with a polite background than his prose. Thomson described his accent as 'common'.[5] Thomson was certainly a biased witness but the American historian, Henry Adams, who met Baker in Samoa in 1891, and who was indeed favourably impressed by him, noted that he was 'doubtful on his aspirates'.[6] The same characteristic was noted by the English traveller and writer, Alfred St Johnston, who met Baker in Auckland in the early eighties and recorded a fragment of his conversation:

> ... into the office bustled a fat, methodistical looking person, with a huge double chin and unctuous countenance, bearing a parcel of documents, which he had according to his own account, been putting through a wonderful series of evolutions and had "on'y jus' got 'em done in time".[7]

Such evidence is not conclusive, of course, but it does throw some doubt on Baker's own version of his early years.

In the second place Baker's story is open to suspicion owing to the difficulty in tracing his father, the Reverend George Baker of London. An exhaustive search in the *Clergy List*, the *Clerical Guide* and *Crockford's Clerical Directory* of the time has failed to reveal any English cleric who could conceivably be Baker's father. The Reverend George Baker's alleged place of work, the Oxford Home Grammar School, London, has proved equally elusive, for the Census of London 1851, Crockford's *Scholastic Directory 1861* and the *London Directory* for the period fail to mention such a school or any other closely resembling it. In fact as evidence of the existence of Reverend George Baker one has to rely on a record of a contribution of one guinea made by Shirley Baker to the Australasian Wesleyan-Methodist Missionary Society in 1870, 'in memory of my father, Revd George Baker',[8] and a record of a remittance of five pounds made by the same Society on Shirley Baker's behalf to the Reverend George Baker, and guardedly addressed care of an uncle, the Reverend Theophilus Woolmer, a Methodist minister in Manchester.[9] In view of the lack of definite evidence to the contrary, it might well be assumed that George Baker was not a Church of England cleric, and that Shirley Baker conferred honorary ordination on his father with a view to improving his own prospects and social standing in Australia; having told his story once, he was stuck with it; it passed into circulation and he was forced to keep it up for the rest of his life.

When Baker spoke of his mother, however, he was on safer ground, and his story is largely substantiated from the Wesleyan archives at Epworth House, London, which show that Samuel Woolmer, Shirley Baker's maternal grandfather, was born at St Neots in 1772, was apprenticed on Lord Harewood's estate in Barbados in 1785 and was ordained a Methodist minister after his return to England in 1797. He married Jane Gray in 1801 and died in 1827, leaving a widow and several children. One of his children was Jane Gray Woolmer, Baker's mother, another was Theophilus Woolmer, who became a Methodist minister and sometime tutor at Didsbury College, and a third was Dr Joseph Benson Woolmer, whose name first appeared in the London *Medical Directory* in 1847. Shirley Baker did, therefore, have an uncle who was a doctor, although not quite so eminent a doctor as he claimed: the *Lord Chamberlain's Department Records,* which contain the names of all medical men employed by the Royal Household, do not mention Dr J. B. Woolmer, a general practitioner of Pimlico.

The most that might be said with any certainty, therefore, concerning Shirley Baker's background is that his mother's family, deriving from humble beginnings, had acquired respectability and middle class status during the nineteenth century. His father's position remains a subject for conjecture, but it seems as if Jane Gray Woolmer married 'below her station', and that Shirley Baker grew up in rather drab circumstances, from which he fled to Australia in 1852.*

The story of Baker's visit to the colonies is also a matter of controversy. According to Baker, his visit was in the nature of a grand tour to call on an uncle, but other sources offer a different version. Baker was befriended on the Victorian goldfields by Joseph Ellis, an immigrant Cornish miner, and Ellis's grandson, the Reverend S. C. Roberts, recorded an entirely different story. According to Roberts, Baker 'found the alluring gold fever so strong that he ran away from them in the old land, hid himself as a stowaway on board a ship for Australia, and worked his passage when dis-

* The postscript to this edition sheds more light on Shirley Baker's background.

covered.'[10] A variant of this account appeared in an article in the Sydney *Evening News* on 21 October 1897, written by A.W. Mackay, the son-in-law of the Reverend J. E. Moulton, a missionary who had known Baker for thirty years:

> Our first trace of this heaven-gifted and erudite compiler of education works, laws and constitutions is as an unknown, uncultured and uncouth stowaway aboard the ship *Statesman* bound from London to Melbourne in the year 1852. Mr Picton, a passenger on the same vessel, employed him on arrival as a cowboy.

The *Statesman* did arrive in Melbourne from London in September 1852, but the list of crew members, among whom a stowaway would have been numbered, has not survived. The list of passengers disembarking at Melbourne has been preserved, however, and it includes a Henry George Picton, which at least partially corroborates Mackay's story.[11]

Little is known of Baker's activities in Victoria between 1852 and 1854. Mackay claimed that as well as being a farmhand he had spent some time as chemist's shop boy,[12] while Roberts suggested that he had tried his hand at mining for gold (perhaps this was the 'loss in business' his father lamented). But by January 1855 Baker had emerged from obscurity to find employment with the Victorian Denominational School Board as the teacher in sole charge of the ninety-one pupils at the Old Post Office Hill Wesleyan School in Castlemaine, a tent and shanty town on the goldfields. It seems that he also acted as druggist for the local community, for Roberts recorded: 'Against the school there was a room where he practised experimental chemistry, and made a studio and laboratory for himself dispensing medicines after school hours'.[13] Roberts also claimed that it was owing to the friendship and patronage of Joseph Ellis, a class leader in the Wesleyan Church, that Baker was given employment as a teacher in a Wesleyan school. Edward Stone Parker, the Protector of Aborigines at Mount Franklin and the Inspector of

Denominational Schools at Castlemaine (the 'Uncle Parker' of the Baker sisters' *Memoirs*) might also have had a hand in the matter, for Baker's qualifications for a schoolmaster's position were very dubious. As a teacher, however, he was quite highly regarded by his superiors, for his educational deficiencies were not very noticeable on the goldfields, while the 'great energy' and 'undoubted ability' which his most bitter detractors allowed him, received favourable notice: in 1859 he was invited by the Board to take their 'Honours' examination and so qualify for a headmaster's position. On 5 May 1859, however, the Board had announced a general reduction in salary for all its teachers and on 15 June 1859 Baker declined the Board's offer; his ambitions were leading him in another direction.

Baker's family connections on his mother's side, his friendship with Ellis, and his position as a teacher in a Wesleyan school had combined to lead him into communion with the Wesleyan Church, and by 1857 his name was on the Castlemaine Circuit Plan as a local preacher. He was thus present at a rally held in Castlemaine on 19 May 1859 to hear an address by the Reverend A. Buzacott, a missionary from Rarotonga who had with him a native Christian, his convert, pupil and disciple. According to the local newspaper, 'Mr Buzacott gave a graphic description of the state of the heathen and of the trials and toils of the various missionaries ... his reminiscences ... were of the most deeply interesting kind'.[14] It was probably this meeting that led Baker to make a momentous decision; a few weeks later he offered himself as 'a missionary to the heathen of the South Seas'.

After June 1859 Baker began to prepare himself for the missionary vocation by taking a more active part in the affairs of the Wesleyan Church, and his name began to appear in the *Castlemaine Advertiser* as the preacher at local chapels and the speaker at meetings of the Band of Hope and the Temperance Society. Another form of preparation was also necessary: the Australasian Wesleyan-Methodist Missionary Society, aware of the temptations of the flesh that faced its agents in the islands, insisted that they be married. Baker proposed to Joseph Ellis's daughter, but was refused. He was more successful with Elizabeth Powell, whom Roberts described as 'a beautiful and accomplished girl from a town nearby'. The couple were married towards the end of 1859.

The story of the wedding party given by the diggers for the young couple was told by Roberts, whose mother was a witness:

> Every available kerosene tin, old bucket or discarded gold dish or anything else that, with the aid of sticks and stones could make a row, was brought into requisition for the serenade to the departing missionary until he could not hear himself speak. Some cake and ale sent out only gave them more vigour and persistency. It was enough to distract a less irritable character. 'Here's some money, now clear off,' he yelled with various adjectives as he threw out a number of pennies he had superheated on the school stove. How many were burned the story does not tell, but the numbers who vouched for the heat of those coppers also vouched for the heat of the serenade, and the still increasing heat of the schoolmaster-chemist's temper. Then he came outside, yelled out something, and threw among them some chemicals which scattered the whole crowd like frightened sheep. The band ceased to play and the report went abroad that he had thrown vitriol in their faces, though nobody showed any scars.[15]

Baker was 'examined for the ministry' on 7 January 1860 and was found to have many of the characteristics considered desirable in missionaries: as well as having his share of natural ability, he had had an active church life, was an accredited local preacher, and, as the *Christian Advocate and Wesleyan Record* noted on 14 July, he 'witnessed a good confession as to his conversion to God and his call to the ministry of the word of life'; he had experience as a teacher, and education was an important missionary responsibility; perhaps most important, he knew a little about medicine and the dispensing of drugs, and on a mission station this would be a most valuable asset. The Missionary Committee, the executive body of the Missionary Society, therefore recommended that Baker be accepted and in April 1860 he was ordered to travel to Sydney to be ordained. His departure from Castlemaine passed unnoticed, for in the same week Robert O'Hara Burke left Castlemaine to lead his ill-fated exploring expedition to the Gulf and the local newspaper was too preoccupied with Burke to notice Baker.

Baker was ordained a Wesleyan minister on 13 July 1860 and was appointed to the mission station at Ha'apai in Tonga. Five days later he embarked with his wife on the schooner *Jennie Dove* and set sail. The voyage took a full month, and in the cramped cabin of the tiny ship conditions must have been wretched, especially for the missionary's young wife who was in her seventh month of pregnancy. A few days out of Sydney the vessel was caught in a gale and was hove to for three days, pitching and rolling, with the sea coming over the decks. After the gale had blown itself out the schooner resumed her voyage only to be overtaken that evening by a sudden squall in which she nearly foundered. Baker described the scene in his first letter home: 'her bows were diving down into the sea, the ladies screaming and everything falling – we expected to go to the bottom'.[16] Finally, however, on 14 August 1860, the schooner reached Tongatapu, negotiated the passage through the reefs and dropped anchor off the village of Nuku'alofa.

From the anchorage the island of Tongatapu stretched as far as the eye could see in either direction, low lying, flat and thickly covered in coconut palms. Nuku'alofa itself was a large village of coconut-thatch houses clustered around a low hill. Opposite the landing place was an open grassed square, the *mala'e*. To the left, along the water's edge, was a group of wooden dwellings which housed the small colony of European traders. To the right, and somewhat more imposing, were two native-style buildings; the first, standing in a large compound on the foreshore, was the palace of King George Tupou; the second, a few hundred yards inland and at the foot of the hill, was the home of the Reverend John Whewell, the Wesleyan missionary. The hill itself was bare except for a large thatch building on the summit. This was Zion Church, the spiritual centre of Methodism in the Friendly Islands.

The arrival of a ship in Nuku'alofa was a big enough event in 1860 to bring the people crowding to the shore or paddling out in small outrigger canoes. Baker left no record of the impression these first Tongans made on him, but they must have looked very much as H. M. Moseley, a naturalist who visited Tonga in 1873, described them:

> The Tongans were naked, except for a cotton cloth round the waist, and one of them a fuller girdle of screw pine leaves … they were remarkably fine men, with all their muscles well developed, and all of them extremely well nourished … the women are large, they have fine figures and are, most of them, handsome. They wear a cotton cloth around the loins, reaching down below the knees. The missionaries have compelled them to cover their breasts, which is done with a flap of cloth thrown up in front. The women, however, evidently have little idea of shame in the matter, and often the cloth is put on so loosely that it affords no cover at all .[17]

With the help of these handsome and friendly people the Bakers and their baggage were transferred from the *Jennie Dove* to the shore and from there to the mission house, where they were to stay as guests of the Whewells until Elizabeth's confinement.

Baker's first obligation after settling into his new quarters was to pay his respects to the king. It was only a short walk from the mission house to the palace, and Whewell probably took the new arrival to meet Tupou on his first day in Tonga. Unfortunately Baker's journal, which would have contained details of this visit and of his first impressions of the king, has been lost, but the scene which confronted him must have been similar to that described by Lieutenant Brenchley, who paid a call on Tupou when H.M.S. *Curacoa* visited Tonga in 1865:

> We proceeded to the palace which stands on a pretty lawn surrounded by a fence of coconut leaves … the royal mansion is

not large but very neatly built and the woodwork of the roof is
prettily wrought after the fashion of the country. The interior is
divided into three compartments or chambers by partitions made
of coconut leaves.

But if the palace was primitive, its occupant, George Tupou,
was very impressive. Brenchley also described him:

> The King is a very tall man with an intelligent countenance and,
> in spite of his colour, has an imposing air. He may be about sixty-
> five years old, and has the reputation of having been in his youth
> a very distinguished warrior. He was extremely reserved and did
> not exhibit to us anything approaching a smile.[18]

Tupou's reputation as a warrior was well deserved, for the
kingdom which he ruled as a Methodist monarch in 1860 he had
created largely by conquest earlier in the century. Known in his
youth as Tāufa'āhau, he had been born the heir to the title of *Tu'i
Kanokupolu*, one of the three great chiefly titles of Tonga. This title,
however, and the two more senior titles, *Tu'i Tonga* and *Tu'i
Ha'atakalaua*, had all but disappeared in the civil war which broke
out in Tonga in 1797 and which continued intermittently for half a
century. Western firearms and cannon were introduced into Tonga
during this period transforming warfare from a relatively innocuous
sport into a serious and bloody business. Ancient stalemates were
broken and the way opened for a political reorganisation. In those
troubled times the title of *Tu'i Kanokupolu* counted for little and in
fact at the time of Tāufa'āhau's birth two pigs had been formally
installed in the office. Later Tāufa'āhau's father, Tupouto'a, and later
still his great-uncle, Ale'amotu'a, had held the title, but without
exercising its authority or prerogatives. The resuscitation of the
office of *Tu'i Kanokupolu* and the reunification of Tonga was the
work of Tāufa'āhau.[19]

Tāufa'āhau grew to manhood in Ha'apai, the central group of
the Tongan archipelago, during the most turbulent years of the civil

war. As a youth he learnt the craft of war by accompanying his father on several expeditions against Tongatapu, and when Tupoutoʻa died in 1820, inherited the position his father had won as ruling chief of Haʻapai. For a decade, however, his authority over Haʻapai was contested by another chief, Laufilitonga, the heir to the *Tuʻi Tonga* title, and it was not until 1830 that he finally gained undisputed control over his inheritance. By that time he had established a formidable reputation as a warrior. At the same time he emerged as champion of a new religion, for during this period he was converted to Christianity.

Christianity had gained its first foothold in Tonga in 1826 when the Reverend John Thomas and the Reverend John Hutchinson of the Wesleyan Missionary Society won the confidence of Aleʻamotuʻa, the chief of Nukuʻalofa. Aleʻamotuʻa was not prepared openly to accept the new faith, but he allowed a church to be built and services to be held in his village. It was on a visit to Tongatapu to attend the ceremonies associated with Aleʻamotuʻa's induction into the office of *Tuʻi Kanokupolu* that Tāufaʻāhau first heard of the Christian God.

On his return to Haʻapai he began closely questioning a beach-comber about the new beliefs, and early in 1828 he returned to Tongatapu to seek a missionary to teach him. Hutchinson and Thomas had their hands full in Tongatapu and could only offer the services of a recent Tongan convert, Pita Vī, who was not even of chiefly rank. It was asking a great deal of a Tongan chief that he should accept instruction from a commoner but, after some hesitation, Taufaʻahau swallowed his pride and returned to Haʻapai with his teacher. A few weeks later he tested the power of Jehovah by beating with the trunk of a banana tree the priestess of the god Haʻehaʻetahi and, when this sacrilege brought no divine retribution, he accepted Christianity and ordered his people to follow. Thomas hastened to Haʻapai to baptise the entire population, and the first to receive the sacrament was Tāufaʻāhau. He took the name George (Siaosi), after the English King; the one wife he retained was baptised Charlotte (Salote), after George's Queen.

After 1830 wherever the influence of George Tāufa'āhau extended, mass conversion of the people followed. His personal ambition became sanctified by religious zeal and his struggle for power assumed the nature of a crusade. In 1831 he visited Vava'u, the northernmost group in the Tongan archipelago, with a fleet of fourteen war canoes, and by a combination of theological argument and armed threat converted the ruler, Ulukālala. When a half-brother of Ulukālala led the heathen chiefs of Vava'u in rebellion, Tāufa'āhau came to Ulukālala's aid, put down the revolt and banished the rebellious chiefs. The new chiefs raised in their place were quick to accept Tāufa'āhau's religion and the population at large followed their example. Thus when Ulukālala died in 1833, with his heir still a minor, Tāufa'āhau was elected by the chiefs of Vava'u as his successor, and Ha'apai and Vava'u became united under the one ruler.

With his position secured in the north, Tāufa'āhau turned his attention to Tongatapu where Ale'amotu'a, who had finally accepted Christianity and been baptised Josiah Tupou, was having trouble with the heathen chiefs who controlled most of the island. In 1833 Josiah learned of a plot to depose him from his office of *Tu'i Kanokupolu* and sent to his nephew for assistance. Tāufa'āhau raised a war party in Ha'apai and Vava'u, sailed to Tongatapu, and in a series of successful engagements in 1837 established the authority of the *Tu'i Kanokupolu* over the whole island. A further revolt broke out there in 1840, and again it was Tāufa'āhau who put it down. Josiah Tupou died in 1845. By this time Tāufa'āhau was the most powerful chief in the group, and of the possible heirs to Josiah's title, he was the obvious choice. He was elected *Tu'i Kanokupolu* in December 1845. The whole group was thus united under one ruler, and at the prompting of his missionary advisers Tāufa'āhau adopted the European title of King, along with Josiah's family name, Tupou. Thereafter he was known as King George Tupou.

For a decade or so after 1845 Tupou's energies were devoted to consolidating his position. One problem was the independence of the chiefs which posed a constant threat to unity. An effective instrument in reducing chiefly powers was found in a written code of laws prepared with the help of the missionaries and promulgated in 1850. Tupou had already introduced a rudimentary written code for Ha'apai and Vava'u in 1839, but the whole kingdom was made amenable to the new laws. Moreover the new code introduced provisions aimed at reinforcing the king's authority over the chiefs by giving him sole right of appointment of all chiefs, governors and judges. Another problem was posed by the two other great titles, *Tu'i Tonga* and *Tu'i Ha'atakalaua*. The latter title had lapsed in 1797 and Tupou suppressed it altogether, compensating the heir with a new title, Tungī, which carried no traditional implications; after much hesitation Tungī threw in his lot with Tupou and became a Wesleyan. The *Tu'i Tonga*, Tupou's old enemy, Laufilitonga, proved more refractory and in 1848 became a convert to Roman Catholicism. He was supported by the people of Pea and Houma and in 1852 these villages revolted. The king raised an army of six thousand men and besieged them until starvation forced the defenders to sue for peace. The surrender marked the end of overt resistance to Tupou. He dared not violate the traditional sanctity of the *Tu'i Tonga*'s person, and even continued to pay him ceremonial homage, but the office was a harmless anachronism. When Laufilitonga died in 1865 Tupou suppressed the title, took for himself its honours and privileges, and compensated the heir with a new title, *Kalaniuvalu*.

The Wesleyan Mission, which had supported Tupou through his long struggle, shared the spoils of victory; chiefs, anxious to show their loyalty to their king, joined his church and brought their people with them. By the 1850s everyone in Tonga was Christian, and the great majority of them were Wesleyans.[20]

In 1860, therefore, Tupou had achieved much. Tonga was reunited and, if old grievances were not far below the surface, they were kept under control by the authority of the King. The religious divisions had also largely disappeared; there was still a Catholic minority, and even among the Wesleyans there were many whose conversion had only been nominal or assumed for political reasons, but for all practical purposes Methodism had become the established religion of Tonga. In both politics and religion Tupou had won peace for Tonga, for the first time in half a century. But peace brought other problems: with peace came European trading and planting interests to exploit the economic opportunities of the country and in their train these interests brought involvements with foreign powers that might prove dangerous to a small and vulnerable state. Tupou was aware of the dangers but was uncertain of the best way of dealing with them. Nor could anyone advise him. His chiefs knew nothing of such matters, and his old allies, the missionaries, had little interest in the question; in fact Tupou suspected that they might welcome the incorporation of Tonga into the empire of one particular foreign power whose virtues they were constantly extolling.

It would be fanciful to imagine that any of this was in Tupou's mind during the civilities and formalities of his first meeting with Shirley Baker. The Misses Baker did claim that when their father was first presented to the king, Tupou took an instant liking to him, but this was possibly merely a romantic conception of an event that occurred so many years before. On the other hand Baker was certainly very impressed by Tupou; in fact everything about Tonga impressed and excited him and in his first letter home, a formal letter to his superiors in the Missionary Committee, he allowed his enthusiasm to break through the otherwise stilted and parsonical prose: 'Tonga is a beautiful place', he wrote, 'and I think I will get on first rate with the natives'.

CHAPTER II

THE KING'S ADVISER

S HIRLEY BAKER plunged into his new life as a missionary with enthusiasm and obvious enjoyment. His early letters abound with references to the satisfaction he found in missionary work, while the belief, expressed in his first letter to Sydney, that he would 'get on first rate with the natives', proved correct. Unfortunately, an ability to 'get on with the natives' was not considered by the missionary brethren in Tonga to be a necessary accomplishment. Tonga had been converted through the military conquests of Tupou, and the missionaries had found little need to develop a grass roots following or to be on friendly terms with their congregations. Moreover, owing to their association with the king, the missionaries had been accorded a high rank in Tongan society and were thus separated from the ordinary Tongans by a great gulf of social distance. They kept aloof, adopting towards Tongans a patronising, peremptory attitude. Commodore Erskine, who visited Tonga on HMS *Havannah* in 1853, noted in his journal:

> I am indeed bound to remark that in respect of their treatment
> of the people here the gentlemen of the Mission do not compare
> favourably with those of the London Society in the Samoan
> Islands. A more dictatorial spirit towards the chiefs and people

seemed to show itself; and one of the missionaries in my presence sharply reproved Vuke, a man of high rank in his own country, for presuming to speak to him in a standing posture.... The missionaries also seemed to live much more apart from the natives than in Samoa, where free access is allowed to them at all times. Here on the contrary the gates of the enclosures were not merely kept closed, but sometimes locked, a precaution against intrusion which ... I never saw adopted elsewhere and which must operate unfavourably to that freedom of intercourse so necessary to the establishment of perfect confidence between the pastors and their flock.[1]

Lieutenant Meade of HMS *Curacoa*, who visited Tonga in 1865, recorded a similar impression:

The Wesleyan missionaries, Messrs. Whewell, Montrose and Stevenson, came off to call on the Commodore. Some of my messmates landed in their boat and were rather disgusted with the specimen they saw of the practical teaching of the religion of love and gentleness. One of the natives had brought down Mr. Whewell's horse to meet him and had ridden rather too fast, I suppose; for, the moment he got off Mr. Whewell ran at him, took the riding whip out of his hand and began laying it about his bare back in a very vigorous style. The native, who was big enough to have eaten him, took his thrashing without offering to raise his hand.[2]

Baker, however, did not accept the local social conventions and almost at once he began seeking Tongan companions to teach him the language. In his first letter to Sydney he wrote: 'I find by associating with the natives and saying to them "ono higoa" – name this – I can get hold of the accent'.[3] By this direct method he acquired a working knowledge of the language very quickly and could inform his superiors two months after his arrival that he was already conducting services in Tongan without a book, and was about to attempt his first sermon in the language.

It was probably not so much his eagerness to learn nor even his lively, slightly coarse sense of humour that won the confidence of the Tongans, but rather his knowledge of medicine. Owing to the Tongan lack of resistance to introduced diseases and the absence of any form of quarantine, Tonga was frequently visited by epidemics which took a heavy toll of the population. Such an epidemic was raging when Baker arrived and had, according to the Reverend John Whewell, 'prostrated nearly the whole population and ... removed many valuable labourers to the rest that remains to the people of God'.[4] The Tongans relied on the missionaries for treatment for their ills, but often they were of little use. The Reverend George Lee wrote in 1857 from Tonga: 'I have no lance or surgical instruments – whether I know or not I must prescribe for them – I am yet a very poor physician – I cannot do without my book.'[5] From all accounts Lee was typical. Baker's arrival was therefore timely, for while his training was not very extensive, he had at least some knowledge of the dispensing of drugs and some practical experience. One of his first patients was his wife, who gave birth to a daughter, Alice, on 20 September 1860. This success probably encouraged the Tongans to seek his assistance – by October he could report that he was attending thirty or forty Tongan patients every day.

Baker's services in Nuku'alofa were evidently considered valuable by the other missionaries for, at their annual District Meeting held in December 1860, they decided not to post him to Ha'apai, as the Committee had recommended, but to retain him in Tongatapu in charge of Mu'a, the old capital in the eastern district of Hahake. This was no easy assignment. Ten years later Hahake was described by the Reverend George Minns as 'the most barren and difficult in the Friendly Islands'. The people of this area showed a decided lack of enthusiasm for the Mission, though the source of the trouble was political rather than religious. The people of Hahake were traditionally opposed to the people of Hihifo, the western part of the island, and regarded the assumption of kingship by the *Tu'i Kanokupolu*, a Hihifo chief, as an usurpation of the rights of the

Hahake chiefs, *Tu'i Ha'atakalaua* and *Tu'i Tonga*. They therefore gave only sullen obedience to Tupou and, at best, grudging lip-service to his religion. As Minns put it: 'While other parts of the District have experienced revivals and reported great material prosperity, Hahake has dwelt in sackcloth and the missionary has mourned over the indifference and unbelief of the people'.[6]

Baker began work in this forbidding district in December 1860 and while his labours made little impression against the apathy of the Mu'a people, his energy and enthusiasm certainly impressed the Reverend James Calvert, a veteran missionary, who visited Tonga in June 1861 and noted in his diary: 'Mr. Baker is likely to do well in the work. I like the look of him'.[7]

In one field Baker did achieve something in Mu'a. He persuaded Tungī to give him an allotment and set to work to build on it a training college for native schoolmasters. It began operations in April 1861 and, although it was a makeshift affair, it fulfilled an important need in the mission education system. Realising this, the Missionary Committee recommended that Baker should be permanently employed in charge of his institution. But he vigorously objected. He had come to Tonga, he said, to hold the high office of missionary to the heathen, not to teach school; he had had quite enough of that at Old Post Office Hill. So the Committee relinquished for the time being the higher education project and appointed Baker to Ha'apai.

Before Baker could take up his new appointment in Ha'apai missionary affairs were thrown into confusion and the Mission's arrangements suspended by a serious dispute that flared up between the Mission and the king. In January 1862 the death occurred of Prince Vuna, the seventeen-year-old heir of Tupou and his only son who was legitimate by Christian standards. All Tonga mourned for the prince and, to show their grief, the people performed a *tukuofo*, a ritual presentation of food and mats to the dead, on the occasion of Vuna's funeral. The missionary who conducted the funeral service was the Reverend W. G. R. Stephinson, a young man of much zeal but little discretion, who was so scandalised by the heathen implications of the *tukuofo* that he publicly reprimanded the king for allowing it. The Reverend Walter Davis, the Chairman of the district, supported Stephinson by invoking church discipline against all who took part and, as a result, relations between the king and the Mission suddenly became strained to breaking point.

Trouble had been brewing between the king and the Mission for some years, for Tupou had been showing signs of growing disquiet at the political influence wielded by the missionaries. While this influence was used in support of his government and against the heathen and Catholic chiefs the king had encouraged the missionaries. When Tonga became involved with European powers, however, the British sympathies of the missionaries aroused Tupou's suspicions. The trouble had begun as far back as 1841, when a French warship had visited Vava'u to demand that Catholic priests be admitted to Taufa'ahau's domains. The incident caused anxiety among the missionaries, who, fearing that Tonga might go the way of Tahiti, prevailed upon Josiah Tupou to appeal to Britain for protection. In 1848 George Tupou had renewed the request. Tupou's faith in his missionary friends was shaken, however, when he discovered that, either through a mistake in translation or through wishful thinking on the part of the missionary who delivered the letter, the British were led to believe that the Tongans wished to become 'not merely the allies but the subjects of the Queen'.[8] When this was more closely inquired into, of course, it was found that Tupou had no intention of surrendering Tonga's sovereignty; but thereafter he viewed the missionaries with some suspicion.

It was Tupou's apprehension that the missionaries might be a fifth column within his own kingdom that led him to seek outside advice. In 1854 an attaché of Charles St Julian, the Hawaiian Consul-General for Australia and the Western Pacific, visited Tonga, and a correspondence ensued between Tupou and St Julian in which Tupou was advised to reorganise his kingdom along Western lines with a constitution and written code of laws. In this way Tonga could win international approval and be recognised as a civilised power. Then, argued St Julian, Tonga would be able to enter into treaty relations with the powers and its independence be guaranteed by international law.[9] The missionaries, however, regarded St Julian's activities as an unwarranted interference in their own preserves and, when they discovered that he was seeking an exequatur to act as the British Consul in Tonga, they petitioned the Secretary of State for the Colonies objecting to the appointment. When Tupou learned of this it further increased his suspicions of missionary motives. By the end of the fifties, therefore, a serious rift was developing between the king and the missionaries. In 1859, when the Reverend John Thomas left Tonga after a stay of some thirty years as the king's spiritual and political adviser, Tupou did not even bother to see him off, and by 1862 the Chairman was openly admitting that the king's religious enthusiasm had waned. He wrote to the Missionary Committee:

> We are not ignorant that for several years injurious influences
> have been at work in the mind of the King. He has had many
> evil advisers and strong temptations and has yielded to
> them ... we have our fears that he has sadly backslided.[10]

Tupou's backsliding was political rather than moral. In 1859 he had decided to dispense with missionary advice altogether and carry out reforms himself along the lines suggested by St Julian. He convened a great *fakataha*, or meeting of chiefs, to discuss the matter. But the task of modernising Tonga and imposing Western civilisation on it was a very complex one and little progress was made. A second *fakataha*, held in 1860, and a third, held in 1861 in Vava'u, were alike unsuccessful. The crux of the matter was the need to reduce the power of the chiefs. The legal reforms of Tupou and the moral teachings of Wesleyanism had between them removed some of the sharper edges of chiefly sanctions, but chiefs still kept tight control over their own people through *fatongia*, the traditional right of a chief to the labour and worldly possessions of all members of his *kāinga*, or tribe. When the products of a commoner's labour were liable to be confiscated by his chief all the exhortations of the

missionaries failed to convince him of the advantages of labouring
and cultivating industrious habits. The accumulation of wealth and
property was further inhibited by the Tongan family system by
which every individual was *fahu*, or higher in rank than, his mother's
brother and his mother's brother's children, and the custom whereby
a *fahu* could authoritatively beg or demand any of the property of
his kinship inferior. So the Tongan commoner did as little as he
could, he saved nothing, he bought little, and he showed no interest
in developing his lands. Yet St Julian had warned Tupou that if
Tongans did not develop their own country and make it productive,
white men would not stand idly by and watch it go to waste. The
solution, Tupou decided, was to abolish *fatongia*, a solution the more
welcome as it would also enhance the king's authority by reducing
the competing authority of the chiefs. Tupou put the matter to the
1861 *fakataha* but the chiefs, led by Tungī, strongly resisted any in-
fringement of their privileges. The project had to be shelved and
little came of the three great *fakataha* except the examination of
certain customs; some of these it was decided, were barbarous and
were abolished, but others, including the controversial *tukuofo* were
approved and retained.

The missionaries regarded the holding of the *fakataha* as an
attempt on the part of the king to manage without their services
and registered their strong disapproval. In 1861 Lee complained that
the meetings merely encouraged gluttony and waste. Davis blamed
them for causing 'spiritual dissipation', claiming:

> The effect of such immense gatherings under circumstances the
> most exciting, and for purposes of a purely worldly character, is
> acting prejudicially on the piety of many who have but lately
> started on their career of holiness, and [has] on the church at
> large [exerted] a most pernicious influence.[11]

The action of Stephinson and Davis over the *tukuofo* was therefore
not an isolated incident, but rather a manifestation of the resentment
felt by the missionaries towards the *fakataha* and Tupou's attempt to

rule without their help. The king recognised that the affair was not
only a personal affront but also a trial of strength between his
authority and that of the missionaries, and his reply was decisive: he
relinquished his church office, revoked his membership and cast the
Mission adrift to shift for itself. Hundreds of his subjects, who had
only joined the church out of loyalty to the king and who had been
restive under the moral prohibitions of Methodism, followed his
example.

For the Mission the situation was very serious and, when news
of the king's estrangement reached Sydney, it caused consternation
in the Missionary Committee, whose members well knew that the
success of the Mission depended largely on Tupou's support. Davis
wrote justifying his stand and declaring: 'We must be prepared to
do battle with the enemy in high places',[12] but Eggleston, the
Secretary of the Committee, dismissed his explanations with scarcely
restrained anger:

> If this means do battle with those who speak evil of dignities and
> bring the discipline of the church to bear upon slanderers and
> backbiters I think you have the word of God on your side ... But
> if 'doing battle' is opposing George and his chiefs in their political
> measures, or giving countenance to their slanderers and defamers,
> neither God nor man ought to wish prosperity to such conduct.[13]

Stephinson was to have exchanged places with Baker early in
1862 but, as his presence in Tongatapu would only further
antagonise the king, he was kept back in Ha'apai and Baker stayed
on at Mu'a. Unfortunately Eggleston's instructions to the missionaries in Tongatapu have not survived, but presumably he enjoined
them to do everything possible to regain the king's confidence and
win him back to the church. This was a task that Baker found
congenial. By 1862 he was already well known to the king. His
medical duties brought him frequently to Nuku'alofa and, as Queen
Salote was chronically ill, he was a regular visitor at the palace.
Evidently he made good use of his opportunities, for at some stage

during the first half of 1862 Tupou sought Baker's advice on how to put his social and political reforms to the *fakataha*.

When Baker later had to explain to his superiors why he had meddled in politics, he described what had happened:

> With regard to the new laws the King asked me my advice and opinions etc. I replied I was a junior minister, it would be better for him to ask one of the senior brethren. He said he would not ask me to do or say anything which might grieve another – he asked me not as a minister but as a friend. I said on these conditions I would give him any advice or anything he wanted – the result is that most of the new laws are the result of my conversations with the King. I wrote them and they are printed almost exactly.[14]

In fact the blueprint for the reforms, and even the general nature of the measures needed, had been outlined by St Julian, so probably all that Baker did was to embody the king's ideas in concrete written proposals; but this was all that Tupou needed. When the *fakataha* convened in Nuku'alofa in May 1862, he put forward a prepared schedule for a new and comprehensive code of laws and demanded that they be approved. Either the chiefs were cowed or they were won over by a promise of a cash pension, for this time, with only token protests from the conservatives, the *fakataha* acquiesced and the code was passed.

In most of its clauses the new code paralleled that issued ten years earlier, although in the new version the king was brought within the law and stress was laid on the duties rather than the privileges of the chiefs. Another innovation was to make school attendance free and compulsory, thus making Tonga one of the very first states to introduce such a measure. The most important feature of the new code, however, was the freeing of the people from the control of their chiefs, or as it became known, (no doubt influenced by the proclamation of the same name issued by Czar Alexander II in 1861) the *Emancipation Edict*. This declared:

> All chiefs and people are set ... at liberty from serfdom and all
> vassalage ... and it shall not be lawful for any chief or person to
> seize or take by force or beg authoritatively in Tonga-fashion
> anything from anyone. Everyone has the entire control over
> anything that is his.[15]

Prior to 1862 the king had relied on *fatongia* to provision his
canoes for voyages, to provide the wherewithal for state feasts and
to carry out such public works as were undertaken. Under the new
laws the only free service the people were obliged to provide was
the clearing and hoeing of public roads along their frontages; all
other services were to be paid for by the government. To provide
an income to defray the cost of these services an annual tax of three
dollars was levied on all males sixteen years and over. It was then
necessary to ensure that the people had the means to pay their taxes.
Baker later claimed that the plan originated from him:

> After I succeeded in getting His Majesty to set his people free,
> one part of my scheme was that every native who paid his taxes
> should have the means of doing so by having a portion of land
> allotted to him.[16]

A provision was included in the legislation instructing the chiefs to
allot farms to each of their followers; so long as a tenant paid his
taxes and an annual rent of two shillings to his chief, he was
guaranteed security of tenure.

The new code was presented to the people on 4 June 1862 at an
impressive ceremony in Nuku'alofa. In the magazine *Missionary
Notices* Baker described the scene in the turgid prose he used for
such occasions:

> It would require a more graphic pencil than mine to picture the
> impressive sight that then burst upon our view, some four or five
> thousand natives of Tonga, Fiji and Samoa clad in garbs of various
> hues, sitting together in solemn silence under the spreading

branches of the Ovava tree ... See in the cool shade of the spreading tree sits in solemn majesty George, King of Tonga ... and if pen cannot describe the sight, how can it describe the feelings of that assembled throng when my respected superintendent gave out the hymn:

> 'Jesus doth reign where e're the sun,
> Doth his successive journeys run.'[17]

It was Baker's great moment. He wrote: 'If ever I felt the burning love of a missionary, it was then'.

Baker's enthusiasm for the reforms was not, however, unfounded and the new code soon began to show results. One of the king's aims had been to demonstrate to the world that Tonga was a civilised state, worthy of recognition, and the code did receive favourable publicity. In both Australia and Britain it received praise in missionary publications as an example of the beneficial effects of the gospel in promoting civilisation. The great powers, however, did not respond immediately in the expected manner, and Tonga remained unrecognised. But when HMS *Curacoa* visited Tonga in 1865, her captain accorded Tupou a twenty-one gun salute and, as British ships in the past had only offered thirteen guns, Tupou may have been satisfied that he was moving in the right direction.

Another important effect of the reform was a reduction of the independent power and influence of the chiefs, which under the old order had been a constant threat to unity and peace. Earlier legal codes had tried to make the chiefs more dependent upon the king, but as long as the chiefs commanded the unquestioning obedience of their *ngaahi kāinga* they were a potentially disruptive force and were only restrained by the military power of Tupou. The new laws sapped the autonomy of the chiefs in two directions. On the one hand *fatongia* was abolished – this was a social revolution and was very slow to take effect but, as the old customs decayed, the relationship between chief and follower began to degenerate towards that between landlord and tenant. On the other hand, the chiefs became financially dependent on the king; to compensate them for the loss of their privileges the king paid them generous stipends out of the tax revenue and they soon came to rely on this cash income. As pensioners dependent on the bounty of the king they rapidly lost the ability, and even the desire, to oppose his will.

Probably the most important effect of the reform was the impetus it gave to an agricultural revolution in Tonga through which subsistence farming came to be increasingly supplemented by cash cropping. In part this was caused by the abolition of *fatongia* and *fahu* exactions which had stifled incentive; in part it was caused by the new demands for money to pay taxes and land rents; and in part it resulted from the security of land tenure which commoners were guaranteed in the new code. In 1879, A. P. Maudslay, the British Consul in Tonga, believed that this last had been the most important factor. He reported:

> In 1862 ... every taxpayer was, under the most solemn oaths taken by the King and Chiefs, guaranteed a good title to his town plot and country land, with liberty to bequeath his title to his heirs and successors. This plan was ... a great success. Feeling secure of their lands the people set to work to plant coconuts with so much industry that in a few years the exports of the country were increased enormously.[18]

The comparative buoyancy of the Tongan economy which followed widespread cash cropping brought many changes. The king had a revenue and spent it largely on public buildings and harbour installations, so that Nuku'alofa began to change from a village of thatch huts to the likeness of a European town. After paying their taxes the people had a surplus and either gave it to the Mission, which spent it on building churches and schools, or used it to buy goods from the traders, who began moving to Tonga in increasing numbers to take advantage of the new opportunities.

The promulgation of the code of 1862 therefore brought important social, political and economic improvements to Tonga and Baker could justly feel proud of his part in it. The other missionaries, however, were resentful at being eclipsed by their young colleague. Davis and Whewell both wrote to Sydney prophesying disaster for the Mission as a result of the changes. The taxes, they argued, were more than the people could afford and they would have nothing left to give to the church, while at the same time church expenditure would increase because in future native ministers would have to be paid a stipend so that they could pay their taxes. 'The result on your balance sheet will be anything but agreeable', warned Whewell.[19] To Baker himself the brethren became acrimonious. Writing some years later Baker recalled: 'When ... I was the means of setting the people free and giving them the laws of 1862 every brother in the district ... opposed it, denounced me, scolded me, did everything but suspending me'.[20] In a mood of resentment and hostility the District Meeting convened in December 1862 and posted Baker to Ha'apai, a hundred miles away from Nuku'alofa and the ears of the king.

Within a few years the forebodings of Whewell and Davis were proved false and Baker was vindicated. In 1861 the cost of maintaining the Mission had been £2,220, of which only £1,874 had been collected locally, £43 in cash and the remainder in the rather inconvenient form of coconut oil. By 1866 local collections had risen to £3,770, of which £533 was in cash, while total expenses still remained at £2,421, the Mission having thus, for the first time, become self-supporting. By 1869 the Mission collected £4,558 in cash and £922 in oil, the total being nearly £3,000 in excess of local expenditure. In 1863 however, all this lay in the future, and Baker was viewed with suspicion and hostility by the brethren. Eggleston, the Secretary of the parent body in Sydney, supported him: 'the reforms,' he advised Davis, 'evince a wisdom that does honour to your King ... he should receive sympathy and encouragement.'[21] But even when the king, his confidence in his missionaries restored, rejoined the church early in 1864, jealousy still rankled among the small band of missionaries.

Baker felt again the edge of his brethren's rancour in 1864. In Ha'apai he spent much of his time attending the sick and, as he had

to buy his own medicines, he made a charge for his services. It is
not clear what his usual fee was, for when an official complaint was
made by E. L. Layard in 1876 that Baker refused to administer even
a single dose of Epsom salts without his fee of a dollar and a half,[22]
Baker protested:

> To say I make a charge is the grossest falsehood. I have never
> done so, saving in cases as other missionaries do, with the natives
> when requiring medicines for a native disease here, and that is
> generally a pig.[23]

Under normal circumstances no one would have noticed Baker
adding a few feathers to his own nest in the process of carrying out
his work as a missionary, but in 1864 he broadened the scope of his
activities by vaccinating three thousand Tongans against smallpox,
and in a program of such magnitude the fees, whether in dollars or
pigs, came to a substantial sum. The other missionaries felt, perhaps
with some justification, that Baker's philanthropy was heavily
weighted with a profit motive, and at the 1864 District Meeting
they told him so in no uncertain terms. Baker confided to his
journal: 'One of the missionaries spoke the most bitter things, also
the chairman. He who judges all knows the motives by which I was
actuated in vaccinating the poor Tongans'.[24] But no matter how
Baker might justify himself, there is little doubt that the other missionaries had touched a raw nerve, and had laid bare perhaps the
worst trait in his character.

If Baker's relations with his fellow missionaries were something
less than happy during these days, he was, it seems, on good terms
with the other European residents. The traders were beginning to
enjoy the increasing prosperity resulting from the reforms of 1862.
Baker, moreover, made a point of never charging his European
patients – a morally peculiar but politically wise arrangement – and as
a sign of their respect the European residents in Ha'apai made him
the secretary of their association in 1864. Of more importance was
the esteem in which he was held by the king, who began making

trips to Ha'apai to visit his young adviser. On one such visit in 1863 he sought Baker's views on a flag for Tonga, having already sought the advice of his chiefs: as the rat was the only indigenous animal one chief had suggested that this would make a good motif; another argued for a rooster. Tupou, however, was not convinced that either of these designs would enhance his dignity, but on applying to Baker he was offered a simple design, a red flag with a white upper quadrant containing a red cross. When it was explained to him that the cross on the white ground stood for the Saviour, and the red field for His blood, shed for Tongans as for the world, the king felt that he had found a worthy emblem. The design was presented to the chiefs at the *fakataha* of 1864, during which Baker assisted the king to draw up a series of Municipal Laws, and Tupou, in return for his services, offered to make him Premier.

Baker refused this honour. The main consideration was the health of his family, which was causing him concern. His second child, Shirley Jnr, had been born at Mu'a in March 1862, and following the confinement his wife was ill almost continuously. In April 1863 he wrote to Sydney that the children were so sickly and his wife's condition was so grave that he doubted they would ever see civilisation again.[25] By the end of that year they were no better and Baker warned the Missionary Committee that if matters did not improve he would apply to return. When the third child, Beatrice, arrived soon after this Baker decided to leave the mission field, at least for a time. Permission was granted him to return to Australia early in 1866, and in April he took leave of his flock. In a private letter he had written, 'a removal down here is no farce, what with trade stores, pigs, fowls, cow, etc., all to be taken care of and provided for and no one to help but these stupid natives',[26] but in writing for the readers of the Wesleyan Missionary Magazine his language was more tactful:

> I can only say that I wept and felt as much in parting from my Ha'apai flock, dark though their skins may be, as though I was parting from a people of my own nation and my own tongue.[27]

Whatever his private feelings were, no one could doubt that he had left his mark on Tonga. The reforms of 1862, for which Baker could claim a share of the credit, were already taking effect and the Nuku'alofa which Baker left in 1866 was not the same village he had come to six years earlier. A fine new church, the biggest yet seen in the Friendly Islands, stood on Zion; near by workmen were busy on a large two-storeyed wooden building which was to be the new Royal Palace; while beside the house of the Wesleyan minister there was considerable activity, for here a college was taking shape under the supervision of the Reverend J. E. Moulton, the newly arrived headmaster. Europeans had been attracted by the new trading possibilities and there were now fifty-four of them on Tongatapu, most of them living in Nuku'alofa. On the *mala'e* a flagpole had been erected and from it fluttered the red and white flag of Tonga.

Baker, too, had prospered. When he first arrived in Mu'a he had complained to his superiors that if they did not see fit to pay him more than stonebreaker's wages he would have to go through the debtors' court but, owing to his training in the chemist's shop and the generosity of his patients he could now afford to remit an occasional five pounds to his father in England and his mother-in-law in Melbourne.[28] Like the more notorious missionaries in Hawai'i, Baker had gone to the South Seas to do good and had done rather well.

CHAPTER III

THE EFFICIENT COLLECTOR

WHEN BAKER arrived in Sydney he found that he was not unknown in Methodist circles. He had, like other missionaries, written frequent despatches to the Secretary of the Missionary Committee and extracts from these letters were published in the *Missionary Notices,* a magazine issued quarterly by the Society for publicity purposes. In the original Baker's letters were disfigured by execrable syntax and an absence of punctuation, but the editor's blue pencil did wonders for them, and when published they provided an exciting contrast to the edifying but rather dull letters that most of the brethren wrote. Baker had a journalist's eye for the bizarre and the romantic; he wrote of storms, tidal waves, shipwrecks, native parliaments and weeping converts – wonderful material for a parson in need of homily or a Sunday School superintendent seeking a story. In Sydney the Committee decided that as Baker was only to stay a short time, it would not give him a circuit, but keep him in Sydney to lecture on the work of the missions and to take up collections. He was thus brought into contact with many of the most influential Methodists of the time. His audiences may have been a little disappointed at seeing him, for Baker was not very imposing, being short and stout, with fleshy features and rather close set little eyes, but his lectures must have been well received because from the collections he took up he was able to build a new hall for Tupou College in Tonga and endow several scholarships there. Between lectures he walked the wards of Sydney Hospital extending his medical knowledge.

Baker spent two years in this pleasant fashion and by the middle of 1868 the Committee began to wonder if he ever intended to return to Tonga. The Reverend Stephen Rabone, the mission secretary, wrote to him: 'I cannot for a moment suspect you of vacillation or of a wish to get free from your obligation ... but....'[1] Baker wished to stay in Sydney until after the Annual Conference of January 1869, which was to elect a new chairman of the Tonga District. Fortunately Elizabeth was expecting another child, and so he was given permission to remain in Sydney until after the confinement, and hence until after the Conference. This meant that when the time came for the Conference to elect a chairman for Tonga they had in their midst one of the contenders. The preferment should probably have been given to Stephinson, who had served loyally, perhaps at times even over-zealously, for twelve years in Tonga. Baker had only been six years in the islands but he had made many valuable contacts in Sydney and had all the advantages of propinquity. When the ballot slips were counted Shirley Waldemar Baker was named as the Chairman of the Friendly Islands District.

By April 1869 the new baby, Laura, had been born and the Bakers embarked on the mission brig *John Wesley* to return to Tonga. With them went the Reverend D. Wylie and the Reverend H. Greenwood, two new missionaries for the district, and a deputation of two senior missionaries on a tour of inspection, the Reverend Stephen Rabone and the Reverend James Watkin.

It is apparent from Baker's letters that the spur which drove him on was a desire, even a need, to make his mark in the world, to be acknowledged as a success. The unfortunate obverse of this was that he regarded any success on the part of one of his colleagues as a personal threat. Almost at once Baker was made aware of just such a danger. The deputation which had accompanied Baker to Tonga carried out their inspection, returned to Sydney and published their report. They scarcely mentioned Baker and they disparaged the reforms of 1862. Their praise was reserved for Tupou College, ('a positive wonder in our eyes'), and for its headmaster, Revd J. E. Moulton, ('a cyclopaedia of accomplishments').[2]

Moulton had left Newington College in Sydney in 1865 to inaugurate higher education in Tonga, a job rejected by Baker a few years earlier. While Baker was absent the college had been built, the grounds laid out, the classes formed and instruction started. By 1869 it was offering courses in Theology, English, Mathematics, Ancient and Modern History, Geography, Chemistry and Astronomy. Moulton was a man of some stature in Methodist circles. His father was a Methodist minister in England and one-time Chairman of the North Shields District. His wife, Emma, was the niece of Eggleston, formerly secretary of the Missionary Society in Australia. One brother, William Fiddian Moulton, was a noted Greek scholar, later to be the headmaster of the Leys School, Cambridge; another, John Fletcher Moulton, became Lord Moulton of Bank, while the third, Richard Green Moulton, was to become the Professor of Literature at the University of Chicago. Being a stammerer and an asthmatic James Egan Moulton had not been to a university, and had worked as a clerk and a chemist's assistant before entering the ministry. He was, however, a scholar, a gifted teacher, and a gentleman.[3]

Against this Baker could oppose only an uncertain background, a few Latin tags – mostly misspelt and used in the wrong places – and a gift for energetic prose, unspoiled by the niceties of formal grammar. Genteel visitors to Tonga quickly appraised the situation, and affected towards Moulton respect and admiration and towards Baker a thinly disguised scorn. For instance, when Mr E. L. Layard, the British Consul for Fiji and Tonga visited Nuku'alofa in 1876 he commented of Baker: 'this gentleman, from his antecedents, is not specially qualified for enacting the part of a legislator',[4] while of Moulton he wrote: 'I saw he was a very different man from Mr Baker. He was apparently a man of education and a gentleman. I called on him'.[5] Similarly, while Basil Thomson described Baker as a 'plausible and not over scrupulous man, half educated but possessed of considerable knowledge of the world',[6] he described Moulton as 'a gentleman and a scholar, full of generous impulses and enthusiasms'.[7] To Baker, so sensitive of his position as Chairman of the District, Moulton appeared as a very dangerous rival, and towards him he began to manifest an animosity that was to become almost obsessive. In many ways the history of Tonga for the next twenty years was to be a running commentary on the vendetta waged between these two men of the gospel.

For the moment, however, they were kept apart, Moulton in Nuku'alofa and Baker in Ha'apai, where his first task was to prove his worth to the Missionary Committee. If he could not give evidence of gentility or scholarship, he could at least provide money, and in 1869 the Society needed funds more urgently than ever before.

It had been the practice, ever since the Australian Wesleyan Methodist Missionary Society had been inaugurated in 1855, for the parent body in Britain to subsidise the Australian Society by meeting its annual deficit, normally between £4,000 and £5,000. In 1869, however, the British Society declared its intention of discontinuing the practice. Notice of this new state of affairs was received in Australia just prior to the 1869 Conference, and the matter was debated at length by that body. The Conference decided to send a deputation to investigate the management of the various mission stations and recommend means of raising their subscriptions – for it was plain that the mission areas would have to bear a larger proportion of their expenses. In January 1870 the *Missionary Notices* announced that areas already converted were expected to make an earnest effort to be self supporting, and exhorted the missionaries to 'adopt a more systematic and efficient plan of collecting'.

Baker had been elected Chairman of the Friendly Islands District by the 1869 Conference, and had been present when the financial problems of the Society were being debated. Furthermore, he had sailed to Tonga in the company of the deputation which had been sent by the Conference to investigate the financial position of the various mission stations. No doubt both the Conference and the deputation took the opportunity to impress upon him the need to be 'systematic and efficient' in the matter of collecting contributions, and so it was to this matter that he first turned his attention in Tonga.

Contributions to the church were made twice a year in Tonga, rather than on each Sunday. At the beginning of the year membership tickets were sold at one shilling each and the proceeds of ticket sales had originally been the only source of revenue. As early as 1836, however, voluntary contributions were collected for mission funds at a special meeting known as the missionary meeting, or *fakamisinale*, held usually towards the end of the year. In 1836 the missionary meeting collection had been £23 3s 2d, but by 1866 it totalled £3,770; it thus not only covered all local expenses, but provided a surplus of over £1,300 for mission work elsewhere. Baker held his first missionary meeting in December 1869, and the results justified the confidence which the Conference had placed in him. The contributions came to £5,450, nearly £3,000 in excess of local expenses and equalling the combined missionary collections of all the Methodists in Australia.

Baker achieved his results by reorganising the method of collection. In each village he gave a few of the most prominent people a 'plate' and made them responsible for soliciting contributions from the other villagers. Each collector then put pressure on his family and friends to make generous contributions and thus ensure that his 'plate' was larger than that of any other 'plateholder'. The intense rivalry which this system generated, and the methods used by 'plateholders' to stimulate contributions were described by Basil Thomson. His description was based on what he saw in 1886 and 1891, but would apply equally well to 1869:

> For some days previously six or seven chosen vessels had been canvassing their friends on behalf of the plates for which they were to be responsible on the great day. There was a keen

> rivalry between them....The tout took care to approach his
> victim in the evening when the house was full of people. He
> would remark that Pita (a neighbour) had promised two dollars
> this year, and would hint that he scarcely supposed the victim
> will allow himself to be outdone by such a one as Pita. The
> unfortunate man, constrained by false shame, promises more
> than he can afford; the amount is noted in a book and has to
> be found by importunity or petty larceny.[8]

The actual presentation of the plates was made publicly in the
church on the day of the missionary meeting. Thomson again
provides a description:

> In front of the pulpit stood a table on which lay a common
> wash-hand basin and an account book. The patrons of the
> basins sat in a stiff row behind.
>
> After the preliminary religious exercises the missionary
> announced the name of the patron in charge of the plate first
> to be filled.... As the name of each patron was called she rose
> in a stately manner and cast her contribution into the basin as
> a nest egg. And now those who had promised contributions
> to the plate just announced, swaggered up the aisle and flung
> their coins into the basin.... When the basins had drained the
> congregation of all their cash, the contents were quickly
> counted and the amount whispered to the presiding teacher.
> In crying aloud the contents of each basin he allowed pauses
> for the cheering, and artistically kept the largest until the last.[9]

Public giving and rivalry between contributors were probably
hallmarks of missionary meetings in Tonga before Baker's time, but
for reasons of propriety earlier missionaries had kept the natural
exuberance of the Tongans in check. Baker on the other hand
allowed them free rein at collection time, and under his governance
the annual *fakamisinale* became the greatest festival in the Tongan
calendar, a gala occasion marked by intense excitement and festive

dress. A trader, P. S. Bloomfield, described the scene in a village on collection day to the British Consul:

> The villages were generally divided into two parties called by the names of different nations such as English and German, and carried, if they were procurable, the flags of the nations they were named after. Each party tried to outdo the other in the amounts they would give and in some cases one village was pitted against another. There was always a considerable amount of excitement, flags flying, kerosene tins beating for want of drums and natives on horseback rushing about with flags in their hands shouting and yelling while exhortations to give largely were being poured forth in the church.[10]

While the organisation described above applied throughout the whole of Tonga, Baker went to even greater lengths in his own circuit, Ha'apai, to ensure that the contribution would be bountiful. In the first place it seems that he let it be known around his circuit that any village which did not contribute fifty buckets of coconut oil, or its equivalent in cash, would be deprived of the services of its native minister.[11] Secondly, he made an innovation which was to be very significant, for in following years it was to spread to other circuits in the group and became characteristic of missionary meeting collections in Tonga. Tongans manufactured coconut oil at collection time with more zeal than at any other time in the year, but many found when the day arrived, that they had not sufficient to provide the sum which, under the stress of the occasion, they felt impelled to give. To these people Baker was prepared to allow credit; their promises were recorded as a gift, and they could subsequently make oil to cover the amount. By these means Ha'apai alone gave two thousand pounds at the 1869 meeting.

Tonga's contribution was received by the Missionary Committee in Sydney with unbounded enthusiasm. In January 1870 the *Missionary Notices* published the full details of this 'noble sum ... contributed in one year by this earnest and devoted Christian community', and the generosity of the Tongans was held up as an example for other Methodists to follow:

> It is hoped that this instance of unparalleled liberality on the part of a people but recently in heathen darkness will not only serve to excite the thanksgiving of many, but also to stimulate those with fuller light and larger privileges, to renewed and increased exertion in efforts and gifts for the Missionary work.

But Baker's efforts were also noted outside missionary circles, and were regarded in an altogether different light. Dr G. H. Kingsley and the Earl of Pembroke toured Polynesia in 1871 and were very critical of missionary activities in the South Seas. They did not visit Tonga, but they received a copy of the *Wesleyan Methodist Missionary Report* for 1870, which contained details of the Tongan contribution in 1869, and on the basis of these figures the 'Earl and the Doctor' published a bitter denunciation of Wesleyan missionaries in general and the Tongan brethren in particular:

> Whatever good the Wesleyans may do 'spiritually', the mischief they work 'commercially', wherever they have a chance, is beyond counting, and the common name of their missionary schooner, 'The Palm Oil Trader', is, according to their own account, well deserved. If the Wesleyan Society had not published the facts themselves I should have hesitated to state them. Can it be believed that out of the kindly credulous Tonga Islanders, just struggling into civilisation, and whose every dollar, hardly earned, should and would be spent on the improvement of their country were it not for these canting sharks, they get 'the noble and astonishing sum of £4489.16.2 ... to assist in sending the glorious Gospel of Christ to the regions beyond'. Beyond where? To those who know the generous excitable nature of the South Sea Islanders, this must be looked upon as sheer pillage.[12]

Most chroniclers have tended to agree with the Earl and the Doctor, but it is necessary to say in Baker's defence that he was not responsible for the policy. He merely improved the techniques of collecting while leaving the theological implications to his superiors, who justified the somewhat shabby means by the end. The Committee, or at least its secretary, the Reverend Stephen Rabone, was well aware of the methods used to raise the collections, for Baker discussed them quite openly in his letters. Baker argued that the coconuts were just lying on the ground and that all he did was to get the Tongans to collect the nuts which would otherwise rot, and press out the oil for the Mission. In return for this small labour the people not only benefited by gaining schools and churches, but also helped bring similar benefits to their less fortunate fellows in heathen lands.

Whatever the ethical justification of his methods, Baker had succeeded in proving his ability as an administrator. As an evangelist he also enjoyed success: in June 1870 Ha'apai was gripped by one of those periodic revivals which were characteristic of Tongan Methodism and Baker could report that more than a thousand new members had joined the church. In his relations with his missionary colleagues, however, Baker was not so successful. He had antagonised Wylie, his assistant at Ha'apai, in some way and relations between the two were becoming increasingly strained. Stephinson felt bitter at the preferment of his junior, and although Baker had left him in charge of Nuku'alofa, the most important circuit, he was not mollified. Affairs came to a head in August 1870, when Stephinson and Wylie sponsored a Special District Meeting to charge Baker with improper conduct towards some of the female members of his congregation.

Charges of this sort were not unknown in Tonga, for temptations of the flesh were something of an occupational hazard for missionaries. One of the reasons for the failure of the L. M. S. Mission in Tonga at the end of the eighteenth century had been the desertion of Vason, one of the brethren, when he was called upon to choose between his faith and a heathen siren. The Reverend James Watkin had been recalled from Tonga in 1837 under a similar cloud. The source of the trouble lay in the attitude of Tongan girls to amorous adventuring, an attitude summed up by Lobase when she explained her indiscretions to Basil Thomson: 'She was born into the world, she said, to enjoy herself, and as the capacity for enjoyment wanes when one is old and ugly, pleasures must all be crowded into the fleeting hours of youth'.[13] The missionaries opposed this philosophy with all the force of civil and ecclesiastical authority, but some, inevitably, fell by the wayside themselves. Whether Baker was one of these will never be known for certain, but the District Meeting charged him with indecent behaviour towards:

1. Elizabeth Kaufo'ou, a young woman of between twenty and thirty, pushing her down nearly flat in the boat, preventing her rising when she made an effort to do so, drawing her hair through your fingers and tickling her neck, it being nearly dark at the time.
2. Also chasing her with a stick on another occasion on the green.
3. Examining the private parts of a young married woman between 9 and 10 pm in a small room, no third person being present. Also acting unbecomingly to the same person on another occasion, to the great indignation of her husband.
4. Pulling the breasts of sundry women, and pricking with a pin the hinder parts of another.
5. Chasing sundry girls around the mission premises and poking them in their sides.
6. Poking and pinching the private parts of a man named Samuela Nauha'amea.[14]

Had these charges been proved Baker's missionary career would have been over, but he managed the affair very skilfully. He insisted, as the Chairman, on presiding over his own trial, then from the chair disqualified Wylie and Stephinson from voting on the grounds that they were witnesses for the prosecution. When the Tongan witnesses proved perverse – probably from a fear of incriminating themselves – Baker was exonerated, though Moulton struck a discordant note by voting 'guilty' on two of the charges. In December Baker counterattacked by charging Wylie and Stephinson with issuing malicious libels against his moral and religious character, and haled them to Hobart for the General Conference to examine the matter. The Conference could only be guided by the decision of the brethren in Tonga, and Baker sailed back to the islands with his name cleared. Stephinson was given permission to retire from mission work and remained in New South Wales, while Wylie was sent to Fiji.

The true facts of the case are no easier to discern now than they were in 1870, though Baker's nickname among the Tongans, *Motu'a Mohetō*, (which means 'an old man who creeps into a woman's hut and commits offences against her while she is asleep') lends some substance to the charges. On the other hand Wylie and Stephinson bore grudges against Baker and were obviously motivated by a desire to have him removed. Wylie, interestingly enough, left Fiji rather hurriedly a few years later, leaving behind some ugly rumours and a pregnant housemaid.

Back in Tonga Baker took over the Nuku'alofa circuit vacated by Stephinson and occupied the mission house, next door to the Moulton's. Relations between the two began very well, for a few weeks after the Bakers arrived Moulton's young son almost succumbed to an attack of quinsy and Baker was able to earn Moulton's gratitude by tending the child back to health. All might have been well had Moulton been willing to allow Baker some authority in the affairs of the college; but here Moulton insisted on complete independence. The deputation which visited Tonga in 1869 had agreed on the need for certain improvements to the college and on the strength of this Moulton spent some hundreds of pounds, merely presenting the bills to the District Meeting without seeking its sanction or approval. He chose the students personally, and on his own account negotiated with the government to allot places in the

college to students who, on completion of their courses, would fill
government positions, completely ignoring the arguments of the
other missionaries that the college was intended to train young men
as assistant missionaries or as teachers in mission schools. Every
Sunday the college students went to church at Zion, which was
under Baker's charge, and Baker had occasion to complain to
Moulton that they were ogling the girls and taking rather more
than their share of the extempore prayers. Moulton replied by conducting his own services on the college premises close by, which
gave the boys the opportunity to sing very loudly, to the discomfiture of their less vociferous rivals up on the hill. Finally, it
came out in a Tongan law court that although the seventh commandment* was preached at the college it was flagrantly not being
practised there, and Baker decided to intervene.

In December 1871 Baker proposed new regulations giving the
District Meeting, through its agent, the Chairman, supervisory
powers over the expenditure and discipline of the college, and it is
perhaps indicative of the extent to which Moulton had alienated
the sympathies of the brethren that the motion was passed. Moulton
resigned and refused to withdraw his resignation unless the motion
were rescinded, or the college moved to Pangaimotu, an island off
the coast of Tongatapu. Realising the trouble that would follow
Moulton's resignation, the brethren agreed to move the college.
Moulton, however, was in the habit of discussing the doings of the
District Meetings with his senior students and news of the proposed
removal soon reached Tupou. So the ship that carried the District
Meeting minutes to the Conference also carried a letter from the
king and the National Assembly of Chiefs seeking a guarantee that
the college would not be removed. Faced with this the Conference
rejected the District Meeting's proposals, ordered that the college
remain in Nuku'alofa and administered a stern reproof to Baker.
The first round had gone to Moulton, but daggers were drawn.[15]

Baker had been very restrained in the past when referring to his
colleague, but after this rebuff he grew virulent. He described the
college as a 'nuisance ... a hindrance to our work ... only causing

* Forbidding adultery.

unpleasantness', and claimed that Moulton's reports were 'giving a false impression to the world as to things taught and accomplished in the college when only some four or five are learning and even those not able to do anything'.[16] Moulton replied by criticising Baker's methods of collecting funds, for though he was very willing to spend mission funds he had a fastidious aversion to collecting them. As early as 1867, when the Missionary Meetings collected only £2,000 and before Baker revolutionised fund-raising, Moulton was murmuring at the amounts raised. 'In some places', he warned, 'it averaged 2/- and in others 3/- and 3/6 per member, and this from those who do not handle four dollars in hard money from January to December'.[17] When Baker reorganised the collections Moulton had much more cause for alarm, for it began to appear that the size of his contribution was the measure of a man's faith. The prestige-conscious Tongan families came to look upon the size of their 'plate' as a status symbol and used all the resources of family obligation and Tongan custom to surpass their rivals. The Godeffroy firm, which had begun operations in Tonga about 1867, gave unwitting assistance by importing quantities of Chilean and Peruvian coin, for it was much more satisfactory for a Tongan 'plateholder' to cast silver dollars into the basin, than merely to have a quantity of oil recorded. The presence of cash also made possible a new and exciting form of collection known as *sivi* (sifting), wherein contributors marched around the tub putting coins in singly until all but one contestant had been eliminated. The winner then cast in his remaining coins, winning applause and admiration from the spectators. At one *sivi* it is recorded that an excited contestant tore off his coat and offered it rather than be eliminated.[18]

To meet the demand for cash at the missionary meetings Baker developed the system of accepting promises one step farther, by actually lending cash from mission funds to the value of the oil or copra promised. The results of this arrangement were gratifying. In 1870 the Mission collected £3,200, in 1871 £4,500 and in 1872 nearly £7,000.

The only place which did not join in the spirit of the missionary meetings was Tupou College. Baker reported after the 1871 collection: 'The College [contribution] last year was £58 – this year £32 and not because they had not the money but because they were told in other words not to give it'.[19] After the clash with Baker in December 1871 Moulton began openly criticising the collections. After the 1872 meeting he commented: 'It's a great mercy the Earl and the Doctor did not come to Tonga or they would have made statements more astounding than they did'.[20]

Perhaps more influential, and certainly more vociferous, were the European traders in Tonga whose profits had been damaged by Baker's collection system. The number of traders in Tonga had grown rapidly since the reforms of 1862. At first they had relied on buying Tongan oil at tax collection time, but the growing importance of the missionary meetings had given them another guaranteed source of income, for at this time Tongans made oil with a will and sold it to the traders. About 1869 the Godeffroy firm began operations in Tonga and introduced the system of buying copra rather than oil. Copra required less effort to make so the people welcomed the change, and as Godeffroys controlled the market outlets for this new product they acquired a virtual monopoly. The local traders were thus forced to accept the position of agents for the German firm, receiving a commission on the amount of copra collected; as long as it passed through their hands, however, they were reasonably content.

Baker's system of accepting promises disturbed this arrangement, for promises were redeemed in copra paid directly to the Mission, Baker in turn passing it on to Godeffroys. This system suited the Mission admirably as their vessel, the *John Wesley*, could not have handled a fraction of the Tongan copra, and it pleased Godeffroys because it guaranteed large quantities of commission-free produce. To the traders, however, it was an attack on their livelihood and was bitterly resented. Matters were made worse in 1872 when Godeffroys reduced their buying price of copra nearly twenty-five per cent. At the new low price the Tongans refused to sell copra to the traders at all, and rather than have no money at the collections, the Mission bought the copra at the old price and sold it to Godeffroys at the lower price. This did not hurt the Mission, as the money they had paid out was refunded immediately at the missionary meeting, but it was ruinous to the traders. Greenwood reported: 'they are embittered towards us, call us traders, say we are endeavouring to injure them etc., etc.'[21] Naturally Baker was the main target for their spleen, and venomous stories about his relationship with Godeffroys began to circulate on the beach.

Even more disturbing for Baker was the decline of his popularity in Sydney. The report of the Earl and the Doctor, describing him as a 'canting shark', was published in 1872, and judging from the many references to it in missionary letters it must have caused a good deal of soul-searching on the part of the missionary fathers and, following as it did the investigations of 1870 and the college controversy of 1871, it began to shake the faith which the Committee had had in the Friendly Islands Chairman. By July 1872 Baker was complaining:

> The work was never in a better state, never had more members, more L.P. [local preachers] and never before raised one third of the amount – we pay all expenses, ask no one for a farthing and yet the Committee and Conference are not satisfied – just because some of the brethren are jealous of our success and a few mean low-lived folk presume to throw dirt at us … it is too hard after one works so hard to get no thanks.[22]

Moreover, while the Committee on the one hand might sanctimoniously shake their heads over his methods of fundraising, on the other they eagerly took all that he was able to raise, and begrudged his spending any of it on his own district. In 1871 Baker set out to beautify Zion, the oldest and most important church in Tonga, by refurnishing it, shingling the roof, and building for it a tower complete with clock and bell. The Committee, however, complained that the project was an unnecessary extravagance, and insisted that Baker collect extra money for it locally. This parsimony irked Baker; it also irked the king. Tupou doubtless felt that with all the money being made out of Tonga the Committee could afford to be generous, and he began to look thoughtfully at the cargoes of Tongan silver slipping over the horizon in the *John Wesley*.

Baker, according to his lights, had been a faithful missionary, serving the Committee ably and zealously; indeed in most cases it was his excessive zeal on behalf of the Committee that had aroused opposition against him. But by late 1872 he was becoming disillusioned. In a letter to Rabone in July he wrote:

> ... all I can say is – I have always brought more grist to the mill than I have taken from it – I have done my duty to the Committee and to Methodism – and if anything I have done too much.[23]

He began looking for a patron less fickle and more appreciative than the Missionary Committee had proved to be. The obvious choice was Tupou.

CHAPTER IV

THE CHAMPION OF AN
INDEPENDENT CHURCH

B ETWEEN SEPTEMBER and December 1872 Baker made the
decision to link his fortunes to those of Tonga and its ageing
king. It was a decision which was to alter his life profoundly, to
lead him into conflict with his church and his country and eventually
to bring him into disgrace. It was also a decision which was to have
a great influence on the course of Tongan history.

Many people, faced with Baker's problems in 1872, would have
simply retired to Australia. In July of that year, indeed, Baker
considered doing this, and wrote to the Missionary Secretary: 'I
sometimes feel tempted to resign and bring those gentlemen (his
critics) to their senses'.[1] He was thirty-six years of age and by that
time had six children. He had spent nine years in the islands and
under his administration Tonga had become the most prosperous
mission in the Pacific. No doubt he could command a pleasant
circuit in Sydney and probably become a member of the Missionary
Committee if he retired from Tonga. In Tonga, on the other hand,
his future seemed unhappy, for there he was a butt for public
criticism, a source of annoyance to the Missionary Committee, and
the centre of unseemly wrangles with his missionary brethren.

To resign, however, would be to admit failure, and Baker's
eagerness to be acknowledged as a success was intense. His resig-

nation, moreover, would mean victory for Moulton, a humiliation he could not accept. Baker's letters to the Missionary Committee give frequent evidence of his jealousy of Moulton. Moulton wanted to be 'top sawyer'; he was a 'spoilt child'; he had 'privileges no other Wesleyan Minister has throughout the world'; he would never rest until Baker was out of the district; he opposed Baker because he was 'in the way of his making a name for himself'.[2] Baker had worked very hard to bring prosperity to the Tongan mission and he meant to keep the credit for it. To hand over the fruits of his labour to his rival and personal enemy was unthinkable.

His reluctance to leave was reinforced by a practical consideration: he was making money in Tonga. By the early seventies Baker was able to lend money to the Tongan government to establish a sugar plantation, and the size of the loan can be gauged by his claim that he lost over £200 when the venture failed, even after receiving compensation.[3] Then in March 1875, because the missionary meeting had not been held, he sent £630 of his own money to Sydney, explaining that he had no other use for it.[4] On a missionary stipend of £150 per annum he could not have saved sums like these, and where the money did come from is something of a mystery. His enemies suggested he received a commission from Godeffroys, but this seems most unlikely. Most probably the source of his new-found means was his medical practice, despite his frequent denials that he had made any profit from treating his patients. One thing is certain: he could not expect to do so well in a suburban circuit in Australia.

There was a solution to Baker's dilemma; if he were to win independence for the Tongan mission, most of his problems would be solved. In an independent church Tongan native ministers would assume equal rank with, and gradually replace, white missionaries, and he could more easily control tractable Tongans than his fractious European colleagues. The Missionary Committee would lose control over Tongan affairs, Baker would be free from its parsimony, and, through local control of finances, those critics who commented on the anomaly of money being raised in Tonga to convert the heathen in Australia would be silenced at the same time. Moreover, Baker needed support and a proposal for church independence would win him strong support in Tonga, for among Tongans there was much discontent over the export of cash. The king, especially, was dissatisfied but he feared to touch the *lotu* directly. Religion was woven into Tongan life and culture, it was intimately connected with the state, and it provided the key to the civilisation that the Tongans sought. An independent church, however, would allow the Tongans to keep the *lotu,* and also keep control over their own money. It combined with this a subtle flattery to Tongan dignity and a recognition of the Tongan's strong desire for independence, in spiritual as well as temporal matters.

The first suggestion that Baker was considering some change in status for the Tongan Mission appeared in September 1872. He wrote to the Committee:

> I believe ere long it will be expedient to take the chiefs more into our advice and confidence than we do now – such a thing must come or else we shall ever be looked upon as foreigners.... I know many pooh-pooh it, but I for one would not object to sit in a financial District Meeting or Committee with King George.[5]

By December he had moved from advocating that Tongans should have some voice in mission decisions, to proposing that the Mission should become a church, completely independent of foreign control.

The first the missionaries heard of this proposal was when Baker read the text of a request to the Conference that the Tongan Church be granted independence, at a missionary meeting towards the end of 1872. Four other missionaries were present but were given no opportunity to discuss the proposal. Baker again read the request at a local preachers' meeting, but as this meeting was composed mainly of Tongans, again the missionaries did not get a chance to object. The District Meeting was the proper forum for discussion of such matters but before it was held Baker sailed for Sydney, where he appeared at the Conference and presented a request claiming to come from the 'agents' in the Friendly Islands that 'Tonga be no longer regarded as a mission'.[6] The request took the Conference completely by surprise, but the members were forced to concede that if graduates of Tupou College could do algebra and mensuration, they ought to be able to manage circuit accounts, and recommended the proposal to the Missionary Committee. The Committee however, refused to sacrifice its main means of support so easily and opposed the proposal. The most it would allow was that for a trial period a home mission fund should be established in Tonga with authority to retain half the juvenile collections and a quarter of the adult collections for local use, the balance to be sent to Australia.

Baker returned to Tonga in April 1873 to find that Moulton had been expressing disapproval of the moves for independence and was, in consequence, out of favour with the king, while his own position was greatly strengthened. He might have been satisfied with this limited success if the other missionaries had not thrown themselves into the arena against him. Moulton wrote to the secretary of the Committee making it plain that the proposals for independence had not come from the 'agents' in Tonga but from Baker alone. He also wrote to the *Advocate* publishing his views:

> The question is not the desirability of such a step nor its advisability at the present time but whether a measure more nearly affecting the missionaries than either King or people should be carried into effect before those missionaries have expressed their opinion upon it according to the Wesleyan system, in District Meeting assembled.[7]

Greenwood, hitherto one of Baker's most reliable deputies, wrote a long memorandum pointing out the difficulties involved in raising native ministers to equal status with Europeans. Tongans were but children, he argued, and handing the church to them would be to make it the tool of the chiefs, for no native minister could align himself against his chief. Only Europeans who were not part of the Tongan social system could keep the chiefs in check. He concluded:

> A great political change will have to take place before the native ministers have that position and influence in the land sufficient to their being left in charge of the Church in Tonga.[8]

The District Meeting convened in December 1873 to discuss the issue and the debate was bitter. Baker wrote shortly afterwards: 'My life at present is a perfect misery ... all I get from my brethren is persecution'.[9] The meeting would not endorse Baker's proposal for independence, but it recognised the value of local control of finances. After meeting local expenses Tonga had still been able to send £4,159 to Sydney in 1873. Money had been provided from the home mission fund to build four mission houses, and this to the missionaries who had previously lived under thatch was probably a persuasive argument. Moreover, Tongan feeling was obviously strongly in favour of the money being used locally, for in Ha'apai all contributions had been made by the children to ensure that half, rather than a quarter, of the collections would be kept in Tonga. The meeting therefore decided to recommend that Tonga be permitted to manage its own finances and the Reverend Jabez B. Watkin was sent to the 1874 Conference to present the case.

At the Conference there was considerable opposition to this proposal – instigated mainly by Stephinson – and eventually a decision was reached to send the Reverend Benjamin Chapman, the Secretary for Missions, to investigate the whole matter in Tonga and report to the following Conference. It seemed that the initiative had been taken from Baker and that the future of the Tongan Mission would be decided between the District Meeting and the Conference.

Baker, however, did not give in easily. In February 1874 the chiefs, probably at Baker's instigation, wrote to the king expressing their wish for the Mission in Tonga 'to be like the Wesleyan Church in Sydney'. Baker discussed the chiefs' request with the king and suggested that the king and chiefs should write a joint letter to the Conference submitting their views. The king and chiefs met in March and drew up their demands:

> This meeting affirms that the time has arrived to fulfil the promise made by the missionaries, and the church appoint trustees and all matters affecting the church be with them to arrange and superintend. With regard to the money raised this meeting justifies the complaining of the people owing to the very large amount of money which is sent from the country ... this meeting earnestly desires that the Committee and Conference ... allow the Church of Tonga to become free such as becomes a people who know the Gospel ... as it is at present it appears that the possession of Tonga has become the property of another.[10]

While these were legitimate Tongan aspirations, there is good reason to suspect that Baker played a larger part in drafting the letter than he admitted. In the first place the letter consisted of a set of peremptory demands backed by thinly veiled threats – this was not the tone used by Tongans in addressing church dignitaries. Secondly, the letter demanded that the Mission 'give up the schools to the Government', and this appears to have more reference to the controversy between Baker and Moulton than to any purely Tongan desire. Finally, the letter concluded by stressing that it was solely owing to Baker's restraining influence that the chiefs were prepared to wait for a decision by the Conference, rather than take matters into their own hands, and this also suggests Baker's hand in the drafting.

Whether or not Baker drafted the letter, it was a formidable weapon in his hands. He forwarded it to the Committee in May, accompanying it with a set of specific proposals of his own, which were less far-reaching than the king's request, but which, he claimed, would satisfy Tongan demands. He proposed that he be allowed to arrange the Mission's leases according to the Wesleyan *Model Deed,* which would, in effect, give the Tongan Mission a constitution, with all the hallmarks of an independent Wesleyan Church; that Tonga be granted control of local finances with native ministers and chiefs represented at financial District Meetings; that European missionaries be gradually replaced by native ministers, leaving only one European in each centre as superintendent; and that government inspectors be allowed to supervise mission schools.[11]

Baker's moderate proposals were much more likely to be accepted by the Committee than the Tongan demands, and by acting as a mediator Baker was in a very strong position. But he worked during 1874 to reinforce his case. The strongest opposition, he knew, would come against his proposals for elevating native ministers and for allowing local control of money. With regard to the former he set out to prove that native ministers could perform the tasks previously reserved for Europeans. Hihifo was vacant and Baker appointed a Tongan to take charge of it, explaining to the Committee:

> We must work our native ministers more, give them a better status and more responsibility and trust them more than we have – in fact it is no longer will we – we shall have to do so – for they are commencing to demand it and we had better do so and give it to them gracefully than have it wrested from us.[12]

By the time Chapman arrived in December 1874 to carry out his investigations, Baker could show that his proposal to use Tongans as fully-fledged ministers was feasible. In proof he could point to Hihifo, which he claimed was doing better than ever before under its native pastor. To answer objections to the local control of finances Baker had to assure the Committee that its income from Tonga would not be threatened; the 1874 missionary meetings were therefore very important. To help his cause Baker began the publication of a newspaper, *Koe Boobooi*, written in Tongan and providing for its readers Baker's views on religious and political matters mixed with selected items of local and foreign news. To enlist local support he began work on at least three European-style churches in Tongatapu, and two new educational institutions, a ladies' college and an industrial school. These measures proved adequate. In 1874 the Mission met all its local expenses, including building costs and the salaries of its schoolmasters and native ministers, and sent a contribution of over £3,000 for Foreign Missions.

Thus when Chapman arrived in Tonga he had little option but to accept Baker's recommendations. They were presented by Chapman to the 1875 Conference, which also had before it a report of the Tonga District Meeting which claimed: 'the proposals will for the present satisfy the wants of the Tongan Church and must eventually lead to its becoming a native church supported by native means and carried on almost exclusively by native agents'.[13] The Conference, therefore, saw the arrangement as an expedient half measure which would give the Tongans the shadow of control while keeping its substance in Sydney, and on this understanding the proposals were accepted.

The proposals which the Conference accepted were those which Baker himself had made in 1874, and Baker knew better than anyone that they did not constitute independence. The king, on the other hand, had come to regard the establishment of his own church as one of his major objectives, and would have lost faith in Baker had he been offered anything less than full independence. Tupou, however, was an old man and saw things in simple terms; Baker evidently told him that the Conference decision meant that independence had been granted and the king, it seems, accepted his word. On 2 June 1875, the anniversary of the Emancipation Proclamation, celebrations were held to mark the inauguration of the *Siasi Tau'atāina* (Independent Church), and when the Parliament met in September the king assured the representatives: 'The Church has been established'.[14]

Baker had apparently purposely misled Tupou and his people,

and in doing so he took a calculated risk. Evidently he felt confident
that the Conference, for fear of alienating the king, would not dare
to contradict him and would tacitly accept his *fait accompli*. In the
meantime he would make acceptance easier by proving that his
church was feasible and viable, and that it was warmly supported by
the Tongans. With this intention in mind he set out to demonstrate
that Tongans could manage their own affairs. He divided Tongatapu
into eleven circuits and put each under the care of a Tongan minister. He kept a close watch on each circuit through regular monthly
meetings of the Tongan ministry, at which he received reports and
issued orders, but the arrangement nevertheless gave the Tongans
an enlarged responsibility and an enhanced prestige. Another major
achievement was made in August, when Baker introduced Tongans
into the Quarterly Meeting. These meetings, at which financial
matters and policy questions were discussed, had hitherto been the
exclusive preserve of the European missionaries, and Greenwood
had prophesied that dire consequences would follow if Tongans
were allowed to participate in them. However, at the August
Quarterly Meeting everything went smoothly, and, according to
Baker, even Moulton agreed that his policy had been vindicated.
Baker reported: 'After the meeting Mr Moulton turned to me and
said, "Well Mr Baker, I congratulate you upon your success. It has
exceeded all my anticipations."'[15]

Baker had also to prove to the Conference that the finances of
the Missionary Committee would not be curtailed if it accepted the
new church which he had proclaimed. He therefore required a large
collection for 1875. In this he was not disappointed. The fact that
the Tongans believed they had their own church was in itself an
incentive to the people to give liberally. And in 1875 there was
another reason for generous giving: the first Wesleyan missionary
had arrived in Tonga in 1826, and the year 1876 had been set apart
as the year of jubilee. Accordingly, the Conference had agreed that
in 1875 Tonga should only remit to Sydney a sum equal to its
average Foreign Missions contribution. All contributions received
at the missionary meetings above this figure were to be retained in

Tonga as a jubilee fund, from which Baker promised to build five new churches and a new college hall, and to create an endowment fund for the Tongan Church. The people were therefore urged to make a special sacrificial effort in 1875, and Baker used all his powers of persuasion and coercion to ensure that they did.

By 1875 Baker had organised the *fakamisinale* into a smoothly efficient mechanism for collecting money. For the jubilee collection he introduced a new technique. Since 1869 the Mission had been accepting promises at the missionary meetings from Tongans, though in theory this was limited to those who had cut their copra but had not been able to dry and sell it in time for the collection. Since 1872 the Mission had actually been advancing cash to the Tongans on the day of the collection to cover the amount of the promises. This system ensured lavish contributions, but it had two disadvantages: the traders were antagonised and the Mission sometimes became involved in embarrassing litigation when the promised copra failed to materialise. The solution would have been for the traders to have advanced cash themselves in return for a lien on the harvest, but the traders were always short of money and had none to spare for loans to the Tongans.

The first missionary to see the possibilities in this situation was Henry Greenwood. In 1874 he lent about £300 to P. S. Bloomfield, a copra trader, who in turn advanced it to the people for the missionary meeting. The money was returned to the Mission on the day of the collection; Bloomfield collected the copra when it was prepared and from the proceeds repaid the Mission the sum he had borrowed.[16] This arrangement proved so satisfactory that Baker took it over in 1875 and expanded it. He made an arrangement with Weber, Godeffroys' manager, to lend mission cash to Godeffroys' agents in return for the firm's bills of exchange; the traders then lent the money to the Tongans on the day of the meeting. The Tongans gave liberally because the traders were less scrupulous than the missionaries and extended almost unlimited credit. The traders collected the copra when it was prepared, and bore any odium that attended the collection of debts. This practice might have been morally dubious, but from a strictly business point of view it was very sound; at the 1875 meetings the Tongan Wesleyans, spurred on by the missionaries' exhortations and assisted by easy credit, gave the almost incredible sum of £15,227.

The final step in Baker's program was to obtain a more formal and legal guarantee that his church was independent than that contained in the resolution of the 1875 Conference. His strongest argument lay in the conditions of the Mission's land leases. The Mission had considerable holdings in Tonga, but the lands had been given piecemeal by Tupou over several decades, and most of the leases were invalid. Baker informed the Committee that the leases were 'not worth a rush', and suggested that to protect the lands new leases ought to be issued in accordance with the Wesleyan *Model Deed*, the instrument under which the Methodist Church held its lands in England and Australia. The *Model Deed*, however, was more than a form of lease, for it contained a definitive statement of the history, organisation and practices of Methodism; it was thus, in effect, a form of constitution. The Committee discussed the matter with its lawyers and found that Baker's information was correct; for the leases to be valid they were required to be vested in trustees, and to elect trustees a proper constitution was necessary. The Committee therefore decided to accept Baker's recommendation and had its lawyers prepare the Tongan *Model Deed*. It was forwarded to Baker in November 1875 and, on 15 December, was signed by Baker, Moulton and two leading Tongan laymen. On the same day new leases were signed by Tupou vesting all mission lands in trustees elected according to the *Model Deed*.

By permitting the signing of the deed the Committee had given tacit approval of Baker's coup and, after 1875, details of affairs in Tonga ceased to appear in *Missionary Notices* or the Missionary Society's annual reports. There was naturally a certain ambiguity about the status of the new church. Although by implication from the *Model Deed* it was independent, yet it was still obliged to remit a stated proportion of its collections to assist foreign missions, and the European missionaries were not controlled by the local body but by the Missionary Committee in Sydney. This ambiguity was to lead to a great deal of contention later but in 1875 it seemed of little importance; Tonga had its church, the king was immensely gratified, and Baker was content with what he had achieved. In February 1876 the British Consul for Fiji and Tonga, E. L. Layard, visited Nuku'alofa and Baker told him that he had achieved one of the two great aims of his life: he had made the Tongan Mission independent.[17]

Baker's other aim, he told Layard, was to make Tonga a nation, accepted by other nations as a sovereign independent state. By 1876 he had not achieved this aim, but he had already moved a long way in that direction.

CHAPTER V

THE CHAMPION OF AN INDEPENDENT STATE

AKER'S DECLINING fortunes during 1872 had led him to seek support from Tupou by championing the cause of independence for the Tongan Mission. His involvement with the king was not confined to religious matters, however, for at the same time, and for largely the same reasons, he began to take part in the political affairs of the kingdom.

Secular matters had long held a fascination for Baker. His goal had always been to 'make a name for himself' and the Tongan political scene offered him unique opportunities to do this. The stumbling block in the way of a political career was an injunction in the Wesleyan Missionary Society's 'Instructions to Missionaries' which forbade them to engage in civil disputes or local politics. Baker's political activities in the 1860s had contravened this rule and as a result he had been censured. Mindful of this he avoided politics when he returned to Tonga in 1869, putting all his energies into his ecclesiastical duties. A *fakataha* was held in Ha'apai while Baker was there in June 1870, but at his trial by the missionaries soon afterwards there was no mention of his interfering in politics, though inquiry was made into a lengthy catalogue of his shortcomings.[1] Another *fakataha* was held in Vava'u in June 1871, but Baker remained in Nuku'alofa. That he was also absent in spirit from this meeting is indicated by the regulation it passed to force Tongans to dress in European clothes, a regulation of which he greatly disapproved, because Tongan money spent on clothing could not be given to the Mission. It seems, therefore, that as long as Baker was securely in the seat as Chairman of the Mission he was not prepared to jeopardise his position by playing politics. By 1872, however, conditions had altered; he began to look to Tupou for support rather than to the Committee, and the way was open for him to indulge his interest in affairs of state.

If Baker needed Tupou in 1872, it is equally true that Tupou needed Baker. The king's policy had always been motivated by a jealous regard for his own independence and Tonga's territorial integrity. He had expected that his reforms of 1862 would have guaranteed this independence by leading to the formal recognition of Tonga by the Powers, but in this he had been disappointed. In the interim Tonga's position had been made more precarious by events in Samoa and Fiji, events of which Tupou could not have been unaware. In Samoa, for instance, it was commonly rumoured in the early seventies that annexation by one of the Powers was imminent, rumours that were persistently voiced in the Sydney press in 1872, and that probably had their origin in an ambitious plan by Theodore Weber, the 'Godeffroy factor' in Apia, to colonise Samoa by Germans, using Chinese as indentured labourers. Large tracts of land had been bought by Weber and the German warship *Hertha* had actually been commissioned to visit Samoa to initiate the scheme when the outbreak of the Franco-Prussian war caused it to be shelved. From the other direction British annexation of the group was being pressed vigorously by New Zealand, and in 1871 both Houses of Parliament in that colony petitioned Queen Victoria on the subject. It seemed only a matter of time before one of the Powers would step in. In Fiji, Tonga's other neighbour, events were equally disturbing. In the decade between 1860 and 1870 foreign settlers there had increased from something under forty to nearly two thousand. By 1868 a quarter of a million acres of the best land had been alienated to these settlers and disputes over land titles had thrown the country into such confusion that visits by British men-of-war and raids by armed settlers were required to maintain the Europeans in possession of their lands. In June 1871 a mixed government of whites and Fijians had been set up under Cakobau, but this had failed to win the support of the settlers. By 1872 Fiji was faced with the prospect of civil war and in desperation Cakobau offered to cede his kingdom to Britain.

By the early seventies British residents in Tupou's own domains, encouraged no doubt by the example of their fellows in Fiji, were beginning to press their case for the Friendly Islands to be included in the Empire. A British resident in Tonga, subscribing himself 'An Unfortunate Settler', published his views in the *Fiji Times* in October 1870. He complained of the 'absurd restrictions' against settlers buying land in Tonga, and warned:

> They will find their efforts to stay the tide of immigration useless … and England, being aware of the justice and importance of protecting, if not actually governing her subjects in these seas, the Anglo-Australian race will settle and find a living in the Friendly Islands, in spite of all the laws passed by Kings and Chiefs.[2]

The provocative attitude assumed by British subjects in Tonga was exemplified by the case of Philip Payne, a copra trader who was brought before a Tongan court and ordered to pay eight shillings damages to the owner of a roll of *tapa* which had been trampled on and damaged by Payne's horse. Payne's defence was: 'It was true the horse damaged the tapa but I did not order the horse to do so'. On these grounds he refused to pay the damages and insisted his case be tried by the captain of a British man-of-war. The judges warned Payne that if he was not prepared to accept the laws of Tonga he would have to leave the country. The court record continues: 'Upon which Philip laughed scornfully at all the judges and said "as if I should pay,

and in case I do not will you be able to send me from Tonga?"'[3]
Tupou answered this question by forbidding any Tongan to trade
with Payne and by giving him six months to quit the country. The
other British residents thereupon petitioned the Governor of New
South Wales complaining of 'the manner Europeans are treated and
what they are subjected to in these islands' and requesting the
Governor to 'define a limit to the arbitrary authority of a government,
which, to say the least, is and only can be semi-civilised'.[4]

Since 1864 Tupou had relied on his secretary, David Moss, in
his dealings with Europeans. Moss had been adopted by the king,
in accordance with Tongan custom, under the name Tupou Haʻapai.
He wrote the king's letters, drafted government regulations and
acted as paymaster and receiver of revenues. But in November 1871
Moss's wife came to Baker seeking treatment for a disease which
was causing her hands and fingers to decay. Baker diagnosed leprosy,
and Moss was suddenly dropped from the king's retinue. Baker
quietly took the vacant place. Exactly when this happened is
uncertain, but it was accomplished by July 1872, for in that month
he reported to Sydney: 'The King could not be kinder – at present
I am his private councillor on matters of importance'.[5] It was also at
this time that Baker began moving for an independent church in
Tonga, and it therefore seems reasonable to assume that the king
and his missionary had come to a tacit agreement: Baker would
assist Tupou in his efforts to maintain his independence; Tupou
would support Baker against his critics and mission superiors. It was
a partnership that was to last for seventeen years and to bring about
great changes in Tonga. At its most fundamental level it was a
partnership based on mutual interest and support, but it grew to be
more than this. Tupou came to rely upon Baker and to have the
warmest affection for him; Baker came to identify himself with
Tupou and his cause – an identification perhaps marred by humbug
and an eye for the main chance, but nevertheless productive of last-
ing benefit to Tonga. It was also of benefit to Baker, who had
become disillusioned with the missionary vocation and found in his

new role a moral armour that enabled him to meet the great on terms of equality. He became a Moses, leading his people to the promised land and able to shake his staff at Pharaoh.

Baker's first acts in his new role were concerned with changing Tupou's public image. Perhaps Baker felt that Europeans would be more impressed by a European-style monarch than by a native chief, or perhaps he was merely concerned with flattering Tongan dignity to secure his own position. Probably it was a combination of both these motives that led him to invest Tupou with the symbols of majesty in 1873. In Baker's view the first necessity for a king was a crown. The 1870 *fakataha* had already investigated this matter. The chiefs no doubt felt piqued when Cakobau of Fiji, regarded by Tongans as a semi-barbarian, had been formally crowned in 1867, and only the cost involved had prevented them from obtaining a crown for Tupou. Baker solved the problem with characteristic simplicity. He had a crown made in Sydney. It was not very costly and it served the purpose very well, despite the verdigris in its flutings. At the same time Baker presented the king with the Great Seal of Tonga and the Royal Standard. The seal, an ornate device containing a cross, a crown, a dove, three swords and three stars bore the legend *'Koe otua mo Toga ko Hoku Tofia'* (God and Tonga are my inheritance). The concept was undoubtedly Baker's, but the drafting was more than likely the work of some unknown Sydney artist, for the sketches of boats and buildings with which Baker sometimes illuminated his letters do not reveal an artistic talent equal to the task. The seal first appeared on government letters late in 1873, though it was not formally accepted until the *fakataha* met in 1874. The Royal Standard comprised the seal motif superimposed on the Tongan flag.

It was probably also at this time that Baker gave Tonga its national anthem. Moulton, some time before 1869, had written Tongan words to the German National Anthem (Haydn, Opus 76, no. 3) and this had been used as the Tongan anthem until this time. Baker replaced this with a beautiful melody of unknown origin to which words were set by 'Unga, Tupou's son. The first reported singing of this anthem dates from July 1874, but it was probably in use earlier.

Crowns, seals, and anthems had something of a comic opera flavour in the Tongan context, and Baker's activities at this stage were regarded by the Europeans as ridiculous but relatively innocuous. In November 1873, however, the traders suddenly found that from January 1874 they were to pay annual licence fees of five pounds for the right to trade, and this was a more serious matter. A meeting of Europeans was called by a Nuku'alofa trader, W. C. Young, to demand 'no taxation without representation' and twenty-three residents petitioned the king for the right to elect two Europeans to the annual *fakataha*. At the same time another of Baker's activities had aroused the indignation of the missionaries. The brethren were already disturbed by their Chairman's independent attitude and suspected that he had misrepresented their wishes at the 1873 Conference. The new affront was the launching of a government sugar plantation, worked under Baker's supervision and financed by Baker's money. The rules of the Wesleyan Missionary Society explicitly stated that 'no travelling preacher shall follow trade' and, accordingly, the missionaries called their Chairman to account at the December 1873 District Meeting. The meeting was a stormy one. Moulton charged Baker with interfering in politics, being virtually Government Secretary and manager of the sugar plantation, and with issuing false information to the previous Conference as to the views of the Friendly Islands' missionaries concerning the formation of an independent church. Baker, faced with the threat of a formal charge being preferred before Conference, agreed to wind up the sugar plantation, have a Government Secretary appointed and avoid direct interference in political matters. To the Committee, however, he defended himself volubly:

> All I have ever done is to give the King advice ... anything that
> has been done has been the King's act not mine. He may have

acted on my advice, but with himself has been the responsibility, and certainly I cannot see any harm in it. Shall I let him in times of perplexity and difficulty let him [sic] be guided by men who are sworn enemies of the *lotu* and all that is good – no.[6]

During 1874 Baker kept in the background. A Government Secretary was appointed. The first was Joseph Cocker, who had filled the post of British Consul in Tonga in the early 1860s. Cocker, however, was a trader and his sympathies lay with the Europeans. After a month or two he was replaced by J. P. Miller, who was a confirmed alcoholic and therefore happy to hold a sinecure and leave the work to Baker. The only real effect of the opposition of the traders and the missionaries was to drive Baker more firmly into the king's camp, where his influence, though exerted behind the scenes, continued to grow.

The Tongan government, under Baker's guidance, was showing a new confidence in its dealings with the Europeans. The most revealing sign of this was to be seen in its reply to the petition of the Europeans to elect representatives to the *fakataha*. The reply was subscribed with Cocker's signature – Baker had won his temporary support by lending two hundred and fifty pounds interest-free to his part-Tongan sons to enable them to set up as traders – but the substance of the reply came from Baker, as he later freely admitted.[7] The petition was refused and the petitioners were informed that only Tongan subjects could sit on the *fakataha*. If ... when Britain recognised Tonga, the petitioners should apply for Tongan naturalisation their request would be reconsidered. In the meantime, they could prove their *bona fides* by paying their taxes promptly. Concerning their protest about 'taxation without representation', they were informed that the Colony of Victoria imposed a heavy head tax on a certain class of aliens, and certainly did not allow them into Parliament.[8] The traders were incensed, and Young wrote in the margin of his copy of the reply: 'Classing us with Chinamen is a gratuitous insult'.[9]

The event which really crystallised Baker's position was the

British annexation of Fiji which occurred in October 1874. This event, long impending, confirmed Tupou's worst fears, and caused him to begin seeking some fuller and firmer guarantee of Tongan independence. Baker responded, and in December 1874 made a formal statement of his views at the Tongan District Meeting to his fellow missionaries and the Reverend Benjamin Chapman, who was visiting from Sydney. He told his audience that the two objects of his life were to make Tonga firstly a self-governing church, secondly an independent nation. These aims were developed and expounded in *Koe Boobooi,* which Baker began publishing late in 1874. The earliest surviving issue, dated March 1875, contained an explicit statement of his new position:

> The flag we have put up has two colours, and on it are to be found these words: Church and Government, which of course means Church and Government of Tonga.... We will no longer hide the purpose of our labour ... our aim is 'Keep Tonga for the Tongan'.

'Tonga for the Tongans' (*'Tonga Ma'a Tonga'*) became Baker's political slogan, and eventually the slogan of the government. Through 1875 Baker continued to expound the proposition. In the May 1875 *Koe Boobooi* he wrote: 'We speak of what we know will be bad for the future, and that is a big wave of incoming Europeans ... if they all settle here what will become of the Tongans? Will they overflow into the sea?' In June he reported the epidemic of measles which the visit of HMS *Dido* had introduced into Fiji in January 1875 and pressed for a quarantine law to prevent a similar occurrence in Tonga. He warned: 'The deaths of these Fijian people [the 40,000 measles victims] were caused by the surrender of the country to Britain'. When the Vava'u Quarterly Meeting of chiefs suggested that chiefs be empowered to grant land leases to Europeans for extended periods, provided the Europeans were 'good men', Baker criticised them publicly: 'It is clear that a man who gives the chiefs strong liquor is a good man in the chiefs' opinion', and when the

Ha'apai Quarterly Meeting elected three Europeans to sit as jurors on cases in which Europeans were involved, Baker lampooned the Ha'apai chiefs for abrogating the sovereign rights of Tonga.

Another aspect of Baker's policy of making Tonga a nation may be seen in his endeavours to introduce some of the 'benefits of civilisation' during this period. In March 1875 it was lavatories that were receiving his attention. Some time earlier the government had enacted that all landholders should build a privy. Baker discovered that one landholder living in Nuku'alofa had built his on his land in Vava'u two hundred miles away, while others used them to cook in or as storehouses for root vegetables. Baker called for rigorous government inspection. At the same time he was making attempts to diversify Tongan agriculture by introducing new cash crops to supplement the staple, copra. In April 1875, for instance, he advised his readers that he had given a consignment of peanuts to the government for distribution to interested landholders. Few of Baker's agricultural experiments actually took root, but a variety of banana is known in Tonga today as *misipeka* (Mr Baker), which is probably a mute testimony to one success (unless it is a snide sexual reference). It was also at this time, and under Baker's aegis, that work was commenced on several public buildings in Nuku'alofa, including a Court House and extensive additions to the Palace. A Government Treasury was also set up, and a Savings Bank was established with capital provided jointly by Baker and the government. This latter venture was of dubious propriety. Its main purpose was, in Baker's words, 'to advance deposits on something like a Building Society principle so as to enable the natives to build houses and get homes for themselves', and he claimed his motives in establishing it were purely philanthropic. He wrote:

> I was led away with the desire to benefit Tonga and the natives and advance the interests of my work ... my other thought, it was teaching the Tonga Government how to manage their finances.... As regards my thinking of making any profit by it ... I must deny in toto that ever such a thought entered my head.[10]

Such protests, however, must be viewed with deep suspicion. As virtual manager of the bank (Thorley, the nominal manager, was a hopeless drunkard), Baker did not let his love for Tonga interfere with ensuring a dividend of ten per cent on his capital. Asaeli Taufa, Makisi Tonga, Leka, and Tevita Lehauli were sold up and their town leases taken by Baker when they became indebted to the bank, apparently through not comprehending the nature of compound interest,[11] and the widow and child of Matekitonga, the late Governor of Vava'u, were left almost destitute when Baker ordered their effects sold to pay the chief's debt.[12] But with a little charity Baker may be credited with having the benevolent motives he claimed, as well as purely commercial ones.

All Baker's political activities during this period were but minor matters, however, compared with his work on a new Constitution for Tonga. This Constitution, which he devised and which was promulgated in November 1875, marked a major step in Tonga's progress towards becoming a modern civilised state, recognised as such by the Powers, and Baker had been working on it since he first began to advise the king. During his visit to Sydney at the end of 1872 he had had discussions about it with Sir Henry Parkes, the New South Wales Premier, and had also visited Edward Reeve, St Julian's successor as the Hawaiian Consul-General, seeking advice and assistance. By December 1873 he had begun work on the draft. During 1874 the draft was completed and submitted to a firm of lawyers in Auckland for rephrasing. In its final form it was presented to the *fakataha* which met in Nuku'alofa in September 1875.

By the time the *fakataha* met, the chiefs had been conditioned to expect some sweeping changes. Baker had made use of the pages of *Koe Boobooi* during 1875 to explain what a constitution was. It was like a Bible for the government, he suggested:

> It is a book of freedom. It is a book of rules for the administration of the country, and how the King must be appointed and his jurisdiction, and also the judges and magistrates.... When a constitution is in writing and in use, then we all are truly FREE.[13]

Moreover, the king made it quite clear in his speech at the opening session that he intended to accept Baker's advice. He told the chiefs:

> You are aware that our country's present form of government is dependent on me. My wishes are the laws. It is only I who select those who join this meeting and I also please myself who shall succeed to the chiefly positions, and I have power to change any title. But it appears to me that this was only suited to the dark period of Government. A new era in Tonga has arrived, an enlightened new epoch and I am prepared to give to Tonga a Constitution and I, with those who shall succeed me, will rule constitutionally and this Constitution will become the protection of Tonga for ever.[14]

The draft was accepted by the chiefs and became law on 4 November 1875.

The new Constitution was a long document of 132 articles. The first section was based almost entirely on the Hawaiian model. It contained a declaration of rights guaranteeing the fundamental freedoms of life, liberty and property, freedom of worship, freedom of speech, and freedom of the press. The equality of all men, chiefs and commoners, Tongans and Europeans, before the law was guaranteed, as was the right of adult males to elect representatives to a Legislative Assembly. In return for these privileges all adult males, Tongan and European, acknowledged the right of the state to exact taxes and jury service.

The second section dealt with the form of government which was to be set up. It was the king's prerogative to nominate the cabinet and governors and to appoint the chiefs. A Legislative Assembly was to be created composed of the cabinet, twenty of the important titleholders, thereafter to be classed as nobles, and twenty representatives of the people, elected by adult male franchise. The judiciary comprised a supreme court and circuit court, to which justices were appointed by the king, and police courts to which magistrates were appointed by the Assembly.

The third section was concerned with land tenure. The prohibition against the alienation of land was confirmed, and remained the first principle of Tongan land laws. Other clauses described a new system of tenure. The land in the kingdom was divided into two categories, town lands and bush or plantation lands. All town land was to be the property of the government who would lease town allotments (*api kolo*) for periods of twenty-one years to Tongans or Europeans dwelling in the town or village concerned. Bush lands were divided into *tofi'a*, or inheritances, vested either in the king or in individual nobles. Farms (*'api 'uta*) could be obtained by commoners by leasing them at rates fixed by the Legislative Assembly from the owner of the *tofi'a* concerned. Titleholders could also lease lands to Europeans, but permission for such leases had first to be granted by the cabinet: 'to prevent any chief acting foolishly in leasing the whole of his land to white residents and driving the Tongese into the sea'.

The Constitution, despite its length and sophistication, was to some extent an extension and consummation of earlier attempts in 1839, 1850 and 1862, to organise effective government in Tonga on liberal Western lines. It did not represent, therefore, a complete break with the past. Many features of the new instrument were completely novel to Tongans, however. One such feature was the arrangement for the succession. Before 1875 the succession to a title was controlled by the senior members of the *ha'a* (lineage), *kāinga* (tribe), or *fa'ahinga* (extended family) concerned, who chose the heir they considered most fitted for the position from among the lineal and collateral descendants or relatives of the previous titleholder. Tupou had received his *Tu'i Kanokupolu* title from his uncle, Josiah, though Josiah's son, Ma'afu, was alive. Thus according to Tongan usage the next heir to the title, and with it the Tongan throne, would probably have been Ma'afu, ruler of the Lau Islands in eastern Fiji. Tupou explained that Ma'afu had become a British subject with the cession of Fiji, and to pass on the succession to him would have endangered Tonga's independence. A lineal succession, moreover, was simpler and less liable to dispute. Tupou therefore nominated his son, 'Unga, illegitimate by Christian standards, as Crown Prince, with 'Unga's son Ngū as next in line. Similar arrangements were adopted for the succession of all hereditary titles, and even for the modest legacies of commoners.

Another new concept which the Constitution embodied was that of a limited monarchy. In the past the *fakataha* had merely served to advise the king, and when the king wished he could override its opposition, as had been demonstrated in 1862 when Tupou had emancipated the commoners despite opposition from the chiefs. Under the Constitution the king, in theory if not in actual practice, vested his sovereignty in parliament. The parliament itself was very different from the old *fakataha*. At the *fakataha* all titleholders were represented; in the new parliament only twenty titleholders, the new corps of hereditary nobles, could sit by right, while an equal number of elected representatives, who might well be commoners, sat with them.

The creation of the new nobility was one of the most surprising features of the Constitution, for it reversed the trends of the earlier codes. Since 1839 Tupou had been trying to limit the power of the chiefs by restricting their privileges over the commoners, by emphasising their duties towards the king, and most of all by assuming ownership of their lands. In the case of twenty of the more influential titleholders this process was now reversed. They were given noble titles and large estates, an hereditary seat in parliament and confirmation of their influence and privilege. A larger body of minor chiefs and *kau matāpule,* those who were not made nobles, were, however, reduced to the ranks in all but title.

The creation of a nobility was probably a move by Baker to enlist the support of the more powerful chiefs, but there is nevertheless a certain consistency in it. In 1862 Baker had tried to free the commoners from the exactions of the chiefs, but in practice this had not worked. The reason lay in the control of land. It is difficult to reconstruct the exact nature of land tenure before 1875, but it would seem that large areas were controlled by powerful chiefs (*hou 'eiki*) who allotted land to dependent lesser titleholders (*foto tehina* and *kau matāpule*) who were the heads of extended families (*ngaahi faʻahinga*), and they in turn allotted it to individual land-holders. Each of these transactions involved obligations on the recipient, so that while chiefs of all ranks had an effective sanction in their control over the distribution of land, the Emancipation Pro-clamation could not be made fully effective. Under the new land laws, however, landholding was a matter arranged directly between landholder and noble at rates specified by parliament, and all the intermediate transactions and obligations were eliminated. The new arrangement was therefore consistent with the 1862 proclamation, and in effect an attempt to make it practicable.

Baker's Constitution was, therefore, a major reform. There were, nevertheless, many who were critical. A. W. Mackay, an anti-Baker propagandist, described it, for instance, as 'the unsuitable, unwork-able and abortive constitution of 1875, which certainly reflects no credit on anyone connected with it'.[15] Alfred Maudslay, the British Vice Consul in Tonga in 1878, wrote: 'I have never met a native from the king down who pretended to understand it, and if one may form any judgment from the English translation this is little to be wondered at.'[16] The harshest criticism came from the British adviser in Tonga in 1890, Basil Thomson, who sneered: 'the constitution ... was written in English that would have disgraced a housemaid'.[17] These were, however, partisan views and reflect an element of intellectual snobbery and perhaps professional jealousy. The Tongans had an entirely different point of view. Tupou had said to the 1875 *fakataha*: 'May it [the Constitution] become the most precious treasure of this country'.[18] Tonga took him at his word. Twenty years later, in the interests of simplicity, Basil Thomson tried to amend some of Baker's phraseology, but his effort met with the most stubborn resistance. In some frustration he wrote:

> The *Konisitutone* [constitution] ... had been introduced by the missionaries and was intimately connected, they believed, with its outlandish fellow *Konisienisi* [conscience] and in some way it elevated their country to the level of one of the Great Powers.[19]

Tonga was proud of its Constitution; in fact as Thomson ruefully observed, 'the Tongans regarded it as Holy Writ'.[20]

In 1875 Baker also promulgated a new legal code. This code passed through the *fakataha* without much comment, probably because it contained little that was new; Baker had merely rephrased existing laws, integrating them in an ordered and comprehensive code. The new code, however, provoked a storm of criticism from British observers and Baker, as its author, was vilified. The main target of the detractors was the social and sumptuary laws embodied in it. For instance, under the new laws fornication and adultery were made criminal offences, and fines of twenty-five dollars and sixty dollars respectively were provided for offenders, causing Alfred Maudslay to say in 1879: 'The laws dealing with the relation of sexes have more the appearance of a missionary wishing to punish sin than a statesman wishing to prevent the increase of crime'.[21] Maudslay's comment was no doubt true, but the particular missionary at fault in this case was not Baker but the Reverend J. Thomas, a predecessor of forty years earlier. The Vava'u Code of 1839, in its first clause, had stated: 'The laws of this our land prohibit – murder, theft, adultery, fornication and the retailing of spirits', and Thomas, not Baker, was Tupou's adviser in 1839. Similarly the Code of 1850 provided three months' hard labour for offenders in each of these categories, and the Code of 1862 punished adultery by twelve months' labour and fornication by two months' labour. It is therefore apparent that the fine of sixty dollars (£12) provided in the new code for these offences was neither new nor, in comparison with previous penalties, harsh.

Other laws in the new code for which Baker was criticised were those prohibiting dancing and wrestling, with fines of five dollars and ten dollars respectively for offenders. Maudslay said of these: 'The most innocent amusements were tabooed, and laws passed especially to limit wrestling and dancing, although the dancing of the Tongans does not in any way offend against ordinary ideas of propriety'.[22] There is no doubt that Baker, like all Methodist missionaries in Tonga, did disapprove of dancing, for the dances, he claimed, were performed nude (by which he probably meant topless) and led, he believed, to lewdness and sexual excess. He was not responsible for the law prohibiting these pastimes, however. The 1850 Code, promulgated a decade before Baker's arrival in Tonga, contained the following clause:

> Let all people know that dancing is strictly forbidden, as well as all Heathen Customs; and if any are found practising such they shall be tried and on being proven guilty, work one month, and in case of repetition, two months.

The most bitter criticism of all was directed at the *Law on Tapa,* included in Baker's Code, by which, between 1876 and 1878, the manufacture and wearing of the native cloth was to be progressively eliminated. Consul Layard, who visited Tonga in February 1876, reported that this law was framed by Baker to ensure the house of Godeffroy a market for cotton cloth, on the sale of which Baker was supposed to receive a commission.[23] Miss Gordon Cummings wrote of her visit to Nuku'alofa in 1877:

> I regret to say that a considerable proportion of the people were like hideously dressed up apes.... Here the influence of certain persons interested in trade is so strong that the manufacture of tappa [*tapa*] is discouraged by every possible means.[24]

Criticisms like these were echoed and exaggerated by others. Yet on closer examination it is evident that not only was Baker not responsible for the *tapa* law, but that he was opposed to it when it was first promulgated. It was Tupou's idea to make his people dress *fakapapālangi* (European fashion) to prove to the outside world that Tongans were 'civilised'; Baker opposed the move because money spent on clothing meant so much less towards the mission collection. In fact, the scheme of forcing Tongans to buy European clothes, by prohibiting the manufacture of *tapa,* was conjured up by those traders

whose profits were suffering from the competition of the missionaries. They put their suggestion to Captain Nares of HMS *Challenger*
when he visited Tonga in 1874 and Nares in turn pressed the idea
on the king, who took it up enthusiastically. Baker's only connection
with the matter lay in his inducing the king to introduce the
measure gradually over a period of two years, and in this fashion it
was incorporated in the 1875 Code.[25]

The social and sumptuary laws were inherited by Baker from
previous legislators and, as his task was merely to rephrase and codify
the laws, they were included in his revised code. Nevertheless, he
was made to bear the responsibility as the 'root and framer of them
all', and his connection with them provided one of the excuses for
Sir Arthur Gordon to have him removed from Tonga in 1879.
Tupou, however, was immensely gratified by his new legal code
and Constitution. In June 1876 jubilee celebrations were held at
Nuku'alofa to mark the fiftieth anniversary of the introduction of
Christianity to Tonga. Here Tupou spoke to three thousand persons
assembled among pavilions and bunting on the *mala'e:*

> There are many things which ought to cause rejoicing today.
> Tonga is still owned by the Tongese. We are not subject to any
> land. Remember how Fiji is lost forever to the Fijians; and in all
> probability Samoa too ... the heathen nation has become
> Christian, barbarous men nearly civilised, churches and schools
> in all islands, a people set free, a Constitution given, laws
> established, Courts of Justice, various offices of Government,
> roads all through the land, stores springing up in every place and
> all the adjuncts of a civilised country. I hardly feel able to express
> my feelings today. I feel my heart burning within me when I
> think what Tonga has accomplished.[26]

Baker could justly claim a large share of the credit for these
improvements of which Tupou was so proud. He had also won a
deserved place in the affections of the king and the majority of

Tongans. His ways may have been devious, and his motives some-times dubious, but it would be difficult to dispute the reality of his achievements.

CHAPTER VI

THE END OF
A MISSIONARY CAREER

TUPOU HAD accepted the legal and constitutional reforms of
1875 not because he saw any moral virtue in surrendering his
autocratic power, nor because he believed that the *fakapapālangi*
(white man's way) was intrinsically superior to the *fakatonga* (Tongan
way), but because he was convinced that the only way to ensure
Tonga's independence was to have it recognised by the Powers,
and that the Powers would only recognise a state which could show
tangible evidence of being 'civilised'. He had learned, in Oliver's
phrase, 'that the only way to remain Tongan is to appear western'.[1]
This assessment proved correct, and within a year of the promulgation of the Constitution Germany recognised Tonga as an independent sovereign state. Similar recognition by the British followed
in 1878. For Tupou this acknowledgment of Tonga's stature was
the fulfilment of a life's work, and the object which he had been
striving to achieve since St Julian had advised him in 1854 that only
thus could Tonga's independence be assured. Most of the credit,
however, belongs to Shirley Baker, for it was he who had created
the political structure which made possible the realisation of Tupou's

aspirations; he who had publicised Tonga's new condition as a 'civilised' state; and he who had conducted, or at least initiated, the negotiations which led to the treaties of recognition.

One month after the promulgation of the Constitution Baker began publishing an English language newspaper, the *Tonga Times,* the expressed intention of which was 'to bring the Friendly Islands more prominently before other parts of the world'. In the first editorial he wrote:

> We believe that when the actual position of these islands is properly made known they will have the sympathy and admiration of all well wishers of native races, for in no other part of the world do we think there is to be found among native races the same desirable state of things as are [*sic*] to be seen on Tonga – that of a native race relying on its own innate strength, trying to raise itself as a Government among the nations of the earth.[2]

The theme was to be developed in subsequent issues.

At the same time Baker began soliciting the representatives of foreign governments, seeking treaties which would recognise Tonga. The first overtures were made to Baron von Schleinitz, the commander of the German warship *Gazelle,* which visited Nuku'alofa in December 1875. A conference took place on the ship attended by Tupou, Baker, von Schleinitz and Theodore Weber. Baker reported in the *Tonga Times:*

> With regard to this interview we must be silent; but we believe we are at liberty in saying that the result of the visit of the man-of-war will be the acknowledgment of Tonga as a nation by the German Empire, and a treaty between Germany and Tonga.[3]

Similar proposals appear to have been made to E. L. Layard, the British Consul for Fiji and Tonga, who visited Tonga in February

1876. Layard, however, was unsympathetic, and Baker did not press him. When a more amenable British official, Commodore A.H. Hoskins, visited Tonga in May 1876, Baker made better progress. The Commodore was impressed with the developments he saw in Tonga and sympathetic towards Baker and his policies. He reported to the Admiralty:

> I feel much sympathy with a native government struggling to become independent and sufficient to itself in a peaceful development formed on civilised usages ... The Government and Constitution of Tonga have never been officially recognised, though it has been the custom of our ships to pay the King the honour of a royal salute.... It might not be without its good effect in their dealings with white men if such a recognition were now officially given to them.[4]

In London Hoskins' recommendation that Tonga be formally recognised was coldly received. The British government was preparing an Order in Council creating the new office of High Commissioner for the Western Pacific and giving this officer wide jurisdiction over British subjects in 'uncivilised' Pacific Island territories. Lord Derby, of the Foreign Office, and Lord Carnarvon, of the Colonial Office, agreed that to recognise Tonga as a 'civilised' state would partly negate the usefulness of that order, and possibly hamper the High Commissioner in the exercise of his judicial functions. On these grounds they decided to withhold recognition.

In the meantime, however, the request which Baker had made to von Schleinitz in December 1875 had been received favourably in Berlin, and as a result the warship *Hertha* arrived at Nuku'alofa in October 1876 to negotiate a treaty, which was signed on 1 November 1876. Its terms guaranteed perpetual peace and friendship between Tonga and Germany, and provided guarantees of freedom of religion, trade, and travel for nationals of one party in the territory of the other, and reciprocal trading and shipping rights. In return for recognising Tonga, Germany was granted the right to establish

a naval coaling station in the magnificent harbour at Vava'u, subject
to the reciprocal right of Tongan warships to refuel in German ports!
Baker's name appeared on the treaty only as interpreter to the
Tongan plenipotentiary, 'Uiliame Tungī, but he was really the prime
mover, a fact acknowledged by Germany when it offered to confer
on him the decoration of Knight of the Red Eagle (3rd Class) for
his part in the proceedings.

News of the German action caused some embarrassment in
London, and in February 1877 the Colonial Office suggested to the
Foreign Office:

> ... as complaints may be expected to arise in the Australian
> colonies if British subjects are not secured for commercial
> purposes in Tonga the treatment of the 'most favoured nation',
> it might be perhaps advisable that a treaty between Her
> Majesty and King George should be negotiated by Sir A.
> Gordon.[5]

The Foreign Office, however, decided that a provisional declaration
securing 'most favoured nation' treatment to British subjects, shipping and trade would suffice, and Sir Arthur Gordon, who was the
Consul General for the Western Pacific as well as High Commissioner and Governor of Fiji, was instructed to secure such a
declaration from Tupou. To this end Gordon visited Tonga in April
1878 but found, to his chagrin, that the king would make no
arrangements without the advice of Baker, who was absent in
Sydney at the time. Gordon spent some time in discussions with
the king, and became convinced that Tupou would make no concessions to Britain unless Britain also conceded formal recognition
to Tonga, and that for his purposes nothing less than a formal treaty
would be necessary. He wrote to Lord Derby:

> [Tupou] is anxious that the Government of Tonga should be
> recognised by England in the same manner that it has been by
> Germany, and with this wish − a very natural one on his part

– it would, I think, be best to comply. Tonga has made
advances in civilisation, and established systems of government
and legal administration which fairly entitle her to such
recognition. Moreover, without some formal engagement of
the nature of a treaty with the Tongan Government it will be
impossible for the High Commissioner's Court to enter into
the exercise of its function at all without dispute and, possibly,
resistance on the part of the Tongan judicial authorities.[6]

Gordon's Vice-Consul and Deputy Commissioner, Alfred Maudslay
took advantage of a temporary breach between Baker and Tupou
to obtain a provisional agreement in September 1878, and when
the British government finally granted permission to negotiate a
treaty Gordon sailed to Tonga to conclude it. The treaty, signed on
29 November 1879, recognised Tonga and declared perpetual peace
and friendship between the parties. British subjects were guaranteed
'most favoured nation' treatment and were made amenable to the
High Commissioner's court for all offences except those against 'the
municipal laws of Tonga not cognisable as such under British Law'.

Thus by November 1879 Tonga had been recognised as an independent sovereign state by the two paramount powers in the Pacific,
and Tupou had been given the reassurance and security he had been
seeking. But the *éminence grise* who had done most to bring about
this consummation was not present to witness the final act. Baker
had been recalled to Sydney a few weeks before the signing of the
British treaty, for while his policies had led to Tonga becoming 'a
nation among the nations of the world', they had brought only
disgrace and humiliation on himself.

By the beginning of 1876 Baker seemed more secure than he
had been at any time since he returned to Tonga as Chairman in
1869. His ecclesiastical reorganisation had proved successful and the
results of the 1875 Jubilee Collections seemed to insure him against
much interference by the Missionary Committee. The missionary
staff itself had been reduced to three; of these the Reverend J.B.
Watkin and the Reverend J. Thomas could be relied upon for loyal

support while even Moulton was being conciliatory. Over the preceding year Baker had been making determined efforts to win Moulton's confidence; he had been made a trustee of the Church leases, and auditor of the Bank of Tonga; while in December 1875 Baker had supported a move to allow him to travel to England at the expense of the Mission for the purpose of translating the Scriptures into Tongan and seeing them through the press. These efforts were succeeding. In May 1875 Moulton had written: 'The folks next door [the Bakers] have been very kind and I hope the gulf is getting bridged over'.[7] In August 1875 he wrote: 'Mr. Baker and myself are working harmoniously in our respective spheres and helping one another where we can'.[8] He had even come to accept the moves towards self-government for the Mission with some good grace.

At the same time, Baker was enjoying success in his political life. The Constitution and code of laws had just been promulgated and Tupou, and apparently all Tonga, looked to him with confidence, respect and even a little adulation.

In his personal affairs Baker was also prospering. His family, by this time, numbered seven children, of whom the eldest boy, Shirley, was at Wesley College in Melbourne. He had acquired considerable means, for at a time when a British working man's wages were less than a pound a week, Baker's account at the Bank of Tonga could at the same time support an investment of £1,500 in the bank, a loan of £1,200 to the government, a loan of £600 to the Mission and an unknown number of private loans to individual Tongans.[9] His new status demanded something more than the coconut thatch house in which he had lived since 1870, so he had begun building a large two-storeyed weatherboard house, the most imposing building in Tonga excepting only the king's palace.

To Baker then everything seemed to be going satisfactorily, and his sense of well-being was adequately expressed in a letter to Chapman, where he wrote:

> For the sake of my family I ought to leave the islands, but I feel as long as King George lives I must stay in Tonga, not

because I am anxious for office, as some say, for I have impudence to think I could fight my way in the colonies, hence it is not also because I feel I could not get on – but from a conscientious conviction I am where the Lord would have me be.[10]

Baker's security was, however, less soundly based than he imagined. His activities, and in particular his connection with the Constitution and code of laws, his methods of fund-raising for the jubilee, and his diplomatic overtures to Germany, had provoked determined opposition from four separate directions: from the traders, from his missionary colleagues, from certain groups among the Tongans, and from the British Governor of Fiji, Sir Arthur Gordon. Over the next four years successive attacks from each of these quarters were to shatter his confidence, destroy his influence, and finally cause him to be recalled from Tonga with his reputation in tatters.

The first assault came from the traders, whose mounting hostility has been described earlier. The reason for their opposition was basically economic: the efficiency of Baker's collecting methods diverted to the Mission, and thence directly to Godeffroys, copra which the traders felt should have passed through their hands. In 1875 they had been forced to borrow money, either from Baker or from Godeffroys, to re-lend to the Tongans on collecting day. This ensured that a share of the trade passed through their hands and that they could stay in business, but their position was precarious; they took the risks, while the Mission reaped most of the rewards. A further consequence of the system was that the Tongans were left with very little surplus money after making their mission contributions, and were therefore unable to buy trade goods, thus depriving the Europeans of their second important source of income. One can hardly wonder that the whites were antagonistic, or that they viewed with suspicion the cordial relations between the Mission and Godeffroys. There is little doubt that Baker gave the mission business to Godeffroys because that firm offered a demonstrably superior service, but the whites were quick to reach other conclusions. They were aware that in Samoa allegations had been made that an American adventurer, Steinberger, had made an arrangement with Godeffroys to give them a monopoly on Samoan copra in return for a commission, and they suspected that Baker had made a similar arrangement. There was even one, Robert Hanslip, a clerk in Weber's employ, who claimed to have seen a draft of such an agreement in Godeffroys' office waiting to be signed by Weber and Baker.[11]

Superimposed on this situation came Baker's Constitution which provided for equality between Tongans and Europeans, made Europeans amenable to Tongan courts and to the rigorous moral restrictions of the Tongan law, prevented them from buying land and made them liable to taxation. If there were any doubts about Baker's intentions he dispelled them in the first edition of the *Tonga Times,* published in January 1876. In the editorial he wrote:

> The object we have set before us and end to be obtained is to try, by training and education, to make the Tongans a nation among nations, governed by Tongans, in fact 'Tonga for Tonga'. We trust our European friends will not be offended by these remarks ... [but] we must ever remember that we are but strangers in Tonga and that the Tonguese [sic] are the only legitimate citizens of Tonga.... With regard to the land we need not remark what are our views for they are well known. We hope the day will never dawn when one inch of Tongan soil shall be alienated by purchase from the Tongans.[12]

'These impertinent remarks of the editor of the Times', Joseph Cocker reported to Layard, 'causes considerable ill feelings, and meets with that contempt it richly disservs [sic]'.[13] They were at least sufficient to cause the traders to put aside their mutual rivalries and unite in a common front against Baker. Their opportunity came in February 1876 when E.L. Layard, the British Consul in Fiji, visited Tonga. He arrived on 12 February and, on 16 February, twenty-two whites petitioned him to appoint to Tonga a consul to 'make a stand against the overweening influence of the missionaries which is rampant here'.[14] Layard was very sympathetic towards the complaints. He had heard in Samoa and Fiji some extraordinary stories of Baker's activities, which predisposed him to accept the accounts given by the 'beach' in Tonga. Moreover, when he asked Moulton, the traders' criticisms were endorsed by an apparently unimpeachable witness. Layard therefore returned to Fiji convinced that the complaints and accusations made against Baker were genuine. He had no authority to take direct action, but in March he wrote a long dispatch to the Foreign Office listing many charges against Baker. Baker, he claimed, ruled the king completely:

> The old King is at least seventy-six years of age and though of vigorous intellect ... is entirely subservient to Mr. Baker's influence. I was informed that Mr. Baker had, on some occasion, saved his life by his medical skill; and this, together with his spiritual supremacy as his religious instructor, has given him his hold over the old man's mind. He will do nothing without Mr. Baker's consent, and as the Chiefs, whether in or out of Council, are subservient to the King, it follows that Mr. Baker is virtually ruler of Tonga.

This power, Layard reported, Baker used entirely for his own aggrandisement and enrichment and to the detriment of every white man, except his own special party, in the islands. In the first place he had conspired with the German firm to give them a monopoly of Tongan copra, in return for a commission; Baker was, he claimed:

> a trader in disguise, and in league with the firm of Messrs. Godeffroy Brothers of Hamburg, in whose favour he obtains (or makes) concessions of every kind, and into whose stores he diverts the streams of copra poured into the mission treasury, receiving a percentage on the same for himself.

Secondly, Baker had used his influence to prevent the appointment of a properly qualified medical practitioner to the government service in Tonga, even though the whites had guaranteed fifty pounds per annum towards his salary. He had done this because he sought to retain for himself the emoluments of the office, which provided one of the most lucrative sources of his private income. Layard asserted:

> Mr. Baker refuses to administer a dose of epsom salts without his fee of a dollar and a half ... on one occasion when an unfortunate native blew his hand off and was bleeding to death from severed arteries he actually declined to attend him until five dollars were given as a fee ... I myself saw a receipt for ten dollars for medical attendance (and medicine) on a European.

Layard was also very critical of Baker's political activities and the organisation he had created. Constitutional government was, he declared, 'a farce', the judiciary was '*ex parte*' and the decisions of the courts 'often most amusingly illogical'. He was equally critical of Baker's legislation. He reported that the inheritance law, making 'Unga, instead of Ma'afu, Tupou's successor, would cause chaos in Tonga on the death of the king. He claimed that the new forms of leasehold which Baker had drawn up, were 'couched in such language that a dishonest landlord might procure the forfeiture of any lease by a little trickery'. He drew attention to the sumptuary law prohibiting the manufacture of *tapa*, claiming that it was an oppressive act, intended solely to increase the profits of Godeffroys by forcing the Tongans to buy the cotton cloth they imported.

Layard's most bitter criticisms were levelled at Baker's missionary pursuits. He reported that Baker had resettled the whole population of 'Ata (Pylstaart) on 'Eua, because it incommoded him to travel to the former island to supervise these people. His major criticism, however, was concerned with the missionary collections. He described in detail the manner in which Baker extracted money from his congregations, his blandishments, the stimulus he provided by lending money at the church door, and above all the iniquities of the *sivi*, Baker's most successful method of fund-raising. Through these knavish means, he reported, Baker had obtained £17,000 from his flock in 1875. He concluded: 'One's ears ring with the denunciation, "My house shall be called the house of prayer, but ye have made it a den of thieves."'[15]

There was more than a grain of truth in many of Layard's charges, but there was also much that was mendacious. Baker did wield great influence, but solely because his advice was given only when it was sought, and when given was shrewd, sound and consistent with Tupou's aspirations. When Moulton, who possessed the same religious authority as Baker, gratuitously offered the king advice, it was ignored.

It was true that Baker sold the mission copra to Godeffroys, but the only evidence that he received a commission on it is the unsworn testimony of Robert Hanslip, one of the least reliable of the whites. On the other hand both Weber and his factor at Nuku'alofa, Thomas Trood, swore affidavits that no agreement existed between Baker and the Godeffroy firm. Weber's denial was positive and unequivocal. He stated:

> I ... solemnly declare and state without any reservation upon my honour and conscience that the Revd. S. W. Baker is not receiving, and has never received in any way whatever, neither from the said J. C. Godeffroy & Sons, nor from myself, nor from any of their representatives, directly or indirectly, any commission, gratification, present or any other like consideration of any description whatsoever, that the said Revd S. W. Baker never has even in the remotest intimated any request to any such effect, and that he has neither ever been offered anything of the kind.[16]

This certainly has a ring of conviction about it; either Baker was innocent or the German Consul-General was a consummate liar. Moreover there is corroborative evidence to support Weber's word.

In March 1875, for instance, Godeffroys detained their vessel, the *Samoa,* for a considerable time in Nuku'alofa to allow two mission families to come aboard, and then transported them to Sydney, all without charge. This, and other favours, were performed by Godeffroys to retain the Mission's good will – hardly necessary if Baker were a paid operative. Furthermore, there was no need for Godeffroys to pay Baker, for the Mission could not dispose of its copra other than through the German firm, and ordinary business principles would prevent Weber paying Baker for produce which would come to him anyway.

With regard to Layard's claims about Baker's unethical behaviour as a physician, it seems clear that while Baker probably did use his influence to dissuade the king from employing a properly trained doctor, and while he probably did enjoy a substantial income from his own doctoring of Tongans, the examples of his avarice cited by Layard were pure fabrication. Baker had accepted ten pounds for treating W. C. Young for a venereal infection, but only when this was pressed upon him by Trood, who considered it absurd to treat Europeans without charging, as was Baker's normal custom. The traders collected the money among themselves, pressed it upon Baker, obtained a receipt, and then with rather transparent guile offered it to Layard as evidence of Baker's cupidity. Similarly, the story of Baker's refusing to treat the boy whose hand had been blown off until he was paid his fee is bogus. An affidavit by Sione Fetokai, the father of the boy concerned, reveals that Baker neither asked for, nor was paid, anything for attending his son. The boy was given ten dollars by a German trader, but he kept it for himself.[17]

Similarly, Layard's criticisms of Baker's political activities included many misrepresentations. It is curious that Baker should have been blamed for the prohibition on *tapa*-making for, as has been pointed out earlier, this measure had been adopted at the request of the traders, and had been included in the new code only on Tupou's insistence, and even then in a modified form.

Perhaps the most absurd item in Layard's report concerned the

'Ata people, who had been moved to 'Eua by Tupou in 1865. The reason for the move, however, had not been missionary convenience, but the ravages of Peruvian slave raiders upon this isolated community.

Layard had been on somewhat safer ground when he criticised Baker's methods of fund-raising, but even this was misrepresented. The 1875 collection amounted to about fifteen thousand pounds, not seventeen thousand pounds as Layard claimed, and this was an extraordinary collection connected with the jubilee of the mission. To report the frenzied collecting which characterised that occasion as if it were normal practice was less than just.

It was because of the patent falsehoods in Layard's charges that Baker was able to ride out the storm. On receipt of the dispatch from Layard the Colonial Office, on the advice of the Foreign Office, communicated the substance of the charges to the Wesleyan Missionary Society in London, which, in turn, sought an explanation from the Australian body. Chapman, the mission secretary in Sydney, informed Baker of the charges and demanded that he reply to them.

Baker had been aware that strictures had been made upon his conduct, for at the end of February 1876 Weber visited Tonga and learned the general nature of the complaints from several German traders who had been party to the petition to Layard. Weber apparently informed Baker of the complaints that had been made and clearly outlined his own attitude in a note to him:

> All the foreigners in these islands are in every regard largely indebted to your exertions, and also the Tongans, whose welfare and progress is owing in a great measure to your zealous endeavours on their behalf, and it must be sincerely regretted that the late unjust proceedings took place at all.[18]

Although Baker was thus forewarned of the complaints made about him, he could not, of course, know the specific charges which Layard would prefer. For several months he could only fulminate generally on the nature of his opposition. Early in May 1876 he wrote to Chapman:

> The Europeans want to have native women and drink *ad libitum,* and because they cannot get it I am maligned, for I am not afraid to speak of their doings and warn the natives against such vices.[19]

A little later he added:

> Whilst I am here no one shall stop my tongue in declaiming against the vices of the Europeans, their brothels, their grog shops which are decimating the natives. Others speak, I know, but do nothing. I both speak and do, and will do all in my power to counteract the grog-selling to the natives. I know I am hated by many an European, let him hate me he knows I am justified and what is the goodwill or otherwise of evil men.[20]

He was particularly bitter about Moulton, who had sided with the traders, and he wrote in June 1876:

> There would have been nothing had it not been for Mr. Moulton, but as he was, so he is, and ever will be – alas that I should be the obstacle in his way of making a name.[21]

In September 1876, however, he finally received Chapman's letter informing him of the precise charges made by Layard. His immediate reactions were summed up in a note which he sent to Chapman soon after:

> I cannot trust my feelings in reference to it now – so disgusted am I – when I see so many names on it who owe their lives to me – others whom I have cured, and some actually doctoring when they signed it for venereal disease – others again

who are living in open concubinage, some with other men's
wives.... W. Parker who drew out the petition and signed it
is a Roman Catholic.[22]

But with the full text of the strictures before him he was able to
answer the charges directly, a task made easier by the many false
and scurrilous statements which Layard had included in his report.
In October 1876 Baker wrote his reply on twenty-seven pages of
closely written foolscap. He dealt with the accusations seriatim,
backing his explanations with sworn statements from the king and
from Weber, and at the end was able to protest, quite convincingly:

> Mr. Layard's whole dispatch is a most garbled statement
> containing in part the grossest falsehoods. It is no use for Mr.
> Layard to say he was informed so – a person in Mr. Layard's
> position, though he may choose to associate with beach-
> combers, yet he has no right to repeat their gossip without
> first ascertaining its truth.[23]

Baker's refutation was not sent to London, but the main points
were included in a letter from Benjamin Chapman to the parent
society defending Baker and the Australian body's management of
the Mission in Tonga. His letter concluded: 'We hope that his reply
to the charges contained in the dispatch will be to you as satisfactory
as it appears to us'.[24] By the time Chapman's letter, forwarded by
the Missionary Society in London, reached the Colonial Office,
support for Baker had been forthcoming from other sources. Commodore Hoskins had visited Tonga soon after Layard, and his report,
forwarded to the Colonial Office by the Admiralty, contradicted
much that Layard had said. Hoskins praised the work of the missionaries in Tonga, especially Baker's alterations to the laws and
Constitution. The discomfiture of the Colonial Office was increased
on the receipt of a dispatch from Sir Arthur Gordon commenting
on the affair. Gordon had taken over Layard's functions, and the
latter, before leaving Fiji, had given him a copy of the charges

against Baker. In October 1876 Gordon wrote to the Colonial Office drawing attention to several inaccuracies and inconsistencies in Layard's dispatch, and expressing doubts as to the impartiality of his informants and the plausibility of their accusations. Faced with this rebutting evidence Lord Carnarvon, of the Colonial Office, concluded that Layard's charges were based upon inaccurate reports, to which a less ready credence should have been given and Lord Derby, of the Foreign Office, sensible of having stirred up a hornets' nest, resolved not to make any further communication upon the subject.

Baker had survived the first determined threat to unseat him, but even before this was apparent he was facing a second assault, this time from his missionary colleagues. He had always displayed a certain high-handedness towards the other missionaries, and the tendency had been encouraged by his growing power and influence. By 1875 he had come to look upon himself as a sort of bishop, with wider powers and more exalted station than the doctrines of Wesley strictly allowed, and among the close-knit and isolated band of missionaries, where small differences loomed large and frustrations found few outlets, it was natural that this attitude should arouse resentment. Layard's inquiries provided the catalyst that set this resentment working.

By 1876 there were four missionaries in Tonga, Baker, Moulton, Watkin and Thomas. Between Baker and Moulton there was an antipathy of long standing, although a partial reconciliation had been effected in 1875. Under Layard's prompting, however, the old discord was revived, and relations between the two returned to normal: a state of open hostility. Watkin, on the other hand, had always supported Baker but, by the beginning of 1876, he too had begun to waver. The occasion was Baker's growing political power and especially his contribution to the Constitution and laws of 1875. Between January and June 1876 Watkin's letters to Chapman all contain complaints about Baker's high-handed attitude in preparing the Constitution without reference to the other missionaries. Then, towards the end of 1876, Moulton visited Ha'apai and stayed for a

Reverend Shirley Waldemar Baker
(1836 – 1903)
Auckland City Libraries (N.Z.)

ABOVE: Zion.
'The hill itself was bare
except for a large thatch
building on the summit.
This was Zion Church,
the spiritual centre of
Methodism in the
Friendly Isles.'
*The Museum of New Zealand
Te Papa Tongarewa
(Burton Bros 7494)*

LEFT:
Elizabeth Baker (nee
Powell): the 'beautiful
and accomplished girl'
who married Shirley
Baker in 1859.
Mitchell Library

Tupou I (Tāufa'āhau), King of Tonga
The Museum of New Zealand / Te Papa Tongarewa
(Burton Bros 7629)

Inside the Tongan-built Church at Lifuka.
Alexander Turnbull Library, F22551 1/2

Tupou College (*c.*1884) 'Although the seventh commandment was
preached at the college, it was flagrantly not being practised there.'
Alexander Turnbull Library, C21952

few weeks as Watkin's guest. Baker later claimed that Moulton used this opportunity to influence Watkin against him, and this was probably the case; certainly by December 1876 Watkin was supporting Moulton and opposing his Chairman.

The most determined opposition, however, came from Thomas, the missionary at Vava'u. Prior to the District Meeting of December his application to return to Sydney had been refused by the Chairman on the grounds that no replacement was available. Thomas's wife was pregnant, and his natural anxiety over this was increased by his isolation at Vava'u and the lack of any proper medical advice. This state of affairs was reported by Baker in January 1876. He wrote: 'Thomas will not remain the year out. He has got unhinged ... he believes his wife has all kinds of imaginable diseases'.[25]

As a result of Baker's refusal to allow Thomas to return to Australia the latter conceived a deep antagonism towards his Chairman, and thus when Layard visited Vava'u in February 1876, he found Thomas ready to confirm the most damaging allegations about him. When a short time later Baker sought to move Joel Nau, one of Thomas's Tongan ministers, to 'Eua, in order to strengthen his own circuit, Thomas withheld the letter for six weeks, and when finally Baker sent a messenger to collect Joel, Thomas wrote to the President of the Conference complaining of victimisation. Finally, Thomas began attacking Baker's policies publicly, and told an audience in Vava'u that while Baker's slogan was 'Tonga for Tonga', his was 'Tonga for Britain'; that he hoped Britain would soon annex Tonga; and that if he remained in the group he would work for that end. Nothing could have aroused Tupou's indignation more effectively, and Thomas left Tonga in January 1877 with a warning that if he ever came back he would be arraigned on a treason charge. Before he left, however, he charged Baker before the December 1876 District Meeting with meddling in the politics of Tonga, with overthrowing the former laws and with being virtually the king. Moulton and Watkin supported Thomas and the meeting resolved that Baker's actions were opposed to the Instructions to Missionaries, and calculated to produce discord among the brethren and to injure the work of God. The matter was referred to the Conference, which was to convene in January 1877.[26]

Baker had no wish to appear before the Conference so soon after the disturbance caused by Layard's complaints, so he excused himself on the grounds that he could not leave the king, who was seriously ill. During 1877 he sought to have the charges dismissed. He described Thomas as 'a young man, green from his market garden without hardly any education', and his charges as 'a lot of frivolous nonsense which any schoolboy ought to be ashamed to put on paper'. From Thomas's successor in Vava'u he obtained very damaging evidence concerning his maladministration and mis-appropriation of funds and forwarded it to the Committee, and from the king he obtained a declaration that if the charges against him were pursued it would be 'tantamount to admitting that your missionaries are in fact agents of your Empire for the acquisition of territories'. The Committee, however, was obdurate and insisted that Baker appear at the January 1878 Conference to answer Thomas's charges.[27]

Accordingly, Baker journeyed to Sydney and attended the Conference, which examined the charges against him in closed session. As a result he was reappointed Chairman of the Tonga District and his right to give assistance to the king was confirmed, though not without reservations. But behind the closed doors he was evidently severely criticised. When he returned to Tonga the newly appointed British Consul remarked: '... although the Con-ference whitewashed him publicly I fancy he caught it in private, and is by no means as firm as he used to be'.[28] In fact Baker's confidence was so badly shaken that he had decided to resign, and in July, shortly after his return to Tonga, he advised Chapman that as soon as he had made proper provision for his current ventures he would retire from the mission field. He added:

> As long as I felt yourself, together with the President and others whose opinions I esteem had confidence in me I did not care what I had to go through or what I had to suffer....

I feel I no longer have that confidence.... I have worked hard,
done my utmost for the Mission cause, but I have never
worked to get the praise of men, but of my Master, had I
tried to get the thanks of the fathers and brethren then I must
confess I have most singularly failed.[29]

Baker was not to be permitted to effect so gentle and honourable
a disengagement. Even while he was discussing his resignation, the
British High Commissioner and Consul-General for the Western
Pacific, Sir Arthur Gordon, was working to have him removed from
Tonga. Gordon's opposition evidently resulted from Baker's flir-
tation with Germany, as a result of which German influence in
Tonga was steadily increasing. It was not that Gordon sought British
annexation of Tonga, for when New Zealand's Sir George Grey
suggested annexation, Gordon protested that it would be scandalous
to interfere with Tonga's independence. Moreover, it was owing to
Gordon's offices that Britain formally recognised Tonga's independence by treaty. Gordon, however, did seek a preponderating British
influence in Tonga, which he felt was essential to safeguard the
British position in Fiji. The home authorities agreed with this view
and Gordon was instructed by the Colonial Office:

... to impress upon the King of Tonga that, as his country is
affected by the interests of Great Britain more largely and more
intimately than by the interests of any other country, Her
Majesty's Government, while deprecating any desire to gain
exclusive privileges in Tonga, considers that he should be
prepared to listen to their wishes, as expressed through you,
with especial favour.[30]

Since November 1876, however, it was the wishes of the
German government to which Tupou seemed to be listening with
special favour. Germany had been granted a naval coaling station in
Vava'u by the treaty through which she recognised Tonga. Shortly
afterwards the management of Tonga's commercial affairs in

Australia was put in the hands of Ludwig Sahl, the German Consul in Sydney, and, in September 1877, the Tongan government sought an exequatur for Sahl to act as Tongan Consul in New South Wales. These indications of the growing influence of Germany in Tongan affairs were deeply disturbing to Gordon. When he discussed the matter with the Marquis of Salisbury in 1879, Salisbury advised him:

> We should do all we can to keep the Germans off Tonga.... The real remedy is to increase your own power there. Political nature abhors a vacuum. If we leave any room in the heart of Tonga for a second affection, Messrs. Godeffroy will fill it.[31]

Evidently Gordon had come to the same conclusion eighteen months earlier, and his visit to Tonga in April 1878 was intended as the first step in a campaign to replace German influence in Tonga with his own. Gordon found, however, that the position of adviser to Tupou was already filled. The king listened politely to his advice, but refused to consider his proposed convention between Tonga and Britain without consulting Baker, who was absent in Sydney at the time, answering Thomas's charges before the Conference. Gordon came to his own conclusions about relations between Tupou and Baker which, he wrote:

> ... reminded me of those between Louis XIII and Richelieu. He writhes under his tyranny, but cannot and will not shake it off. That he had no love for him is plain enough; but he is bound to him partly by fear and partly by feelings of gratitude and honour. His fear is twofold. He dreads the debacle Baker's removal might cause.... But his apprehensions are also personal; for Baker, who is his doctor as well as his chaplain, prime minister and banker, has instilled in him the belief that he will certainly die if Baker be not at hand to prescribe for him. He feels also, and it is true, that Baker has served him zealously, if not well, and has strong claims on his forbearance and support.[32]

Gordon undoubtedly concluded that he would have to rid Tupou of this turbulent priest in order to improve his own position in Tonga. Any scruples he might have had about taking such a step were overcome by the distaste he felt for Baker's activities, the evidence of which was everywhere to be seen.

Baker's policies in Tonga were the antithesis of Gordon's ideals. Baker was a missionary, and accepted without hesitation the axiom that a missionary's task was to 'alter' and 'improve' the people among whom he worked. To Baker, as to most missionaries, the model for personal behaviour was the earnest, non-conformist Englishman, while the model of enlightened government was British parliamentary democracy; he had tried to reconstruct Tongan society to conform to these criteria, his efforts being embodied in the Constitution and code of 1875. Gordon, on the other hand, was opposed to the missionary objects of 'progress' and 'improvement', where these meant sudden change. He believed that the way to maintain native vigour and self-respect was to retain, with as little alteration as possible, native customs, social and political institutions, and patterns of authority. He had written:

> It is manifest that the more native policy is retained, native agency employed, and change avoided until naturally and spontaneously called for, the less likely are these results [loss of self respect, industry and vigour] to follow. Most of all it is essential to abstain from seeking hastily to replace native institutions by unreal imitations of European models.[33]

His policy in Fiji was based upon these principles. Gordon viewed with repugnance the changes Baker had wrought in Tonga. The best he could say of Nuku'alofa was: 'it somewhat resembles a small colonial or American watering place'; of the population: 'they wear chiefly European clothes and ape, more or less successfully, European manners'; and of the law courts: 'they were less defective than I had anticipated'. But what really antagonised Gordon and provoked him to angry denunciation was Baker's Constitution and code. These,

Gordon wrote, were 'singularly harsh and impolitic', had been 'pressed with inconsiderate haste and enforced with inconsiderate rigour', and were, therefore, in their operation 'singularly harsh and oppressive'. [34]

Gordon gave Tupou the benefit of his views before leaving Tonga, and the king promised that at the forthcoming parliament the worst errors of which he complained would be rectified. Gordon also wrote to Baker on the same subject, and in answer received Baker's assurance that he was not responsible for many laws which Gordon criticised. Baker wrote:

> With regard to the various charges made of late years in Tonga, there are some, though placed to my credit, yet nevertheless have been opposed by myself both in private and public.[35]

Had Gordon's only concern been to protect Tongans against oppressive legislation, then his task was successfully completed. Baker was anxious to please, and the king had promised to review the laws. Yet even after these assurances Gordon continued to engineer moves against Baker designed to destroy his influence and bring about his recall. This confirms the view that Gordon was opposing Baker not merely because his laws were objectionable, but mainly because his continued presence in Tonga was incompatible with Gordon's wider political ambitions.

Gordon opened his campaign against Baker as soon as he returned to Fiji. His first action was to write a critical report on Baker's activities for the British Secretary of State for Foreign Affairs. The text of this report was then apparently leaked to the press, for on 8 May 1878 the *Fiji Times* carried an article on the Governor's visit to Tonga which quoted verbatim the criticisms made in Gordon's official dispatch. When Langham, the Chairman of the Wesleyan Mission in Fiji, protested that a full inquiry had been made into Baker's activities by the recent Conference, and that as a result of that investigation it was evident that the Governor's

strictures were unfounded, Gordon warned Langham that Baker
would have to be removed from Tonga, otherwise he (Gordon)
'would take further action'.[36] Then, in July, Gordon returned to
England on leave, calling at Sydney on the way. The purpose of his
stay in Sydney is revealed in his journal:

> I was of course very busy all the time seeing people, especially
> Dr Chapman and Dr Smith, the heads of the Wesleyan body
> in N. S. W., and sought to persuade them of the iniquity of
> Mr Baker's ways, but they are dull of hearing.[37]

Gordon also decided to keep a permanent representative in
Tonga, and to this end sent Alfred Maudslay to Nuku'alofa in June
to act as his Deputy-Commissioner and Vice-Consul. The presence
of such an officer would, in itself, inhibit Baker's activities, but it
seems clear that Maudslay was given private instructions to under-
mine Baker's influence and to find means to have him removed.
This was recognised by the beach, for one of the traders, discussing
Maudslay's appointment some time later for readers of the *Fiji Times,*
commented that the move was part of Gordon's 'laudable design of
relieving himself of a dangerous antagonist by hoisting Baker out of
Tonga'.[38] It was recognised by Langham, the senior missionary in
Fiji, for he wrote to Baker warning him: 'There is no doubt in my
mind that the Governor wants to put his hand into Tongan affairs
and considers you in the way'.[39] It was even recognised by Baker,
for when he went on board to welcome the new arrival he was
coldly rebuffed by Maudslay, and commented: 'from the first it was
apparent that his instructions were to snub us in every respect'.[40]
Furthermore it was tacitly acknowledged by Maudslay himself – in
his first letter from Tonga to Gordon he made the revealing
comment: 'Mr. Baker has offended everybody, and is playing, as far
as I can see, right into my hands'.[41]

Baker had indeed offended many people, and this made Maudslay's
task easier. The opposition of the traders and the missionaries has
already been discussed, but there was also a growing discontent

among certain groups of Tongans who had been adversely affected by one or other of Baker's activities. First of all there were those who had become indebted through borrowing money for the missionary collections, especially for the jubilee collection of 1875. Large sums had been borrowed on that occasion, but severe hurricanes in 1876 and again in 1877 had blown the nuts from the palms before they were ripe, thereby preventing the Tongans from making the copra with which to repay their debts. Late in 1877 Godeffroy and Sons, to whom the debts had been transferred, began taking out distress warrants against those most heavily indebted and, by order of the courts, the houses and chattels of several families were sold at public auction to meet their debts. These warrants were executed, in the main, while Baker was in Australia, and on his return to Tonga he used his influence to stay the proceedings. But a great deal of ill feeling had been aroused by the Godeffroy action, and Baker lost much support.

A second source of discontent was the new code which Baker had drawn up in 1875, and in particular the sumptuary provisions which it contained. As has been shown there was little that was new in this code, but unlike earlier codes, this one was effectively administered. In 1850 a law had been passed decreeing that 'Chiefs, Governors, and people shall clothe', but Meade noted on his visit to Tonga in 1865 that little notice was taken of this law. Similarly fornication had been made a criminal offence in 1850, but in 1862 Davis, the missionary at Ha'apai had reported: 'scarce a man marries a virgin'.[42] Baker reaffirmed these laws in his new code, but he also created the machinery to enforce them. The office of Minister of Police was set up by the Constitution, and this official, at the head of a freshly recruited constabulary, pursued transgressors with relentless zeal. The result was a startling increase in the criminal classes, and a growing disaffection towards Baker and his policies.

A third group opposing Baker was described by Gordon as the 'Vaka-Tonga Party', a faction made up of conservatives who preferred Tongan ways and customs (*fakatonga*) to the European ways

(*fakapapālangi*) which Baker was actively sponsoring. Their complaints were given by Semisi, a magistrate at Vavaʻu:

> We Tongans have but one ambition – to get black clothes and wooden houses.... The women do nothing now that 'masi' [*tapa*] making is forbidden. To get money for the missionary collections is the great object of everybody. The women's object is to vie with their friends and neighbours in showy European dress. We all see we are mistaken.[43]

The acknowledged leader of this group was 'Uiliame Tungī, the chief of Hahake and heir to the extinct *Tuʻi Haʻatakalaua* title. Tungī was no doubt a genuine conservative, but he also had other reasons for opposing Baker. In ancient Tonga the *Tuʻi Haʻatakalaua* was a more senior title than the *Tuʻi Kanokupolu,* and until the promulgation of the Constitution Tungī, aware that 'Unga was extremely unpopular and that Maʻafu had become a British subject, probably entertained hopes that the succession would pass to him on the death of the aged Tupou. The Constitution, however, had decreed that the succession should pass to 'Unga and his direct heirs. This was probably a contributory reason for Tungī's disaffection towards Baker, his Constitution and all things *fakapapālangi*. At least it is certain that after 1875 Tungī became Baker's most active opponent, and his people at Muʻa a perennially dissident and factious minority.

Opposition from Tongans was, however, mostly inarticulate, and while Baker enjoyed the support of Tupou it was impotent. But by July 1878 Baker had offended the king too, and discontent among the Tongans assumed a new significance. The reason for the strained relations between Tupou and Baker is not clear. Maudslay believed that Gordon had persuaded the king that his adviser's ways were iniquitous, and that this was the reason for the coolness that existed between the two. A more likely explanation is that because of his censure at the 1878 Conference Baker had decided to have nothing further to do with Tongan affairs and had refused to give any further advice to Tupou. Wilkinson, Maudslay's assistant, reported:

> Much that Mr Baker has done since his return ... surprises
> me much – I gave him credit for more ability and tact. He
> has seriously offended the King and seems to be acting like a
> spoilt child after a whipping.[44]

The king had come to trust Baker completely and the latter's
desertion at this point left him to face alone the negotiation of a
treaty with Britain and the revision of the laws which he had
promised to Gordon; he was understandably displeased.

With Baker's influence removed Maudslay was able to negotiate
an arrangement with Tupou with little difficulty, and by 30
September 1878 he could report that Tupou had signed an agreement which provided the framework for a treaty between Britain
and Tonga. It contained an 'extraterritoriality' clause which in effect
negated all Baker's efforts over several years to make whites in Tonga
amenable to the local courts.

The revision of what Gordon had termed the 'intolerably irk-
some and repressive legislation' proved more difficult. Maudslay
made a promising start, however. He began by seeking the support
of the conservative chiefs, who were a natural focus of opposition
to Baker. His behaviour was ostentatiously *fakatonga*. He chose as
the consular ground an *'api kolo* in Kolomotu'a, the exclusively
Tongan quarter of Nuku'alofa and built on it a consulate constructed
of reed thatch, in pointed contrast to the weatherboard cottages of
the 'progressive' chiefs and the whites. He frequently invited chiefs
to dine with him and sought their co-operation. He had only been
in Tonga a fortnight when he confided in a letter to his cousin: 'I
find myself becoming a rallying point for a conservative reaction'.[45]

Maudslay's most valuable ally, whom he took particular pains to
cultivate, was Tungī. David Wilkinson, an officer of the Fijian
government who had accompanied Maudslay to Tonga, advised
Maudslay that Tungī's influence in Tonga was second only to the
king's, and that he had no love for Baker. Maudslay therefore

frequently entertained Tungī at the consulate, and after dinner pressed his views on his guest. Reporting one of their nocturnal discussions Maudslay wrote:

> We talked away last night for about three hours, and at last I apologised and said that he must not go away with the notion that I wanted to lecture him on the things we talked about. Tungi replied: 'Tell the Consul that's all humbug, he does lecture me, and it is the lectures we get here that has done us all so much good'.[46]

Tungī was the Speaker in the Assembly and, when the parliament met on 18 July 1878, encouraged by Maudslay's 'lectures', he pressed for a complete revision of the laws. Baker refused to have anything to do with the parliament. He wrote to Chapman: 'I have not written one line to it, or sent one message to it, or given any advice whatever',[47] and Tungī confirmed this when he told Maudslay: '... this is the first Parliament which has been free from outside pressure. We talk about things like Tongans now, and don't have new things shoved down our throats'.[48] The result was that Tungī's influence prevailed and the *fakatonga* party was able to carry through an extensive revision of the laws. Legislation was framed limiting recoverable debts to one pound per man, allowing people to dress as they pleased, repealing the *tapa* laws and removing the legal penalties on adultery and fornication. Only the king's signature was wanting for the measures to become law.

In the meantime, however, Baker had begun to reassert his influence. He had effaced himself between July and September, but by the end of the latter month it had become evident that Maudslay's intention was to discredit him and procure his recall, and Baker took up the challenge. On 30 September Maudslay noted: 'Baker has been working like a horse to put things right with the people, and I believe, if left alone, would reinstate himself in a few months'.[49]

He began by denouncing Maudslay from the pulpit and on 26 October preached to the Quarterly Meeting of ministers a telling sermon on the text: 'Oh foolish Galatians, who hath bewitched you?' He bridged the gulf that had grown between the mission house and the palace through Wellington Ngū (who, as 'Unga's son, suspected Tungī's motives), and Ngū began relaying Baker's advice to the king. Finally, Baker called in the aid of his German friends. Towards the end of October Weber visited Nukuʻalofa and spent most of his stay closeted with Baker. Before he left Baker, Weber, and the captain of the German warship, *Ariadne,* had a private interview with the king, and soon after that meeting – and probably as a direct consequence of it – it was announced that Tupou had rejected nearly all the proposals put forward by the parliament; the *tapa* law was relaxed and laws regulating clothing and prohibiting smoking were modified, but otherwise the code and Constitution were left intact. It was also announced that Tupou would appoint as his secretary, to replace the completely derelict Miller, not Thomas Trood, as suggested by Gordon, but someone to be nominated by the Emperor of Germany. Maudslay's efforts had been completely eclipsed, and Tungī retired to Muʻa, to sulk amongst his own people.

Maudslay's other main task was the investigation of Baker's alleged malpractices. His inquiry into the affairs of the Bank of Tonga did not prove very fruitful. Gordon had been told of Baker's banking interests during his visit, and had formed the impression that the profits Baker had made were outrageous. Maudslay was able to examine the books of the bank, and as a result reported to Gordon that he had been somewhat misled; however improper it might have been for a missionary to engage in financial speculation, the speculation itself had been legitimate and the profits (amounting to about ten per cent on paid up capital) were not usurious.

Inquiries into the methods used by Baker to raise funds for the Mission proved more rewarding. This task was begun soon after the Consul and his party arrived in Tonga, and was conducted mainly by David Wilkinson and Taniela ʻAfu, a Tongan Wesleyan minister who had spent many years in Fiji and had accompanied Maudslay to Tonga for the specific purpose of questioning Tongans about mission collections. Maudslay sought and received from Tupou permission to inquire into Tongan indebtedness to Europeans, and under this pretext Wilkinson and 'Afu visited several villages in Tongatapu, including Mu'a, Fua'amotu, Vaini and Kolovai, and took statements from the people concerning the manner in which collections were made, the indebtedness of the people caused by the jubilee collections, and the distress warrants that had been executed by Godeffroys. It was when news of this investigation reached Baker that he threw off his lethargy and began taking steps to counteract Maudslay's influence. He had already prevailed upon Treskow, the Godeffroy agent, to stay the execution of further distress warrants, but at this point he settled all the outstanding debts himself, using mission funds. He also warned the villagers, through the local preachers, that no information was to be given to Wilkinson unless a written authority from the king was produced. Three church officers who had already given information were dismissed from their posts. These steps were effective enough, but were too late to prevent Wilkinson gathering some very damaging statements.

Meanwhile Maudslay had sought corroborative evidence from the Europeans, and Charles Baker, Washington Simpson, Philip Payne, Francis Payne, and P. S. Bloomfield, all of whom had lent money to Tongans for mission collections, swore affidavits revealing some of the shabbier aspects of the *fakamisinale*. That of Bloomfield is typical:

I, P. S. Bloomfield, make oath and say as follows: In the year 1874 I gave out money for the Missionary collections, but not to a large amount. In 1875 I gave money to the natives of Kolovou [Kolovai], Kalago [Kolonga], Afa and Havehiuli [Haveluliku], Manuka, Navutoka and Talafou [Talafo'ou]. I went round to these villages with Mr. Baker meeting him at Talafou by arrangement; at each village money was given to me at the minister's house, at the church door, and sometimes in the church itself. If I ran short of money I called Mr. Baker out of the church and asked him for more. I gave Mr. Baker orders on the firm of Godeffroy and Son as I drew the money from him. I advanced about $5,000 in the year 1875.... It was clearly understood by the natives that the advance was to be repaid in copra.[50]

Finally, in August 1878 Maudslay sailed to Niuafo'ou, an isolated island two hundred miles north of Vava'u, which was included in the Tongatapu circuit. Because it was nearly inaccessible and was seldom visited by outsiders, Maudslay suspected that it was Baker's pet hunting ground and his visit confirmed his suspicions. He was told that the population, numbering only three hundred taxpayers, made an annual subscription to the Mission of from $10,000 to $12,000 (£2,000 to £2,400), that the people were at the time some $6,000 to $7,000 (£1,200 to £1,400) in debt, and that they had been driven to the extremity of picking unripe nuts to make copra for their creditors.

By September Maudslay had all the evidence he required and wrote to the Missionary Committee in Sydney reporting his findings. He reminded Chapman of the assurance he had given to Gordon that Baker would be recalled if it could be shown that he had organised the payment of subscriptions in borrowed money and, on the basis of the evidence he tendered, he invited the Committee to redeem this pledge. He indicated very plainly, moreover, that if the Committee did not comply, he would bring a public scandal about its ears.[51]

The Committee was in a dilemma. In the first place, Maudslay's letter uncovered nothing that the Committee did not well know. Chapman himself had attended the 1874 meetings, and the method of raising subscriptions was frequently referred to in missionaries' letters.

In the second place, Tonga was the Missionary Society's most important single source of revenue. In the nine years since Baker had taken charge, Tonga had sent £39,375 to Sydney and, after subtracting the cost of missionaries' salaries and Tonga's share of the expenses of the *John Wesley,* a surplus of £16,451, or nearly

£2,000 per annum, was left. This surplus had made it possible for the Society to balance its books, and in 1873, for the first time, it had not needed assistance from the parent body in Britain. In 1875 a new mission had been opened by the Reverend George Brown in New Britain, and this too was made possible only by the finance provided from Tonga. When sending his 1875 remittance Baker had commented: 'surely Tonga lays golden eggs.'[52] This was an apt allusion, and the Committee was well aware of the implied moral.

In the third place the members of the Committee had grave doubts about the motives of Gordon and Maudslay. Langham had written to Chapman from Fiji: 'It is singular and suspicious that they are content to do nothing if only Mr. Baker is removed from Tongatabu'.[53] Chapman agreed. He wrote to the Reverend M.C. Osborne in London:

> Mr. Brown had [a visit from?] a gentleman occupying a principal position in Her Majesty's service whose name I don't want to give at present.... At last Tonga was mentioned and the gentleman said: 'Sir Arthur Gordon wants to drive away Rev. S.W. Baker from Tonga because Mr. Baker governs Tonga and Sir Arthur Gordon wants to govern it himself.' This is the opinion of many of us here. If Mr. Baker could have been relied upon to advance British political interests I do not believe any complaint against him would have reached us from British officials.[54]

Moreover the Committee had recently concluded an investigation into Baker's affairs, and had officially approved his conduct. Under these circumstances, the Committee probably agreed with Langham, who advised: 'Baker cannot be dealt with in the summary way that would suit Sir Arthur.... If Baker is right with the people, stand by him, and do not be the Lord High Commissioner's catspaw'.[55]

Yet Maudslay's threat was serious, and something had to be done. The Committee decided to shift the responsibility to the District Meeting of the missionaries in Tonga, which was instructed to inquire into the Consul's charges. In Tonga, however, the missionaries had realised what Maudslay was doing, and recognising that an attack on the collections system involved them all, they had closed their ranks. Moulton had left for England by the time the District Meeting met in December 1878 so Watkin took the chair; Maudslay's charges were read and Baker's explanations given. The meeting then unanimously resolved that the charges were without foundation. When Baker announced his intention to resign at the end of the year, the meeting passed a resolution expressing its sympathy and support for Baker, 'under the trying circumstances in which he had been placed through the exaggerated, and in many instances false reports which have been circulated against him'.[56]

Baker's decision to retire from Tonga had been given to the Committee before the meeting began, and Chapman had passed it on to Maudslay. Maudslay, however, could not accept such a compromise solution. By January 1879 his plans had been completely upset, and he had been made to look foolish both in European and Tongan eyes. His attempt to remove Baker had failed, his proposed alterations to the laws had been rejected and the king had agreed to accept a German secretary. His most important ally, Tungī, had retired to his village discomfited, while 'Unga, who had been well disposed to him when he first arrived, had become convinced that he sought the succession of Ma'afu and had therefore been won back to his old alliance with Baker. Baker had also gained considerable support from the Tongans by personally settling outstanding mission debts, and by encouraging the already widespread suspicion that Maudslay's attempt to discredit him was the first step in a plot to subvert Tongan independence.

To avoid complete humiliation Maudslay carried out the threat he had made to the Missionary Committee. In January 1879 he wrote three long despatches to the Marquis of Salisbury, Britain's Secretary of State for Foreign Affairs, on the subject of Baker's delinquencies. The first dispatch was an indictment of Baker for his political activities, and detailed what Maudslay considered were the faults in the Tongan Constitution and laws. It repeated most of the criticisms made by Gordon a year earlier, and drew special attention to Baker's relations with the Germans, as exemplified by the announced appointment of a German secretary. The second dispatch concerned the mission collections. It gave an outline of Maudslay's proceedings and presented a résumé of the evidence he had collected, together with statements from Tongan debtors and affidavits from the Europeans. The third dispatch described Baker's commercial activities, especially his association with the long-defunct sugar plantation and the Bank of Tonga, and alleged that he virtually controlled the finances of the Tongan government. Maudslay also reported his belief that a mutually rewarding understanding existed between Baker and Godeffroys. He concluded: 'I trust that in this and the two previous despatches I have given sufficient grounds to justify the wish I have expressed that he (Mr. Baker) may be speedily removed from the islands'.[57]

Once official sanctions were invoked events moved quickly towards a climax. The task of dealing with Baker was referred to Gordon, who was in Britain at the time, and who had the power to remove troublesome British subjects from the islands under the Order in Council which had created the office of High Commissioner. Gordon was aware, however, that if he deported Baker himself he would provoke hostility from missionaries everywhere, and understandably preferred to work through the Wesleyan authorities. Accordingly he brought Maudslay's accusations under the notice of the Wesleyan Missionary Society in London. This body had been largely prepared for Gordon's overtures by Moulton, who, from his vantage point in England, had been doing some effective sniping at his old enemy. Moreover, the London authorities were greatly concerned that Gordon might make Maudslay's despatches public, as he had implied he would if his demands were not met, for they recognised that such adverse publicity could do great damage to the whole missionary cause. They therefore pressed upon the Sydney body a 'fraternal statement of views' which concluded:

> Under these circumstances we cannot but feel that the usefulness of Mr. Baker as Chairman of the Tonga District is at an end. A civil investigation, even with the best issue, would

disturb the interests of our missions all over the world, and
with any issue but the best would seriously wound those
interests. The prompt removal of Mr. Baker seems to us
desirable, equally for local and general reasons.[58]

The Missionary Committee in Sydney received this advice in
July 1879 and, despite the misgivings it had, decided to accept it.
Baker was therefore informed that he was recalled. He was further
advised that a deputation would investigate Maudslay's charges in
Tonga, though it would in no way affect the Committee's decision
to recall him. He was, in fact, to be punished first and tried later.

The investigation of the charges against Baker was conducted by
the Reverend Benjamin Chapman and the Reverend William
Clarke, the special commissioners of the Board of Missionary
Management. It began on 8 October 1879 and continued for three
weeks; Maudslay acted as Prosecutor and Baker conducted his own
defence. Baker was charged with being an agent for Godeffroy and
Sons, with conducting the business transactions of the Tongan
government, with interfering in political matters, and, under three
heads, with encouraging Tongan indebtedness at missionary meetings. It was, therefore, an investigation of all the charges that a long
series of complainants had levelled against Baker. It was also the
only investigation that had been held *in situ,* at which accused and
accuser stood face to face, and at which evidence was tested by
cross-examination. Its findings, therefore, offer the most reliable
testimony to the truth or falsehood of Baker's alleged malpractices.

The result of the investigation, as the most hostile witnesses had to
admit, was an almost complete vindication of Baker. Commenting on
the trial some time later, a European trader from Tonga (probably
Robert Hanslip and certainly no ally of Baker's) wrote in the *Fiji Times:*

The contest was ... too unequal. Sir Arthur Gordon's baby
began to flounder from the outset, and the exhibition of
weakness became so lamentable that Baker fairly played with
his opponent, by offering him evidence to support his case, so

that the prosecution might present something like a respectable
obstacle for him to demolish ... so that at the end, though he
might have returned a perfect conviction as to the truth of
every charge laid against the accused, the Rev. Statesman's
worst enemy could not conscientiously have failed to give a
verdict of not proven on every charge but one.[59]

The one point which Maudslay was able to substantiate concerned the collections. It was proved that Baker had lent money to
several traders on the understanding that it would be redistributed
to Tongans for the missionary meetings. Baker readily admitted that
this was true, and further admitted that the practice had been ill-
advised, but in his defence claimed that he lent money only because
there was a shortage of coin in Tonga and that the system had been
abandoned since the difficulties that attended the 1875 collections
had been discovered. He claimed that, but for the hurricanes, there
would have been no difficulties, the Tongans would have quickly
repaid their debts and no distress would have been caused. As it was
he had done everything in his power to alleviate the distress, even
to the extent of paying the outstanding debts. In his zeal for the
cause he admitted he had been guilty of a peccadillo, but his motives
were above reproach.

All Maudslay's other charges Baker denied completely. He defied
Maudslay to offer any evidence to indicate that he was in any way
an agent of Godeffroys, and the Consul was obliged to protest that
the charge was not of his making and that, although he had heard
rumours to that effect, he had never reported that Baker was
connected with the German firm. To counter Maudslay's charges
that he controlled the financial affairs of the Tongan government,
Baker produced a signed statement from 'Unga, the Premier,
denying that Baker played any part in these affairs; and to counter
the charge that he was 'virtual ruler of Tonga' he produced a
statement from Tupou declaring that his only function was that of
a trusted and valued adviser. On this charge Baker put his own case
very competently. He told the inquiry:

> That I have great influence with the Tongan Government, I
> don't deny; that I designed their flag, I admit; that at the
> King's request I compiled the original draft of the Con-
> stitution, I admit; that at his request I assisted him in reference
> to the laws, I admit; that I corrected the proof copies of the
> laws, I admit; that at his request I planned the present system
> of Police Courts and Debtors' Courts and a system of regis-
> tration I admit; that as long back as 1862 I drew out the
> charter of their liberty I admit; that I was editor of the *Boobooi*
> and the *Tongan Times* I admit; that I used my influence to
> compel, or to enforce, or to interfere, I deny. I have given
> my opinion, but I have never pressed my views either on the
> King or on the chiefs, which His Majesty's letter to the
> committee proves.[60]

Maudslay was unable to produce any evidence to contradict him.

As a result of the investigation Baker was confident that his
actions would be approved and his recall negatived. He told the
inquiry:

> I appeal to the world wherever civilisation is to be found, to
> pronounce their verdict ... and I fear not what the verdict
> will be ... I feel I can confidently leave the matter with a
> clear conscience to the judgement of my brethren and of my
> fellow citizens and in the hands of God.[61]

So confident was he that he had disproved the charges that he
printed a résumé of the evidence and circulated it among the members of the Conference, before which he appeared in 1880. The
Conference, however, while it resolved that nothing had been
proved against his 'moral and religious character', nevertheless
confirmed his recall. Despite the wording of the resolutions, it was
clear to Baker and to everyone that his missionary career had ended
in disgrace, and that all his efforts to build a reputation for himself

had come to nothing. Instead of retiring from mission work amid the expressions of esteem and praise which he felt his twenty years of service in the field deserved, he had been summarily discharged.

He refused to accept an appointment in New South Wales from the Conference. He would seek employment where his talents were appreciated.

It is a fairly simple matter to describe the processes by which Baker was pulled down but it is rather more difficult to weigh the justice of these proceedings. Any attempt to do so must comprehend the sequence in which the events occurred.

Baker was challenged in 1876 by Layard, whose accusations were based on the flimsiest of evidence culled from the least reliable of sources. Inquiry into these complaints resulted in complete exoneration for Baker. Layard's charges, however, undoubtedly influenced Thomas, who, for personal reasons, made similar charges in 1877. As a result of the inquiry into these charges by the 1878 Conference, Baker was again exonerated. Baker was challenged for a third time by Sir Arthur Gordon, and his subordinate, Maudslay, in 1875, and when these charges were investigated by the District Meeting in December 1878, Baker was again cleared. In this case it may be argued that the tribunal was not impartial; but neither were Gordon and Maudslay.

By 1879, therefore, Baker's activities had been investigated at three inquiries, and on each occasion he had been vindicated. Yet without further inquiry he was recalled in October 1879. The reason for his recall was the intervention of Gordon, who wished Baker out of the way and was prepared to use a little blackmail to enforce his wishes. The Missionary Society, realising that it stood to lose more from a public scandal than it stood to gain from Baker's collections, offered him as a propitiatory sacrifice to avert the wrath of the High Commissioner. There was, in a strictly legal sense, little justice in such a proceeding.

It may be argued, however, that Baker's recall, while not just, was justifiable; that his behaviour was improper – even pernicious – and that he deserved to be humiliated. It must be admitted that Baker was not a heroic figure. He was pompous, equivocal, plausible, self-righteous, venal, and probably lecherous. Few people liked him, and outside his own family (which was intensely loyal) the only friends he ever had were Tupou and Watkin – and even they vacillated. He was guilty of many lapses from the accepted standards of missionary behaviour; he used his medical skill to supplement his stipend; he lent money, and charged interest on the loans; he meddled in politics; and he was not over-scrupulous about the methods used to raise money for the Mission. Yet to offset these deficiencies he had considerable ability and a great capacity for hard work, and these talents were used in the interests of the Mission and Tonga as much as in his own interest. As a result of his political meddling Tonga had become recognised by 1879 as an independent sovereign state, worthy of entering into treaty relations with the Powers, while the money he had collected had been used to build numerous churches in Tonga, to provide increased educational opportunities for Tongans, and to lay the foundation for the Mission to become an independent self-governing church. Moreover, in developing his system for collecting subscriptions he had only been obeying the instructions of the Missionary Committee, given when he first took charge of Tonga, to be 'more systematic and efficient' in raising contributions. Until Gordon's intervention this system, which had kept the Society solvent for a decade, was recognised and tacitly approved by the Committee. The responsibility belonged to the whole Missionary Society as much as to Baker who was, in reality, made a scapegoat, a role for which his personal shortcomings made him particularly suitable.

The only other possible justification for Baker's recall is the claim that the Tongans themselves would benefit from his removal, and wished him out of the way. This was the feeling of Gordon, who said: 'I have seldom seen a population so deeply and profoundly discontented, or where there was more cause to fear from a sudden and lamentable uprising against a system, the pressure of which was too heavy to be borne'.[62] Maudslay had come to the same conclusion. In his dispatch to the Marquis of Salisbury seeking Baker's deportation he had stated: 'I feel sure ... that should his removal be effected it would be looked upon as an act of deliverance by the greater number of both whites and natives on this island'.[63]

This accusation was answered by the Tongans themselves, who were in a much better position to judge the value of Baker's influence than either Gordon or Maudslay and who gave a verdict that must have surprised the paternal British officials. Tupou replied to Baker's removal by declaring all Wesleyan leases in Tonga null and void until there should be in Tonga a free and independent church, allowed to manage its affairs without intervention from Sydney, and to Chapman and Clarke he wrote: 'This is what is plain to Tonga, Mr Baker goes, not because he is wrong, but because of his love for Tonga'.[64] That many of Tupou's subjects were of the same mind was shown when no fewer than 2,275 of them signed a petition asking that Baker be permitted to remain. They wrote: 'Our minds are greatly grieved for it to be said Tonga dislikes Mr. Baker. It does not. For is there one we love so much as Mr. Baker'.[65] Even allowing that neither of these views were spontaneous their testimony cannot be dismissed. Baker gave what seems to be a reasonable explanation for the attitude of Tupou and the Tongan petitioners. He explained in a letter to the deputation:

> The King and the people well know that I was tried at last D.M. [District Meeting] for what the Deputation are now come down to investigate, and that no Church court has been held since, and that it is solely in consequence of pressure brought in the Committee by Sir Arthur Gordon that I am now recalled. They are persuaded that it is because of my expressed opposition to the annexing of Tonga to Fiji that I am thus wanted out of the way. They feel that it is not because of what I have done that I am leaving, but because I am their friend.[66]

And despite all the reservations that may so easily be made about Baker and his works this is probably a closer approximation to the truth than any other explanation.

CHAPTER VII

THE KING'S
FIRST MINISTER

WHEN BAKER left Tonga at the beginning of November 1879 he took David 'Unga with him to New Zealand so that the prince might seek medical attention for a liver ailment. The treatment was unavailing, however, and 'Unga died in Auckland on 18 December 1879. Baker wrote to Tupou advising him of his son's death and promising to escort the body back to Tonga; then, leaving instructions for the prince's remains to be embalmed, he sailed for Sydney to attend the Conference.

The Conference confirmed Baker's recall from Tonga and offered him an appointment in New South Wales. Baker asked instead to be made a supernumerary, receiving no salary but with leave to live in New Zealand. The Conference complied. Baker then informed the session that he intended to return to Tonga to take back 'Unga's body, for not to do so would constitute a grave breach of Tongan etiquette. While in the group he would also collect materials for a memoir of Tupou which he intended to write. There was some feeling at the Conference that he should be forbidden to revisit Tonga, and a resolution to that effect was canvassed among the delegates, but was dropped when Baker promised that his visit to the scene of his former labours would be only of short duration, and that while there he would try to calm down the excited feelings which had been aroused in connection with his recall.

Baker presumably returned to New Zealand shortly after the termination of the Conference in early February 1880, but though numerous vessels arrived in Tonga from New Zealand during the ensuing four months, Baker and the body of 'Unga remained in Auckland. The cortège did not arrive in Tonga until 30 May 1880, but when it did arrive the reason for the delay became apparent. Baker had used the influence he enjoyed with the German establishment in Polynesia to seek a favour, and 'Unga was borne back to his native land not in the hold of a copra schooner but aboard the German warship *Nautilus*.

The German ship remained in Tonga for the funeral, which was held in 'Uiha, Ha'apai, on 10 June, and her presence added greatly to the pomp of the occasion. Her guns fired a salute at minute intervals and forty-five of her marines, slow-marching to muffled drums, acted as pallbearers. Even Maudslay's successor, James Blyth, vainly trying to uphold British dignity in the face of such overwhelming odds, had to admit: 'The ceremonies were marked by the greatest solemnity and decorum', though he added: 'They were also marked by the ostentatious prominence given to the Germans'.[1]

Tupou was deeply moved by the solicitude shown by Baker, and by the respect which the German Empire, at Baker's instigation, had shown to Tonga. When the parliament met a month later, the king in his opening speech publicly acknowledged his gratitude. He told the Assembly:

> ... I stand here today to thank Mr Baker for what he has accomplished – in bringing David to be buried in the land of his ancestors. Thanks to Mr Baker and his love, and I am also truly grateful to the Captain of the German man-of-war and the Emperor of Germany because of David being brought in the German vessel of war, and also for the respect which was shown him – a proof of our being a nation.[2]

Baker and Tupou visited Vava'u after the funeral, but Blyth

returned to Nuku'alofa where he began to hear persistent and disturbing rumours that the king had given Baker an appointment in the government. On 21 June these rumours were confirmed when Blyth discovered that a German trader had received an official letter from Baker in which the latter described himself as the Minister of Foreign Affairs and Comptroller of Revenue. Tupou returned to Nuku'alofa on 1 July and the next day Blyth requested an interview with him to determine the truth of the matter. He reported to Gordon:

> I said that I had heard some time ago that Mr. Baker had received an appointment from His Majesty but did not believe it ... The King said, 'It is true'.
> 'What is the appointment?'
> King, 'Minister of Foreign Affairs.'
> 'Is that the same as Premier?'
> 'No, it is distinct — there will be a Premier also.'
> Then I continued ... that I could not see how such an appointment was consistent with His Majesty's promises to Your Excellency and Her Majesty's Government.
> The King said ... 'Surely I can govern my country in my own way, and appoint Mr Baker if I please. I do not know if he is friendly to his own country or not, but I think he will do for me.'[3]

Worse news was in store for Gordon. On 23 July Blyth called on Tupou to share a bowl of *kava* and reported to Gordon: 'His Majesty was quiet and, I thought, more restrained than usual.'[4] On the following day parliament opened and the reason for Tupou's restraint towards the British Consul was explained, for the king told the assembled representatives:

> I wish to refer to ... Mr Baker again visiting Tonga. I am greatly pleased — for who helped us make the laws and other arrangements of the Government and what we have accomplished. Even this Parliament Meeting was his work. I have

asked him to help me.... I have asked him to represent me in your Parliament Meeting and inform you as to my wishes.[5]

The office of king's representative and spokesman was an informal one; in more formal terms Baker was nominated Prime Minister, Minister for External Affairs and Minister for Lands. In seven weeks he had completely resurrected his fortunes: when he returned to Tonga on 30 May he had been completely discredited and degraded, by 24 July he had been raised to a position of unambiguous authority and standing. It was perhaps only natural that he should gloat over the powerful adversaries whom he had outmanoeuvred. Blyth reported:

> Several times in bringing forward a new 'motion' Baker is said to have interrupted himself with a small laugh saying, 'But I must be careful what I say in case someone comes from Fiji and takes me away'.[6]

Among the Tongans Baker was known by a new nickname: *Motu'a Mohetō* (the old night creeper) gave way to *Ta'emangoi*, meaning 'the irrepressible one', or 'the one who surmounts all difficulties'.

With his position in the government established in positive and explicit terms Baker was in a position to take up the policies he had advocated when he was merely the king's unofficial adviser, and pursue them with vigour. Between 1876 and 1879 he had been under continuous attack and had gradually withdrawn from political life. Even his newspaper, *Koe Boobooi*, was abandoned in November 1877. As a result many of the reforms which he had introduced in 1875 had either never been properly implemented or had ceased to function through lack of administrative supervision. The department most affected by the lack of surveillance was the Treasury, which between 1876 and 1879 had been left to its own devices, assisted only by J.P. Miller who was, as has been mentioned, an alcoholic when he was appointed Government Secretary in 1874; by 1880 he was completely derelict and the Treasury was in chaos. In November

1879, when Gordon visited Tonga, he took with him Dr William McGregor, the Fiji Government's Receiver-General, to examine the Tongan Treasury records and to recommend measure to keep the government solvent. He found the task very difficult for Miller had never bothered to prepare annual statements of account or strike annual balances. He did conclude, however, that one of the main problems was the dilatory methods of collecting taxes and licence fees; the revenue from the poll tax varied enormously from year to year, and in no year did it bear any relationship to the number of taxpayers, while collection of licence fees had been so perfunctory that by 1879 revenue from this source had dwindled to half of what it had been in 1876. By 1880, therefore, it was apparent that the Tongan government was heavily in debt. Because of the inadequacy of the records the extent of the indebtedness was difficult to estimate, but Blyth's guess in July 1880, based on information supplied by Miller, was that the government was in the red for $33,000 (£6,600).[7]

Baker attacked the problem of the finances with determination. His first measure was a piece of financial jiggery-pokery. At Baker's request the 1880 parliament declared the Chilean silver dollar legal currency in Tonga, and officially valued it at 4s English. Intrinsically the dollar was worth only 3s 3d English, but Godeffroys undertook to exchange government silver, at its nominal value, for bills of exchange on Sydney, Auckland and San Francisco. Thus the Tongan government's holdings in silver dollars, and future tax revenue collected in the same currency, were appreciated very considerably. The measure also had important secondary consequences. Godeffroys had given Baker valuable support, both during the investigations of the previous decade and over the affair of 'Unga's funeral and, by making the Chilean silver legal tender, Baker was able to do them a favour in return. Godeffroys were the sole importers of the coins, and made a profit of about twenty per cent on the transaction. Furthermore, as the coin was not accepted outside Tonga, private traders had to exchange the coins for Godeffroys' bills of exchange, on which the firm charged a further five per cent 'drawback'. The

English traders were therefore seriously disadvantaged, for they were forced to accept at nominal value a currency on which they lost about twenty-five per cent when purchasing from ports outside Tonga. But as the English traders had been his most persistent adversaries, Baker was not sympathetic about their difficulties.

Baker then turned his attention to the taxes. The 1875 parliament had established the poll tax at $7 (£1 8s) per year for every adult male, and had imposed a further indirect tax by declaring all town lands to be the property of the government and charging a rental (evidently at the rate of 4s per year) to the tenant. In 1850 the parliament returned all town lands to the nobles and abolished the rents payable on them; thereafter the 2s per year payable to the noble for an 'api 'uta was the only rent Tongans would pay. To compensate the government for the loss of revenue which the surrender of the town lands entailed, the 1880 parliament raised the poll tax to $8 (£1 12s) per annum. This made no difference to the Tongans for they paid the same amount as before but after 1880 they paid it all as poll tax. The real change introduced by Baker lay in the thoroughness with which he collected the taxes, a change which had a marked effect on the balance sheet. In 1879 the poll tax had provided a revenue of £5,880; when Baker published his first statement of revenue and expenditure it was revealed that for the year ending September 1881 the poll tax had yielded nearly £13,000. There were, in consequence, some murmurs from the Tongan taxpayers and the British Consul reported in September 1881 that many of the people were refusing to tend their plantations, saying they would rather go hungry than see the fruits of their labour taken by the government. It seems likely, however, that the Consul exaggerated: Tongan Wesleyans gave freewill offerings of $10, $20 and even $50 at the annual missionary collections, and in comparison the annual tax of $8 (£1 12s) seems neither harsh nor unreasonable.

On the other hand Baker introduced new licence fees which applied almost exclusively to Europeans, and these were certainly harsh and in some cases prohibitory. The 1880 parliament decreed that wholesale traders were to pay $70 (£14) per year for a licence and retail traders $25 (£5) per year; a license to sell liquor to other Europeans cost $100 (£20) per year, to own a billiard table $30 (£6), a buggy $5 (£1) and a horse $1 (4s). Perhaps the most vindictive of the new fees was the $100 (£20) per year required from an auctioneer. Robert Hanslip, Maudslay's interpreter and the chief prosecution witness at the 1879 investigation, was the only auctioneer in Tonga, and the whole profits from his business hardly covered the licence fee. When Blyth pointed this out to Baker the fee was reduced to $50 (£10), a mere fifty per cent of Hanslip's profits. Baker was not a generous victor.

Baker's financial measures were completely successful in restoring solvency to the Tongan government. Despite an enlarged expenditure, when a balance was struck in September 1881 the revenue exceeded expenditure by nearly $10,000 (£2,000), and when the next parliament sat in September 1882 the king could inform the representatives that the government's debts had almost all been liquidated.

A second problem which faced Baker in July 1880 was the question of land tenure. In 1862 the chiefs had been ordered to distribute land to their people, though the size of the holding was left to the chiefs to determine, the king merely advising that the amount of land given should be proportional to the size of the tenant's family. Once land had been granted to a tenant, his right of tenure was guaranteed by the government. A considerable modification of this system was envisaged by the 1875 Constitution, which divided all plantation lands into *tofi'a* or inheritances belonging either to a noble or to the king. *Tofi'a* holders were to lease lands to individual tenants at rates specified by the government for terms of twenty-one, fifty or ninety-nine years, but no regulation of the size of holdings was made, and the chief was under no obligation to lease lands to his followers unless he so desired. In fact, owing no doubt to Baker's preoccupation with his personal affairs after 1876, the delineation of *tofi'a* was never carried out and not a single lease was ever issued. The people continued to work their traditional lands, but because of the uncertainties introduced by the new laws, ceased to improve them or replant their coconut groves.

It was apparent that the 1875 legislation was inadequate to bring about the situation Baker desired, namely a peasantry with secure tenure of portions of land adequate to satisfy their needs and free from chiefly demands and encumbrances, and a nobility with holdings large enough to satisfy their relatively higher demands for status and remuneration. It was to implement this policy that Baker accepted the portfolio of Minister for Lands in 1880, and the parliament session of that year, under Baker's direction, began reconsidering the whole land question. Deliberations were not fully completed during the sitting and many matters were left to be resolved by the next parliament, but several alterations, including the payment of a stipend of $100 (£20) per year to nobles, the elevation of ten additional chiefs to the nobility, and the surrender of the town lands by the government to the nobles, were accepted. The next parliament, which met in September 1882, completed the revision of the land laws, and its resolutions were embodied in *The Act to Regulate Hereditary Lands,* published in November 1882, and the revised Constitution which was published in April 1883.

Under the new laws the *tofi'a* of the thirty nobles and the six chiefs, who though not nobles were granted hereditary lands, were delineated and all lands not specifically granted were declared to be the *tofi'a* of the king. Each tax-paying Tongan was to be granted by his chief an *'api kolo* in a designated town and also an *'api 'uta* in the countryside measuring 100 fathoms by 100 fathoms (about eight and a quarter acres or three and a third hectares). In Hihifo and Ha'apai, where land was comparatively scarce, an *'api 'uta* of fifty fathoms by fifty fathoms was allowed. In return for his lands, which were to be hereditary, the security of tenure being guaranteed by the government, each land holder was to pay two shillings per year rent to the holder of the *tofi'a* in which he resided. No Tongan could possess more than one *'api 'uta* or *'api kolo* and, as in earlier legislation, surplus lands of a *tofi'a* could not be leased to Europeans without the consent of parliament.

The new land regulations helped to stabilise Tongan society, for

nobles and commoners were each guaranteed a secure place consistent with their levels of aspiration. The only Tongans who had
reason to resent the laws were those minor chiefs who had chiefly
aspirations but no title of nobility. One of the results of the 1875
land laws had been to threaten the status of the minor titleholders,
foto tehina and *kau matāpule,* and it is probable that one of the reasons
for the non-implementation of those laws had been the opposition
and obstruction from members of this group, from whom the ranks
of government positions were mostly filled. The new laws made a
much more serious attack on their position, for not only was the
basis for the authority of minor chiefs over their people destroyed,
but the amount of land they could hold was reduced to eight and a
quarter acres, exactly the same size as that of their most lowly
retainer. Naturally the *foto tehina* and *kau matāpule* vigorously opposed
the new laws, and even before they were promulgated the *kau
matāpule* of Mu'a – evidently motivated by the rumoured changes –
began a movement of opposition which grew to very serious
proportions.

Another policy which Baker had advocated while he was a
missionary was the transformation of the Wesleyan Mission into an
independent church, and as Premier the attainment of this objective
ranked high among his priorities. Church independence, like political independence, was a matter of deep concern for Tupou, and
he had expressed great satisfaction in 1875 when the Tongan *Model
Deed* had been signed, believing that by this instrument his church
had been established. The recall of Baker in 1879, against the king's
wishes and contrary to the verdict of the local inquiry, had shown
that the church was not in fact independent, but in all important
matters controlled from Sydney. Tupou's response at the time, no
doubt prompted by Baker, was to threaten to revoke the Wesleyan
leases unless really effective independence were granted to the
church. When Baker returned to Tonga the leases were not revoked,
but at the opening of the 1880 parliament the king announced that
he would give no financial support to the Wesleyans until full
independence had been achieved. Baker moved the Address in
Reply supporting the king's attitude. Then, in December 1880, as a

further earnest of his determination, Tupou issued a proclamation forbidding all members of his family and all government employees to subscribe to the church or help it in any way, warning at the same time that if the proclamation did not achieve the desired effect he would take other measures.

In Sydney the news that Baker had accepted government office, and that he had lent moral support to Tupou in the moves against the Mission caused considerable indignation, and he was summoned to appear before the Committee of Discipline to answer for his behaviour. Baker declined to appear, claiming that as he was not a missionary the Committee had no authority over him. He did present himself, however, before the Conference which met in Sydney in 1881, and at this meeting his conduct was denounced. It was obvious that he would be expelled, and to avoid this he tendered his resignation from the ministry. But he returned to Tonga bereft of all sympathy and affection for the cause for which he had worked for twenty years. He had not been defrocked, but only his resignation, tendered most reluctantly, had prevented this from occurring.

The 1881 Conference also decided to recall Watkin, who had returned to Tonga in 1879 to fill the office of Chairman vacated by Baker. The Conference decided that Watkin was too much under the influence of his friend and erstwhile superior. As the new Chairman they appointed Moulton, Baker's most tireless opponent and personal enemy, who had returned to Tonga from England in June 1880 and had taken up his old post of master at Tupou College. Watkin received word of his recall early in March 1881, and began packing. But on 2 April 1881 Baker returned to Tonga and on 5 April Tupou wrote to Watkin *ordering* him to stay. On 28 May Baker sent a telegram to the General (All-Australian) Conference then meeting in Adelaide:

> King and Chiefs enraged at Watkin's recall. Decided to establish national church and get Watkin as first Minister ....
> This is the King's ultimatum: Tonga to be an independent district like Auckland; Watkin to be reinstated; Tonga to be

attached to New Zealand. Grant this, peace. Reject, one
secession. Don't be deceived. The secession will be universal
and popular.[8]

In fact this dramatic threat was not necessary, for the General
Conference, which had finished its sittings before the receipt of
Baker's telegram, had already decided that after 31 December 1881
the Friendly Islands District should no longer remain under the
Board of Missions, but become a district in connection with the
New South Wales and Queensland Conference, and in response to
a panicky letter from Moulton, the President of the New South
Wales and Queensland Conference had overruled the decision of
his own Conference and appointed Watkin to the vacant station at
Ha'apai.

Baker's demands had not been fully met, for Tonga remained
attached to Sydney instead of Auckland and Watkin, though retained
in Tonga, was still deposed from the office of Chairman; but the
compromise was sufficient to prevent Baker from putting his secession threat into effect. It was not sufficient, however, to prevent
him from putting into operation a plan that the king had long
contemplated, the nationalisation of the schools.

As early as 1874 the king had demanded that the Wesleyan
Mission surrender its schools to the government. The resolutions of
the Quarterly Meeting of Chiefs held in Tonga on 24 March 1874
endorsed by Tupou and forwarded to the Conference, included the
following:

> Whose are the schools? Are they not the schools of the
> missionaries only? The missionaries arrange and rule over
> them; the Government has nothing whatever to do with them;
> therefore this meeting says, give up the schools to the Govern-
> ment and then the Government would assist in a manner
> worthy of the Government.[9]

At the time Baker had given guarded support for the proposal; by
1881, influenced by the treatment he had received from the

Conference, he supported it wholeheartedly.

Accordingly, in June 1881 it was proclaimed that all subsidies paid by the government to the Wesleyan schools would be discontinued, and that the government would set up its own primary schools under the personal supervision of Baker, who assumed the additional portfolio of Minister for Education. Attendance at the government schools was to be compulsory for all children between five and sixteen years of age. Furthermore, the establishment of a State-run college, which all aspirants for government appointments would be required to attend, was announced, and the services of J. H. Roberts, a Victorian schoolmaster and an acquaintance of Baker's from his early days on the Victorian goldfields, were obtained to fill the position of 'professor' at this new institution. Roberts arrived in Tonga on 23 August 1882, and three weeks later the Tongan Government College was formally inaugurated.

The taking over of the schools marked a significant turning point in the relations between Baker and the Wesleyan authorities. Hitherto he had confined himself to polemics, but the Schools Act demonstrated that he was capable of deeds as well as words. He had chosen his ground carefully. Moulton's prestige depended largely on his reputation as a teacher and, with the eclipse of Tupou College, which became merely a theological training school, his influence began to decline. Moulton, however, had little room for complaint because Tupou College had been set up specifically to train Tongan clergy, and had only acquired its more general functions through Moulton's personal authority. Similarly, the Methodists in New South Wales who were the most ardent opponents of state aid to denominational schools in that colony, found it difficult to argue with conviction against the abolition of state aid in Tonga. Baker therefore won his first skirmish with little difficulty but the struggle was really just beginning.

Another policy which Baker had developed while a missionary, and which as Premier he could implement more effectively, was that of making European residents subject to Tongan law and amenable to Tongan courts. The 1875 Constitution had declared:

'There shall be but one law in Tonga, one for the chiefs and
commoners, and Europeans and Tongese', but in practice the
Tongan courts had had little success in enforcing judgements made
against Europeans. For instance, Philip Payne had received forty-
four pounds from a Tongan for a draught horse some time in 1876
but had neither delivered the horse nor repaid the money, despite a
ruling against him by the Tongan Supreme Court in November
1877. Cases like this made the police very reluctant to press charges
against Europeans. Under Baker's administration things began to
change. An English trader at Mu'a, whose real name was Clarke
but who had altered it to Von Hagen for what he described as
'trading purposes', operated a profitable sideline in smuggling. Baker
hauled him before the Supreme Court, obtained a verdict and then
put the onus on the British Consul to extract the fine. Von Hagen
was a ne'er-do-well who, according to the Tongan court records,
had a talent for obscene language and a penchant for indecent
exposure so the case aroused little indignation among the Europeans,
but Baker also challenged E. W. Parker, the grazier on 'Eua and the
most substantial European settler in Tonga. Parker was eminently
respectable; he had been nominated by the other residents in 1876
to fill the post of British Consul, and probably would have been
appointed had the king not informed Gordon that his appointment
was unacceptable. Tupou looked on the nomination with disfavour
because for many years there had been an altercation between the
Tongan government and the Parker brothers, the latter claiming
that the 'Eua people continually butchered and ate their sheep. In
November 1880 Parker made a claim for £13,669 against the
government as compensation for 23,338 sheep which he claimed
had been stolen between 1869 and 1880. He arrived at this figure
by comparing the number of sheep he actually had in 1880 with
the number he calculated he ought to have had if the flock of 5,580
sheep bought in 1869 had multiplied unmolested. To inquire into
the matter Baker set up a Royal Commission, which brought down
a verdict in September 1881 that 'the Tongan Government dis-
claimed responsibility for acts done by individuals', and that

therefore compensation would not be considered. Ngu wrote to Symonds, the British Consul through whom the claim had been submitted, in wording that was unmistakably Baker's:

> His Majesty thinks that even when Jacob shepherded Laban's flock on the plains of Pandanaram they hardly equalled your calculations.... His Majesty cannot but say that in his opinion the whole case is a trumped up affair ... which would, if it had taken place in any civilised land, be considered a disgrace to all parties concerned.[10]

It was Baker's determination to impose Tonga's laws on its European settlers that brought him into serious opposition to Sir Arthur Gordon. Of course Baker regarded Gordon as the one responsible for his humiliation in 1879, and this no doubt played some part in the petty incidents which marred British-Tongan relations during the early part of his premiership, and which gave Blyth so much material for his consular correspondence. But the main problem was Baker's opposition to the treaty which Gordon had negotiated with Tupou and which contained extraterritoriality clauses inhibiting the jurisdiction of Tongan courts over British subjects. The treaty had been signed in 1879, while Baker was absent from Tonga, but its ratification was required by the 1880 parliament. When the parliament came to discuss the treaty, however, it became clear that Baker opposed ratification, and so effective were his criticisms of some clauses that the members refused to make any recommendation at all, leaving the whole question to be decided by the king.

Gordon was convinced that Baker intended to dissuade the king from ratifying it, and in July 1880 he sought permission from the Secretary of State for Foreign Affairs to warn Tupou 'that Her Majesty cannot permit him to offer Her the affront of refusing to carry out his promise to ratify the treaty'.[11] The case was difficult because the British government had been dissatisfied with the original text of the treaty and required further time to consider a re-draft. Tongan agreement had therefore to be sought for an alteration in the wording of the treaty and for an extension of time, and Gordon realised that this would provide an excuse for a Tongan refusal. In September Gordon wrote to Tupou asking that the ratification date be postponed, and in reply received a grotesquely evasive answer. Tupou wrote:

> I am glad to hear that Your Excellency and friends in Fiji are well. I and my friends in Tonga are enjoying good health also. My letter is short. There is no need for it being long as it might only burden you.[12]

However, when H.F. Symonds (who had replaced Blyth in August 1880 as the British Vice-Consul) sought from the king the purport of this strange reply, he was told that, because the British government had had ample time to prepare the Act of Ratification, and had not done so, the Tongan government would refuse to grant the required extension.

On receipt of Symonds' dispatch Gordon wrote a curt letter to Tupou remonstrating against so gross an act of discourtesy to the Queen and warning of the most serious consequences which could follow a Tongan refusal to ratify the treaty. HMS *Alert* was despatched to Tonga to carry the High Commissioner's letter. Six days later Gordon received telegraphic instructions from London to warn Tupou that a refusal to ratify the treaty would be considered as an unfriendly act and to notify him that he would do well to consider seriously whether it was in his interest to offend a powerful nation which had always behaved to him in a friendly manner. On receiving these official instructions Gordon sent to Tonga J.B. Thurston, the Secretary to the High Commission aboard yet another warship, HMS *Danae,* to press the warning in more explicit terms. The *Alert* had been delayed on the voyage, and arrived at Nuku'alofa only twenty-four hours before the *Danae,* so that when Thurston arrived his words were backed by the formidable authority of two British warships riding at anchor in the lagoon. Moreover Baker, the real cause of the king's reticence, was not in Tonga at the time. He had accepted the office of Premier on the condition that he should be free to spend some time each year in New Zealand, where he could enjoy his new social standing in a wider society than that offering in Tonga and, in August 1880, he had sailed to Auckland to launch his family on the giddy social whirl of pianoforte recitals and suburban at-homes. Left to face the British warships alone, Tupou assured Thurston 'that there had only been some misunderstanding about the treaty, nothing more', and an exchange of notes postponing the ratification was hastily arranged.[13]

Shortly after this Gordon left Fiji for Wellington to take up his new office as Governor of New Zealand, and on the way passed through Auckland. Baker was still in Auckland and, having apparently received news of events in Tonga and realising that he had no arguments to match the High Commissioner's gunboats, he decided to seek an interview with Gordon in the hope of arranging some *modus vivendi*. Accordingly a meeting was arranged for 25 November 1880.

The meeting between Gordon and Baker was the first occasion on which the two had met, although they had been bitter adversaries for three years. The talks continued for two days and, by the time they concluded, an understanding had been reached. Gordon admitted that meeting Baker was very different from hearing about him, and agreed to co-operate with him in furthering the interests of Tonga. He protested that neither he nor the British government had any intention of annexing Tonga, though he claimed that British interests in Fiji required that German influence be not allowed to predominate in so near a neighbour. With regard to the extraterritoriality provisions in the treaty, he argued that they gave the Tongan government a greater measure of control over British subjects than it had had before, for under the treaty provisions British subjects were made amenable to the 'municipal law of Tonga', which did not mean regulations by town boards, but all local laws not cognisable under British law. This provision, he pointed out, was more liberal than Britain allowed either to China or Turkey in her treaties with those countries.

Baker was reassured and mollified. He undertook to return his Knight of the Red Eagle accolade and to refrain from actively promoting German interests in Tonga. As an earnest of his good faith he promised that the legislation which Gordon had suggested in 1878, and which Tupou had rejected in 1879, would be re-submitted to the Privy Council for approval. Baker kept his word and in October 1881 he reported to Gordon that all the recommendations had been approved: debts recoverable from Tongans had been limited to £3 per person; the *tapa* law had been suspended; the divorce law had been modified; a subsidy of £500 per year had been granted towards the cost of a steamer to operate between Auckland and Tonga; a more efficient system of bookkeeping had been introduced, and it had been decided to publish six-monthly accounts of government revenue and expenditure in the *Tonga Government Gazette*. A little later Baker informed Gordon that another of his recommendations had been accepted and that the services of a qualified medical practitioner had been secured to act as medical and quarantine officer under the Tongan government.

In May 1881 Thurston again visited Tonga to seek Tupou's agreement to the altered wording of the treaty, and the cordial reception he was given clearly indicated that the reconciliation bet-ween Baker and Gordon was complete. Thurston reported to Gordon:

> I deem it my duty to inform Your Excellency that His Majesty assented to the proposed alteration without hesitation, and that the Reverend Shirley W. Baker, who as Your Excellency is aware has been appointed Premier of the Government and Minister of Foreign Affairs, gave an active and cordial assis-tance in expediting the business that brought me hither.[14]

And in June 1882 when Gordon visited Tonga to exchange rati-fications of the treaty, the formalities were conducted smoothly and amicably. It seemed that the quarrel between Baker and the British authorities was finally buried.

The first two years of Baker's administration in Tonga had been very fruitful. The state finances had been reorganised and placed on a secure footing; the land laws had been simplified and embodied in a revised and more workable constitution; a new state-run education system had been implemented; the Wesleyan Church in Tonga had been granted a considerable measure of independence including complete control over its funds; and finally, amicable relations had been resumed between Gordon and Baker, the result of which had been the ratification of the treaty by which Tonga's independence and sovereignty was finally recognised by Britain. These were very concrete gains, but they had not been won without cost. In the process of achieving his objects Baker had alienated the Wesleyan body in Australia and an influential group of minor chiefs in Tonga, while the animosity which Moulton and the traders had always felt towards him was exacerbated and intensified. By mid-1887 the fruits of this hostility were already beginning to ripen.

~~~~~~

CHAPTER VIII

THE AFFAIR OF
THE MUʻA PARLIAMENT

DURING HIS FIRST two years in office Baker had succeeded
in bringing order and stability to Tonga but, on the other
hand, had aggravated the opposition from the traders, alienated
the Wesleyans and created a new focus for opposition among the
Tongan minor titleholders. Towards the end of 1881 these factions,
each with their own separate reasons for opposing Baker, coalesced
into a united front, forming an opposition party. The resulting
struggle was bitter and Baker was never fully to recover from its
effects, for, although he was to maintain his position in Tonga for
several years afterwards, they were years of makeshift responses and
diminishing prestige.

The dissension was sparked off by a minor incident which
occurred in July 1881. Six young chiefs of high rank had violated
one of Baker's laws – probably that prohibiting fornication – and to
avoid the consequences they applied to H. E. Symonds, the British
Vice-Consul, asking if they might take the oath of allegiance to
Queen Victoria and become British subjects. It was not that they
were disloyal to their king, they assured Symonds, but to Baker,

who made laws to suit himself and ground down the people he professed to call free.

Symonds naturally refused the request and the matter was dropped. News of the incident, however, reached the government, and four of the young chiefs, who were officers in the militia, were arraigned before a court martial on a charge of high treason. It seems that the intention of the government was to frighten the young men into making a public recantation, but the youths defied the court and reiterated their demands. The court dared not sentence youths of such high rank to execution, the penalty for treason, so the charges were dropped.

The protest of the young chiefs was merely a dramatic gesture by a group of high-spirited young aristocrats who resented the prohibitions of the rigorous Tongan social laws, and in itself the incident was unimportant. The weakness of the government's response, however, encouraged another group of dissidents to protest openly, and so begin a movement of much greater significance. This was the so-called 'Mu'a parliament'.

The Mu'a parliament began at a *faikava* in Mu'a attended by a number of minor chiefs and *kau matāpule,* many of whom bore personal grievances against Baker. For instance 'Usaia Tōpui, a member of Tungī's family and the most influential member of the group, had borrowed $900 from the German firm and had expected to repay this sum from the income from his lands at Holonga. When Baker's land laws became operative, however, Tōpui, not being a noble, could expect his lands to diminish to an eight-and-a-quarter-acre farmlet. He could thus anticipate utter ruin if Baker remained in office and the rumoured land redistribution became effective. Another member of the group, Tupouto'a, was in a similar plight. He was a chief of high rank and had precedence over many who had been made nobles, but his title had not been included among the nobility. He had thus been relegated to the commonality, and could expect only eight and a quarter acres as his inheritance. Two other members, Eliasa Leka, a *matāpule,* and 'Asaeli Tāufa, of unknown rank, had been partners in a business enterprise which had borrowed money from Baker's bank in 1875. Their trading venture had failed after about eighteen months and Baker had confiscated their stock, their horse and cart and even their town lands in settlement of the mortgage. Two other members, Tēvita Tonga, a *matāpule,* and Tēvita Valu, a minor chief, had held a piece of land which Baker required as a site for his new government college, and as they held no title for the land, Baker had resumed it without compensation.

Some members of the group opposed Baker because of his increasingly hostile attitude towards Moulton and the Wesleyan Church. Among these were probably Lavuso and Tonga, who were members of the staff of Tupou College, Tonga having been Acting Principal during Moulton's absence in England. Tōpui himself was a leading Wesleyan layman and had given evidence to Maudslay in 1878 about the jubilee *fakamisinale* at Mu'a. But while individual members had special reasons for opposing Baker, the group as a whole had a common reason. All of them appear to have been holders of minor titles. The members were described by an observer as 'chiefly heads of families', which in Tongan terms meant *kau 'ulumotu'a,* and these were almost exclusively holders of minor titles, *kau matāpule* or *foto tehina.* These titles had held a secure place under the old regime with a sanction in the control of land. They all stood to suffer from the implementation of the land laws which Baker had proposed to the 1880 Parliament.

As was inevitable at such a *faikava* the discussions turned to Baker and his laws, but on this occasion the group decided to form a society to debate the questions which had been raised. Tōpui was elected president, Leka was appointed secretary, and a list of grievances was drawn up with a view to petitioning the king to have them redressed. Before a petition could be submitted, however, word of the affair reached the government in Nuku'alofa. Tupou took the matter very seriously, not so much because the group questioned the government but because it came from Mu'a, the traditional centre of opposition to Nuku'alofa, and because it was connected with Tungī, his most dangerous rival. When Tupou had nominated Baker as his Premier in 1880 instead of Tungī, the latter's fortunes had suffered a severe blow, but his prospects had suddenly improved with the death of Maʻafu in March 1881. Symonds explained the position in a letter to Gordon written at the time:

> Maafu was the last of the elders of the Kanokobolu who could have succeeded the present king, and the family is represented now by Gu [Ngū] the present Crown Prince. Although by act of Parliament Gu is appointed to succeed his grandfather, yet the people always looked upon Maafu as the rightful heir and successor, and had he lived until the death of King George and contested the throne the people would, to a man, have declared themselves for him. Although about twenty-six years of age Gu is, in reality, only a boy and very unpopular with the majority of the people, and should the king die before he, Gu, has attained in the eyes of the natives years of discretion, I feel sure that the people will never submit to be ruled by him, unless strong outside influence be brought to bear, and in default of any elder of the Kanokobolu family existing, will no doubt seek a king from the other race of hereditary rulers, the Haatakalaua family, the present head of which is Tungi, the speaker of the Legislative Assembly, one of the most powerful chiefs of the group.[1]

The chief obstacle in the way of any ambitions Tungī might have entertained was Baker, the author of the Constitution which had formally excluded him and his family from the succession and the friend and supporter of the heir-apparent, Ngū. It was this situation which made Tupou very suspicious of any act by Tungī aimed at Baker, and noting that the members of the Muʻa society were mostly Tungī's relatives or dependent minor chiefs, he concluded that a rebellion was under way. A Privy Council meeting was held to discuss the matter and it is said that Baker, ʻAhomeʻe, the Chief Justice, and Tuʻuhetoka, the Minister of Police, advised that an armed force should be sent to sack Muʻa – though this rumour was later emphatically denied. It was, however, finally decided to order Tungī to suppress the movement or accept the consequences. A messenger was accordingly sent to Mu'a to ask Tungī if he were tired of governing his people. If that were so, Tupou assured him, he had only to say so and the government soldiers would march against the rebels.[2]

It is doubtful whether Tungī had actually encouraged the movement before September 1881, but the direct challenge issued by Tupou forced him to take a stand, and he took it with his own people in defiance of the government. He dismissed the king's messenger with a firm assurance that he was not tired of governing his own people, and forthwith took the society under his own patronage and protection. The society then drew up a petition calling the king's attention to a number of grievances. To help in phrasing the petition Tōpui called on Robert Hanslip, a self-styled lawyer, and one of the leaders of the British community. Hanslip had been fourteen years in Tonga, much of which had been spent at Mu'a as a trader. He had married, or perhaps merely cohabited with, a Mu'a girl, and was a confidant of Tungī, who had given him an allotment on his own town section at Fasi, Nuku'alofa. Hanslip was an ardent supporter of Tungī's claim to the succession and probably hoped to establish himself as adviser if the latter became king. He was also a close associate of E. W. Parker, whose legal affairs he handled, and a friend of the British Consul, Symonds, with whom he had been associated under Maudslay's consulship, the one as clerk, the other as interpreter. He had, moreover, been concerned in every attempt to dislodge Baker over the preceding six years. Once Hanslip had joined the movement it began to take shape as a united front, with the minor titleholders, the Moulton faction, and the British traders uniting in opposition to Baker.

Hanslip helped Leka and Tōpui draw up the petition to the king and, probably through his advice, the complaints made did not specifically refer to the problems of the minor titleholders but to problems of more general interest: the extra $1 per year poll tax, the licence fee of $1 per year on horses and the 'different regulations pouring down upon us like a waterspout'. There was really little justification for these complaints. The tax on horses was possibly a real grievance, but the poll-tax increase had been offset by the abolition of town land rents, and most of the vexatious regulations which had attracted Gordon's attention in 1878 had already been repealed. The real core of the complaint was opposition to Baker. The Europeans in Tonga, however, were quick to claim the movement was seeking redress of intolerable burdens, and Symonds, in his official despatches, claimed the society was evidence of the increasing impatience of the Tongan people towards heavy taxation and severe laws. The affair was similarly represented in the *Fiji Times*, whose 'own correspondent' in Tonga was E. W. Parker. Fortunately for Baker there was an impartial observer in Tonga at the time, R. S. Swanston, an adviser to the late Ma'afu, who had come to Tonga in an unsuccessful bid to find employment under the Tongan government. When a report appeared in the *Fiji Times* claiming that the Mu'a movement was widely supported by a suffering and exasperated populace, Swanston scoffed that the article was 'so coloured and exaggerated that the people of the country he writes from would laugh at him did they know what he had written'.[3]

Tupou, however, did not laugh at the petition. On the contrary he took the matter very seriously. He ordered the members of the Mu'a society to attend a *fono* in Nuku'alofa and lectured them at length on their actions. He told them plainly that he would allow only one parliament in Tonga; he strongly reaffirmed his confidence in Baker; and he refused to let them leave until they had all solemnly promised never again to interfere in the affairs of the government. The episode might have ended there (despite the powerful influences which were beginning to mobilise behind the Mu'a group), but Baker was piqued at being criticised by Tongans and determined to reply to such effrontery. He left Tonga for New Zealand in September 1881, but before sailing he issued an edition of *Koe Boobooi* alluding to the Mu'a affair. He derisively referred to the Mu'a parliament as an organisation of debtors, thieves and ex-convicts. 'Is that the class of persons to discuss the laws?' he asked.[4] This was too much for the men from Mu'a. Despite their promise to the king and in defiance of the threats to use armed force against them, the petitioners met again to draft a reply to Baker. They answered Baker's claim that they were debtors and thieves by calling attention to his promise to build a church in Mu'a from the money collected there in the Jubilee Year, a promise he had never fulfilled, and retorted, 'Your criticism is like a pot blaming a frying pan'. They then reiterated all the complaints they had made in their original petition and concluded with a demand that Baker be removed from office.[5]

When word of this latest meeting reached Tupou he determined to take strong measures. Police were despatched to Mu'a to bring in the representatives to stand trial on charges of high treason and breach of agreement. The trial was held in Nuku'alofa in October 1881. The magistrate could find no law that the petitioners had broken, so they were acquitted. But after pronouncing this verdict the magistrate, Maka, washed his hands and then addressed the petitioners:

> I have nothing to do with what I am about to tell you. I only do it because the chiefs have ordered me. After this day you are not to meet together any more. If you do ... some of your number will be hanged and the rest banished.[6]

The king had made his attitude very clear. Any further action by the Mu'a parliament would be treated as rebellion. Yet within a few weeks of being acquitted the Mu'a men were secretly planning another move. They were incited to continue their agitation by Robert Hanslip, probably acting on behalf of all the English residents. Hanslip had attended the trial, and a few days after the verdict had been handed down he published the first edition of a Tongan language manuscript newspaper, the *Niu Vakai* ('Look-out Coconut Palm'). In a long article entitled 'The Mu'a Parliament' he reviewed the course of events which had led up to the trial and defended the

legality of the actions of the Mu'a men. He condemned the actions
of the government, claiming that Tupou had acted illegally in calling
the men to a *fono,* that Baker had issued malicious libels in his article
in *Koe Boobooi,* and that Tu'uhetoka had trampled on the Constitution by bringing the men to trial. Hanslip evidently accompanied
his public pronouncements with private communications with the
Mu'a men, for on 7 November 1881, less than three weeks after
the trial had ended, Leka and Tupouto'a wrote to him seeking
advice about a new and bolder move. They wrote:

> Please do another thing for us and tell us if you think we
> should put the question to all Tonga as to whether they are
> willing that Mr Baker should rule or not. If it is a good thing
> write and tell, and if not, never mind, we will give it up.[7]

Hanslip evidently thought it was a 'good thing', and the members
of the society began paying visits to their villages to ask all the
taxpayers whether or not they supported a move to have Baker
removed. Not unnaturally the villagers hastened to agree with their
hereditary leaders and a large number of names was collected. When
Tōpui had thus obtained two thousand names he wrote to Hanslip:

> We write to inform you that we have finished our work –
> the list of people opposed to Mr Baker.... We are much
> obliged to you Mr Hanslip, and we hope you will be good
> enough to inform us what is proper to do.[8]

On Hanslip's advice a petition was addressed to Queen Victoria,
requesting her to order Baker to leave Tonga. On 5 January 1881
Hanslip delivered this petition to Symonds; it was translated from
Tongan into English by Moulton and forwarded to Sir Arthur
Gordon on 6 January.

The presentation of the petition to the British Queen had been
done clandestinely, but reports that the Mu'a group had been
canvassing support in the villages had reached Tupou. On 29

December 1881 Ngū sent off a report to Baker, who was still in Auckland:

> The Minister of Police, Tuuhetoka, has been investigating the petition they are getting up about removing you. When the King heard about it he was terribly enraged and said without any hesitation that it is to try and dethrone me, not for the Premier's banishment, and looks like the work of a white man.[9]

The king was sure that the country was in revolt and that several powerful chiefs were concerned. Not trusting the local judges he left for Ha'apai on 11 January 1882 to bring back judges to try the men who had defied him. On 22 January the judges arrived in Tongatapu together with a large band of Ha'apai police, and on 30 January the leaders of the Mu'a parliament were brought to Nuku'alofa, put in irons and thrown in prison. Then, on 11 February 1882, Tupou arrived back in Tongatapu with four vessels filled with fighting men from Vava'u. On the two succeeding days a number of boats arrived from Ha'apai whose crews performed a *laka-laka,* or war dance, on arrival to a chant composed especially for the occasion:

> This country has become depraved.
> It needs a club or two!
> This country has become wrong headed.
> An axe or two will fix that![10]

Under conditions that amounted to martial law an investigation was held to decide whether a *prima facie* case could be made against the petitioners. Even the Ha'apai judges, however, could discover no law that the petitioners had broken, and told the king so. But Tupou had lost patience with legal niceties. Declaring that if the law would not hang the men, they should be hanged without it, he ordered them to be removed to Ha'apai and summarily executed.

By this time, however, the European residents had begun to organise support for Tōpui and his followers, and when news of the king's declared intention reached them, they petitioned Symonds to demand a fair trial for the men in Tongatapu. The British Consul protested to the king, threatening the most serious consequences if the men should be hanged without a trial. Finally Tupou agreed to bring the men back to Tongatapu later to stand trial. He then left for Ha'apai, where he was not only king, but also hereditary chief, where the loyalty of his people was beyond question and where there was no British Consul to interfere in his decisions.

Meanwhile the petition had reached Gordon in Wellington on 15 January, accompanied by Von Hagen, who had been entrusted to deliver it and urge its prayers upon the High Commissioner. Von Hagen also released the details to the New Zealand press, and Gordon therefore felt obliged to send a copy of the supposedly secret document to Baker, who had been in Auckland since the previous September. Baker knew little of what had been happening in Tonga and could offer no explanation for the petition. He pointed out that he had recently repealed most of the laws that had been considered too harsh; the only new law was the *Cricket Law* which forbade the game except on Thursdays and Saturdays – it had been introduced because cricket had become so popular that the copra rotted in the plantations and taxes remained unpaid while the population engaged in an endless series of test matches – but this was hardly sufficient to cause such a fuss. He suspected that there were deeper influences at work, that Tōpui and his friends were really just pawns in the hands of certain white settlers with whom he had been compelled to come into collision.[11]

Baker returned to Tonga early in April 1881 and found that what had been a minor disturbance when he left in the previous September had grown during his absence into a major crisis, with a large section of the Tongan population, the Wesleyan Church, the English community and the British Consul confronting the government with open hostility.

When the Mu'a parliament had begun agitating against Baker

the majority of Tongans paid little attention. The Mu'a group represented the interests of the minor titleholders; members of other classes, comprising the vast majority of Tongans, had every reason to support the redistribution of the lands which Baker's laws envisaged. Between September 1881 and April 1882, however, the issue had grown vastly more complicated. In the first place the petitioners were people of Mu'a, the traditional focus of opposition to the central government, and when the king moved against them he had aroused all the latent hostilities which the people of Hahake felt towards Nuku'alofa. Secondly, Tungī's involvement in the movement had revived the traditional rivalry between Tungi's lineage, the *Ha'a Takalaua*, and the lineage of the king, the *Ha'a Tui Kanokupolu*. It seems also that other lineages had lined up with one side or the other, with the powerful *Ha'a Havea* supporting Tungī. Thirdly, the introduction of Ha'apai and Vava'u warriors had injected into the situation the suspicion and hostility that had always existed between Tongatapu and the other islands. Tungī, it must be remembered, was a paramount chief of Tongatapu, while Tupou's hereditary fiefs were Ha'apai and Vava'u. The situation had been further aggravated by the visits of the petitioners to the villages, and by the provocative statements in *Niu Vakai,* which appeared regularly, trumpeting praises of the Mu'a men and condemnation of the government. The appearance in March 1882 of yet another newspaper, *Koe Taimi o Toga (Tonga Times),* edited by Ngū and supporting the government, had only added fuel to the controversy and supplied Hanslip with material to criticise. In March 1882 Symonds had reported that, but for his intervention and the promise which he had extracted from Tupou, an armed attempt would have been made to free the petitioners. The disturbance had thus assumed so threatening an aspect that civil war seemed possible.

The whites, or at least the British faction among the Europeans, were also deeply involved in the dispute. Until February 1882 only Hanslip and Von Hagen had overtly acted on the petitioners' behalf, but they were almost certainly fully supported by the other British subjects, all of whom would have welcomed any move to dislodge

Baker. By March all the British residents had openly declared for the Mu'a group by their petition to restrain Tupou from summarily executing the prisoners.

The Wesleyan Church had also become involved in the controversy. Moulton had probably played no part at all in the original petition of the Mu'a group, but since it had been presented he had given it his support. Soon after Baker left for New Zealand, Moulton had published a statement in his *Local Preachers' Paper* concerning the two leading members of the Mu'a parliament, Tēvita Tonga and Tēvita Valu, whose land had been resumed as a site for the new college. This article implied support for the Mu'a group, but in March 1882 Moulton was forced to take a completely unequivocal stand on the issue. The occasion was the arrival of the Ha'apai and Vava'u men in Nuku'alofa. Moulton went to the king to remonstrate, and it was during this exchange that Tupou learned who had translated the petition into English for presentation to Gordon. The king was furious, and Tu'uhetoka, who was present, roundly condemned Moulton as a traitor. When Tupou sailed for Ha'apai soon afterwards he swore that he would not return to Nuku'alofa as long as Moulton was there and the ingenuous missionary was forced squarely into the camp of the Mu'a parliament supporters. He began cooperating with Hanslip and openly supporting the cause of the petitioners.

The odd coalition of Tongan malcontents, British settlers and the Wesleyan Church was further strengthened by the support of H. F. Symonds, the British Consul. Symonds had participated in Maudslay's attempt to overthrow Baker in 1879 and his attitude towards Baker had been formed under those circumstances. He was on friendly terms with the British residents, particularly E. W. Parker and Hanslip, and had also become identified with the cause of the Wesleyan Church by marrying Moulton's daughter. Symonds identified himself so closely with the cause of the Mu'a parliament that when Tupou removed the prisoners to Ha'apai, Symonds asked Gordon to send a warship to Tonga to ensure a fair trial for the petitioners. In fact his attitude was so partisan that the German

Consul-General, Zembsch, accused him of sponsoring the petition himself to provide an excuse for British annexation, and even his own superior, Sir Arthur Gordon, felt moved to warn the Secretary of State for the Colonies not to give his despatches much credence.

Baker inherited this extremely difficult situation when he returned to Tonga in April 1882, and the full responsibility for calming down the excited passions which the events of the previous six months had aroused devolved on him. He had considerable success in dealing with the unrest among the Tongans. His first step was to withdraw from circulation *Koe Taimi o Toga,* which he realised was only adding heat to the controversy. Then he issued a promise that the petitioners would be given a fair trial before the Tongan Supreme Court, a conciliatory gesture that probably did much to reduce the political temperature. On the other hand he suppressed agitators with firmness, and Vaea, a chief who had been very critical of the government, was arraigned on a charge of sedition. Vaea was acquitted, but the case no doubt dissuaded other malcontents from acting rashly. By July 1882, when Gordon visited Tonga, the crisis was over, although a great deal of discontent remained. Gordon noted: '... that there is very strong feeling against Mr Baker on the part of a large section of the population is certain, but I do not think it is quite so general as Mr Symonds supposes'.[12]

By September Baker felt that it was safe to convene parliament, though he took the precaution of having the king come down from Vava'u for the occasion and, in his opening address, warn the members against holding wrong views as to the meaning of the word 'liberty'. Despite Tupou's warning, however, the members were very obstructive and, for the first time in his political career, Baker experienced great difficulty in getting any of his measures accepted. In fact parliament proved so uncooperative that Baker finally walked out and tendered his resignation to the king. Tupou then summoned the members to a private interview. What was said is not recorded, but when the members reconvened Baker resumed his office and business proceeded very much more smoothly.

It was not until February 1883, however, that Baker felt secure enough to hold the trials of the Mu'a men. These presented many problems. On the one hand, Tupou insisted that the 'rebels' should hang; on the other hand, Gordon had warned Baker that he would be held personally responsible if the men were punished for petitioning Queen Victoria, and had instructed Symonds to sever relations with Tonga if the men were hanged. Baker persuaded the king to accept a compromise that would not seriously offend the High Commissioner. The petition to Victoria had included a statement that Tupou was 'advanced in years and under Mr Baker's influence', and on the basis of this statement the men were tried and convicted on a charge of libelling the king. To avoid being personally concerned Baker left for New Zealand before the trials began (though he left very explicit instructions for Fehoko, the judge who was to try the case) and, to preserve the fragile peace that had been established in Tongatapu, the trials were held in Ha'apai. Twelve of the men were sentenced to five years, and two to three years hard labour. By Tongan standards these sentences were relatively mild and, had it not been for the activities of the Europeans, Tongan interest in the Mu'a parliament would probably have completely expired.

Baker had not been successful in dealing with the Europeans, and the British settlers were making every effort to embarrass and, if possible, to remove him. In May 1882 they petitioned Gordon seeking Baker's deportation, but the High Commissioner refused to comply with their wishes. He explained his reasons to the Secretary of State for Foreign Affairs:

> Mr Baker's government is that of a narrow-minded, selfish and ignorant man, unfettered by any check whatever. It is therefore a bad government. But even a bad government is better than none, and it appears to me that were Mr Baker dispossessed of power at the present moment, the government must fall into the hands of some lower or more unscrupulous foreign adventurer, or that anarchy must at once ensue.[13]

Failing in this move the whites turned their attention to the press and a regular series of articles, written by Parker and Hanslip, but modestly ascribed to 'our own correspondent' or 'a correspondent', began appearing in the *Fiji Times,* directing praise on the Mu'a parliament and scathing criticism on Baker and the Tongan government. In Tonga the issues were kept alive by *Niu Vakai,* which continued to appear regularly in 1882.

Baker could do little about the *Fiji Times,* but he did begin writing articles himself for the New Zealand press. He also made strenuous efforts to suppress *Niu Vakai.* Affidavits from Tu'uhetoka and Ngū were obtained concerning Hanslip's part in the Mu'a parliament and, when Gordon visited Tonga in July 1882, Baker offered these as evidence in support of a formal request that the High Commissioner deport Hanslip as one dangerous to the peace and good order of the Western Pacific. Gordon examined the case and expressed strong disapprobation of Hanslip's interference in native affairs, but he found nothing properly illegal in his activities and refused to deport him. Baker tried again in September 1882 by putting an *Act Relative to Newspapers* and an *Act Relative to Sedition* through parliament, the one making an editor liable for the contents of his newspaper, and the other making it an act of sedition, punishable by up to twenty-four years imprisonment, for anyone to speak or print libels against the king, to attempt to influence anyone to rebel against the laws of the kingdom, or to do anything to produce hatred towards or contempt for the government. This second attempt to silence *Niu Vakai* was also frustrated by the High Commissioner. In the interim Gordon had retired to England and the office had been filled by Sir William Des Voeux, who was relatively new to Fiji and knew little of the circumstances of the case. Symonds described *Niu Vakai* to him as a paper: '... edited by an Englishman and supported by the British residents who ... naturally look upon the press as the most legitimate means of expressing their views,'[14] thus leading Des Voeux to believe that it was an English language paper circulating among the English community, rather than a Tongan language paper written for Tongans by an English provocateur. On the basis of Symonds' information Des Voeux instructed that Tupou should be asked to repeal the laws or at least not to use them for the suppression of legitimate criticism upon the acts of his chief adviser. The laws were not repealed, but Baker dared not invoke them against Hanslip, and the *Niu Vakai* continued to appear.

Soon after this exchange Baker held the trials of the petitioners and, while this event virtually marked the end of the Tongan disaffection, it served only to reinvigorate the Europeans. In the first place Tupou had promised Symonds that the trials would be held in Tongatapu, and the Consul regarded the decision to hold them in Ha'apai as a personal affront and as a direct blow at British prestige. Secondly Baker had sent Fehoko, the judge who conducted the trials, very detailed instructions as to the procedure to be observed and even the punishment to be inflicted. Symonds was somehow able to obtain a copy of this letter, and with this written evidence that the case had been prejudged he put a strong plea for British intervention to Des Voeux. Accordingly Commodore James Erskine visited Tonga on HMS *Miranda* in June 1883 to investigate the matter. At the time of Erskine's visit Baker was absent in New Zealand and the king was in Vava'u. A gale prevented the *Miranda* from sailing to Vava'u and so Erskine's only source of information was Symonds, whose account of the situation the Commodore accepted without question. Erskine had no authority to intervene, but on Symonds' urging he interviewed Ngū and issued an ultimatum that unless the prisoners were released Britain would break off relations with Tonga. This was probably all that Erskine threatened, but a rumour circulated that he had also warned Ngū that he would return and bombard Nuku'alofa if his demands were not met, and this rumour encouraged the whites to redouble their efforts.

When Baker returned to Tonga in August 1883 the behaviour of the Europeans was so threatening that he took extraordinary precautions to secure his own safety. Symonds reported:

He invariably stayed at night on board his vessel although he
has a large furnished house here, and I am informed upon
good authority that before his departure for the north a
portion of the Tongan soldiery was disarmed and the rifles
taken aboard the *Sandfly* ... [one night] he placed a woman in
irons for having struck a light on board the vessel. This would
point to the conclusion that a quantity of powder was on
board.[15]

There were other signs that the whites were making a concerted
effort to bring matters to a conclusion. In October 1883 Hanslip,
Parker and Moulton made yet a further petition to Des Voeux
seeking Baker's deportation, and supported it by lengthy affidavits
testifying to Baker's pernicious influence in Tonga. In November
Dr A. G. Buckland, the Tongan government medical officer, signed
a medical certificate asserting that Tupou was suffering from 'inci-
pient softening of the brain' and this information was widely
circulated among the Europeans, even finding its way into the *Fiji
Times*. Early in December Symonds and a group of Europeans took
matters into their own hands when a piece of land belonging to the
king, but over which Frederick Coventry claimed a title, was leased
to a Tongan and planted with yams. According to Fifita, the lessee,
their behaviour was most arrogant. He swore:

We had cleared our land ... and planted our yam patch....
Whilst we were engaged in our work the Consul, Mr Symonds,
came with Mr Percival, Mr Coventry and some others. When
he came up to the ground he demanded to know at whose
command we had planted on their ground and ran at once and
trampled under foot one row of yams and then ... another
row. We went to him and said, 'Mr Symonds, why are you
thus destroying our garden ... for it is the land of the king on
which we are residing?' Mr Symonds replied, 'If there is anyone
here wishes to fight let him come and we will fight.... This is
a portion of Britain which we possess'.[16]

The sequel to this incident occurred in March 1884, when Coventry's store in Nuku'alofa caught fire. Wellington Ngu, who was a bystander, ordered his people not to assist the Europeans to put out the blaze, and the Tongans stood by cheering while the building was razed.

Meanwhile there had been other signs that the tensions were increasing. In December 1883 seven British residents gave formal notification to Symonds that they were determined to pay no further taxes to the Tongan government 'until the existing state of affairs is altered'. A campaign of abuse was also launched against Baker, best exemplified by a long doggerel 'poem' on the subject of Baker's iniquities which was circulated on the beach. Two sample stanzas are sufficient to show the general theme:

> Professing to preach of the word of our Saviour,
> Teaching to tread on the path that he trod;
> He showed by the fruits of his filthy behaviour,
> How hypocrites deal with the Gospel of God.
>
> A thing with a licence to cheat and to plunder,
> To lie, to deceive, to bamboozle, to rob;
> The cloak of the Gospel to hide his deeds under,
> And lastly a humbug, a cad, and a snob.[17]

Baker was also subjected to personal indignity. On one occasion when he and his wife met Hanslip in Nuku'alofa, Hanslip turned his back, lifted his coal tails, and presented his buttocks to the Premier – an insult by any standards, but a particularly coarse one according to Tongan usage.

Baker's efforts to deal with the growing opposition from Moulton and the Wesleyan Church were equally unsuccessful. Moulton had begun giving overt support to the petitioners in March 1882 and, when the British residents petitioned for Baker's removal in the following May, he had assured E. W. Parker that, though he was unwilling to sign the petition, he agreed with its contents and was prepared to give oral testimony in support of it to the High Commissioner. At about the same time he sent one of his Tongan ministers, Tēvita Fīnau, to remonstrate with Baker over the case of three Tupou College students who had been convicted on a charge of stealing. Fīnau's protests were apparently couched in insulting language, for Baker thrashed him with a riding whip. The next Sunday Moulton denounced Baker from the pulpit, comparing his act to Saul's attack on David, and declaring:

> Was such a thing ever heard of, here or elsewhere? For Mr Baker was a good man, a minister, had a position. We all of us ... acknowledge that he was useful to you; but how do we see him now? Isn't his goodness gone? ... he has fallen into evil. He has not retained his goodness; he has an evil spirit.[18]

Then in July 1882, when Gordon delivered judgement on the application to deport Hanslip, Moulton printed Gordon's verdict on the mission press, and circulated it as a pamphlet. A little later he helped Hanslip to convert *Niu Vakai* from manuscript to print by lending mission type. When Baker began putting pressure on Moulton by tightening the school regulations and thus preventing new students from entering Tupou College, Moulton responded by writing, printing and circulating an open letter to the king complaining about the favouritism shown to the government college. Following the visit of HMS *Miranda* Moulton again went into print against Baker, publishing in the *Tupou College Magazine* an article denouncing the Tongan government's current attitude towards Britain and advising Tonga to choose a premier who could keep on good terms with so powerful an ally. Finally, in October 1883, Moulton joined in the petition to the High Commissioner seeking the removal of Baker as one prejudicial to peace and good order.

Baker acted decisively against Moulton when the Tongan District Meeting convened at Ha'apai on 24 October 1883. Through Watkin he brought a long series of charges against Moulton, alleging that he was disaffected towards the government and encouraged unrest and sedition. Watkin took over the chair for the hearing of the charges, and the meeting, voting separately on each of the twenty-one charges, gave a majority of votes against Moulton on each charge. The decision was then sent to the Conference for ratification. At the same time the king wrote to the Conference outlining his objections to Moulton and earnestly begging that he be recalled.

The New South Wales and Queensland Conference met in January 1884 and appointed a special committee to consider the controversy in Tonga. Baker appeared before this committee and stressed that, while it was common knowledge that he and Moulton were enemies of long standing, he had not brought the charges for personal reasons, and that the only question at issue was 'Mr Moulton's political and obnoxious conduct to the king and his Government'. But Baker was pleading a lost cause; by his *Schools Act* he had completely alienated Wesleyan opinion in Australia and, in spite of Tupou's plea and the recommendations of the Tongan District Meeting, the committee rejected every charge and expressed its conviction that the well-being of the Church in Tonga required the presence there of the Reverend J.E. Moulton. A public censure was given to Watkin for his handling of the affair.

Baker left Sydney for Tonga, denouncing the decision of the committee as 'unfair, discourteous and unjust', and when Watkin received word of the censure that had been made upon his conduct he wrote to another missionary warning that he did not intend to submit quietly to the way in which he had been treated. Moulton, on the other hand, returned to Tonga in triumph, although this was somewhat diminished when he called at Vava'u to acquaint Tupou of the Conference decision. The king refused to see him.

By mid-1884 it was becoming plain that Baker was unable to control the opposition of the beach and the Church. At the same time outside influences were pressing matters to a climax. Symonds had been constantly urging Des Voeux to take direct action against Baker and in August 1883 the High Commissioner decided to follow his advice. He informed the Secretary of State for Foreign Affairs

Affairs that he had determined to send a warship to Tonga to free the prisoners and deport Baker. This dispatch was referred to Gordon for comment. Gordon advised that any change in the government in Tonga could only be a change for the worse, and urged that Des Voeux be restrained from rash action. Lord Derby concurred, and the High Commisioner for the Western Pacific was instructed not to proceed with his plan. However Des Voeux was determined to make some show of force in Tonga and in July 1883 Captain Sir Cyprian Bridge, commanding HMS *Espiègle,* was ordered to proceed to Tonga to demand the release of the Mu'a men and to seek satisfaction on several matters of dispute between Tonga and Britain. But when Bridge reached Nuku'alofa he found that he had been forestalled. Baker, apparently realising that his position was no longer tenable, had sailed for New Zealand, and before leaving had issued, as a mark of his 'great love for all the natives of Tonga', a full and free pardon for the Mu'a petitioners.

CHAPTER IX

THE TONGAN REFORMATION

D URING THE EPISODE of the Mu'a parliament Baker had behaved, on the whole, in a moderate and conciliatory manner, and had tried to compose the troubles by reasonable compromise. By late 1884, however, it was clear that this policy was bankrupt, that the opposition parties had outstripped him and that his eclipse was imminent. There were in fact only two alternatives: to submit meekly, or to risk everything in a desperate bid to regain the initiative. For the *Ta'emangoi* this really left only one option. The traders and the Tongan dissidents were the most active elements in the anti-Baker coalition, but the strength of the movement lay in the support of Symonds and Moulton and the interests which they represented. Characteristically, Baker directed his attack against the real core of the opposition: he challenged simultaneously the British establishment and the Wesleyan Church.

The visit of HMS *Espiègle* provided the excuse for Baker to move against Symonds. Captain Bridge had visited Tupou at Vava'u in the company of Symonds, and had demanded of the king the repeal of the press law, the treason and sedition laws, and the law prohibiting Tongans from bringing cases before the High Commissioner's Court. He had also demanded an apology for alleged discourtesy shown by the Tongan government to Symonds, and an undertaking that, in future, British officials in Tonga should be treated with respect. Tupou had protested that the Constitution did not permit him to repeal laws that had been passed by parliament, but Bridge, backed by the authority of *Espiègle's* guns, had insisted. The king was then obliged, under protest, to give the required undertakings.

Baker prepared a long formal protest about the actions of Bridge and Symonds, forwarding copies to the Secretary of State for the Colonies and the High Commissioner and at the same time publishing the text as a Tongan Government Blue Book. He pointed to many inaccuracies in Bridge's statement which had their root in misleading despatches sent by Symonds. For instance Bridge had objected to the press law because in its English translation there was no mention of a trial to assess the guilt of a defendant. Baker pointed out that in the Tongan original, which was the version used in the courts, this ambiguity did not occur. Bridge had demanded the repeal of the *Law Relative to Treason* on the grounds that it contravened the British treaty, but Baker showed that this law had been passed in 1875, long before the signing of the treaty, and that in any case the law specifically exempted foreigners from its application. On the question of Tongans bringing cases before the High Commissioner's Court, Baker had sought advice from two eminent colonial jurists, Sir Wigram Allen and Sir Frederick Whitaker, and forwarded their opinion that the Tongan government's interpretation of the treaty was correct and that the British government had no reasonable ground for complaint. Finally, Baker countered the charge of discourtesy to Symonds by counter-accusing him of gross breaches of courtesy towards the Tongan government, instancing in particular his procuring and publicising a statement that Tupou was in his dotage and suffering from 'softening of the brain'.[1]

Baker's complaint was effective. His evidence showed British policy to have been founded on false premises and erroneous information, and Des Voeux was furious at being caught so badly off-balance. He wrote to Lord Derby explaining that he had merely inherited the situation, and that the real blame belonged to Gordon, who had encouraged Symonds to pursue a policy of continual meddling with native affairs. Symonds was on leave in England at the time of the complaint but when he returned to Tonga in 1885 Des Voeux's temporary successor, William McGregor, gave him some very pointed advice, and strictly enjoined him to refrain in future from taking any part in the domestic political squabbles of Tonga. His teeth were drawn, and though he remained in Tonga during 1885 and 1886, he was merely a bystander. In June 1886 he sought a transfer, and in the following October he was appointed to Samoa.

Baker's protest had an equally chastening effect on the High Commissioner. No formal apology was offered for the *Espiègle* affair, but when J.B. Thurston, the then Acting High Commissioner, visited Tonga in September 1885, he came with ostentatious humility, not on a man-of-war but on an island cargo steamer. For the time being at least Baker had the advantage and British interference in Tongan affairs was suspended.

With Symonds disabled, Baker turned his attention to the Wesleyan Church. In January 1885 he managed to provoke a wholesale secession of the Tongan Methodists from the Sydney Conference; it was a deliberate and decisive blow which completely disrupted and almost destroyed the Wesleyan Church in Tonga. He gave adequate warning of his intentions: in August 1884 Ngū wrote on behalf of the king (but almost certainly at Baker's instigation) to the President of the General Conference telling him that Tupou was 'grieved and annoyed' that the New South Wales and Queensland Conference had not acceded to his request for Moulton's removal, and asking that the General Conference exercise its authority and remove Moulton in order to prevent the secession which must otherwise take place.

At the end of September Baker himself formally applied to the General Conference seeking the removal of Moulton, whom he claimed had become a political partisan opposed to the king and the Tongan government; if Moulton were removed, he promised, no schism would take place. That a schism would occur if Moulton were not removed was not stated, but was clearly implied.

The Australasian General Conference met in Christchurch, New Zealand, in November 1884 and Moulton attended to defend his position. It was decided that a deputation should visit Tonga to inquire into its problems, but no action was taken against Moulton, and he returned to Tonga with his status and authority unimpaired. Baker noted in his journal: 'It is a matter of regret that the General Conference held in Christchurch did not accept the compromise proposed by the King'[2] – but perhaps the regret was not very keenly felt. By careful manoeuvre he had placed himself, according to his own lights, 'in the right'. It only wanted a favourable opportunity and he could, with a clear conscience, carry out the threatened secession.

The opportunity came at the beginning of 1885. Baker received word that both Watkin and Tupou were ill in Vava'u and he sailed there to attend them. On his return he called at Lifuka, Ha'apai, where he found the Wesleyan congregation torn with dissension over the suspension by Moulton of the resident Tongan minister, Paula Vi, for being too outspoken a supporter of the king in ecclesiastical matters. This was just the chance Baker had been waiting for. On 4 January he called an open air meeting and invited Paula Vi to preach – about five hundred people attended. In the afternoon another service was held and this time the congregation numbered about a thousand. Encouraged by this support, Baker called a meeting on the following day of all the people 'who loved the king more than Mr. Moulton', and at this mass meeting announced the inauguration of a new church, the Free Church of Tonga, Wesleyan in doctrine, but independent of the Sydney Conference.

Baker then returned to Vava'u to acquaint the king of the developments at Ha'apai. According to Catholic sources Tupou was greatly displeased with his Premier for taking matters into his own hands, and only after Baker had humbled himself, Tonga-fashion, by a ritual presentation of a *fei'umu* of baked food, would the king listen to his explanations. Eventually, however, Baker won Tupou's support for his coup, and on 14 January the Free Church was established in Vava'u by proclamation of the king. On the following day Watkin severed his connection with the Sydney Conference and accepted the office of President of the Tongan Church.

In Vava'u the establishment of the Free Church met no opposition whatever, and almost without exception chiefs, clergy and people defected from the Wesleyan Church to join the church of the king. From the Tongan viewpoint this was not a reprehensible desertion of their faith, but merely obedience to a lawful demand of the king. One minister, who had given long and faithful service to the Wesleyan Church, explained his defection to the Reverend Lorimer Fison:

> King George is our Chief, and we are bound to obey all his
> lawful commands. He expressed his will that we should join
> the Free Church of Tonga. Was that command lawful or
> unlawful? If he had told us to go to the Church of Rome or
> in any way to abandon Methodism, we would have been
> justified in refusing, and we would have taken the conse-
> quences of our refusal. But he did not do this. The Free
> Church is a Methodist Church. We have the same Bible we
> had before, the same doctrine, the same discipline, the same
> worship, the same God and Saviour Jesus Christ, our Lord.
> The only difference is that we are independent of outside rule.
> Therefore the King's command was a lawful command, and
> to disobey it an act of rebellion.[3]

The people of Ha'apai received the king's proclamation in very much the same way as the people of Vava'u. Baker called in at Lifuka on his way back to Tongatapu, to acquaint the chiefs of the king's proclamation, and he had the satisfaction of seeing the great majority of the people formally join the Free Church. In Tongatapu, however, Baker met considerable resistance. Moulton had visited Ha'apai to attend a District Meeting on 6 January, the day after Baker had held the inaugural meeting of the Free Church, and had hastened back to Tongatapu to warn his people of what had occurred, and to stiffen their resistance. At a public meeting in Zion Church he announced: 'There is a new thing happened in the land; there is a new religion set up'.[4] He exhorted his flock to stand firm and, thus encouraged, large numbers began rallying to his support – the majority for reasons that were genuinely religious, but a significant minority for reasons that were purely political. The sudden conversion of this latter group Moulton regarded as a special manifestation of Providence. In February he reported 'numbers of the wild young men have had their hearts touched and have joined the Society', and in March he recalled how 'God had poured his Holy Spirit on irreligious young men and women who joined in such numbers that the loss of the old adherents was scarcely felt'.[5] It seems, however, that Moulton did not allow sufficiently for profane influences. Prominent among 'the wild young men' were Tōpui, Leka and Tupouto'a, who soon became the unofficial leaders and spokesmen of the Wesleyans in Hahake. Many others seem to have been political partisans who had supported the Mu'a parliament, and who saw in the religious dispute an opportunity to reaffirm their opposition to Baker and his government. Thus from its inception the confrontation of Free Church and Wesleyan in Tongatapu was exacerbated by political differences and, at least in part, developed into a bitter struggle between the government and its political opponents. Caught between this hammer and anvil were those Tongans who for the sake of conscience and conviction remained loyal to Moulton and the Wesleyan connection. Their lot was desperate.

Baker and Watkin arrived in Tongatapu on 27 January and by that time the opposition movement was well established. A meeting of all chiefs and government officials was held in Nuku'alofa and

Baker read a letter from the king which ordered, 'If you have any love for me join at once the Wesleyan Free Church of Tonga and set it up in your respective towns.'[6] All who refused would lose their title and government office. Under these conditions the majority of the notables embraced the new church, but several refused. Kēlepi 'Otuhouma, a chief and the magistrate at 'Eua, refused to turn, and justified his decision in a calm and dignified statement which encouraged other waverers to stand firm. The general tenor of his reply was given to a later inquiry:

> I said I loved the King, and prized my position in the Government, and my pay, and my inheritance and title possessed by my ancestors, but that I would not barter my religion for these things. I wished that the King's word touched some worldly matter, a war for instance. In that I would do my best for the King. Or a public debt – I would help. The difficulty was the King gave orders about the lotu. That concerned myself alone.[7]

Others followed 'Otuhouma's lead. Tēvita Lātūkefu, the Town Officer of Kolovai, told Baker:

> I wished to remain a Wesleyan because I obtained spiritual light in that Church. The one thing that was clear to my mind was that it was not the part of the Government to set up a Church, but that it was the work for priests.[8]

Altogether eleven notables, five of them hereditary chiefs, refused to join the Free Church, and Baker, acting on the king's authority, deprived them of their titles and dismissed them from office.

Following the meeting with the chiefs and officials, Baker and Watkin visited several important towns, holding *ngaahi fono*, reading the king's proclamation and exhorting the people to join the Free Church. However they met with very limited success. The people were confused by the conflicting arguments put forward by Moulton and Baker, and hesitated to commit themselves. Moulton's

most recent move had been to publish a circular letter to the people
of Tonga warning that Baker's *ngaahi fono* were contrary to the
Constitution and violated the British treaty. He promised that a
British man-of-war would intervene to humble Baker and secure
the rights of Wesleyans. This letter was intended to encourage
Wesleyans to stand firm, but it had another very significant effect:
Baker wrote an angry reply to Moulton's letter ridiculing the idea
of British intervention, but nevertheless he immediately relinquished the direction of the campaign to establish the Free Church to his
Tongan associates. Evidently he feared that Moulton's threat might
contain a grain of truth, and wanted to give no grounds for the
High Commissioner to exercise his powers of summary deportation
against him.

Once the task of carrying out the king's orders had been dele-
gated to Tongans, the campaign assumed a much more coercive
character. Towards the end of February Ngū held a *fono* in
Nukuʻalofa, and ordered the people in blunt and peremptory terms
to join the Free Church. He expressed his determination to hold
ngaahi fono all over Tonga to bring the matter to a successful
conclusion, but he was not permitted to carry out this intention.
On 11 March 1885 Ngū suffered a heart attack and died.

The body of the Crown Prince was taken to ʻUiha in Haʻapai
for burial, and the ceremony was attended by all the principal chiefs
and officials in the group. Despite the solemnity of the occasion the
church controversy frequently intruded: Wesleyans were excluded
from the *faikava* ceremony, which was an important part of the
obsequies, and for the religious service Wesleyans were sent off to
worship by themselves at Felemea, while the church at ʻUiha, in
spite of loud protests from the Reverend E.E. Crosby, was taken
over for the use of the Free Church worshippers. After the funeral
the king held a *fono* and told the gathered chiefs that he was
determined that the Free Church should be the only Methodist body
in Tonga. He gave his people until the end of May to join his
church, at which time, he informed them, he would come to
Tongatapu accompanied by loyal warriors from Vavaʻu and Haʻapai,

to deal with any Tongan who had not complied with his wishes. He added: 'If I say there will be mischief, there will be mischief'.[9]

The king's *fono* at 'Uiha marked the beginning of real persecution in Tonga. The chiefs had received direct personal instructions from the king and felt justified in making their own arrangements for carrying them out. They began holding *ngaahi fono* as soon as they returned to Tongatapu. The first was held at Nuku'alofa on 27 March; others followed in rapid succession in all the towns and villages. Halaholo, the chief of 'Eua, held his *fono* on 30 March and told his people:

> The King's will is that you should change your religion. And don't you delay. If any of you hold on and hinder you will find yourself in an evil case. We can do what we like with you.[10]

Many joined the Free Church on the spot and were allowed to go home. Halaholo then turned his attention to the recalcitrants. Lūpeni Fehi'a gave evidence at a later investigation:

> I remember Halaholo thrashing a man called Josepha Mau because he would not join the Free Church.... Halaholo took a stick and thrashed him. He broke one of his ribs. While beating him he asked him if he would change over. Josepha refused. Halaholo kept on thrashing him until he said he was Free Church. Josepha is still an invalid [two years later] from the effects of the beating.[11]

Even after treatment such as this, however, many refused to join the Free Church. A young woman, 'Akanesi Kaufo'ou, testified:

> I am from 'Eua. I was beaten for refusing to be Free Church.... After I was bound the order was given to beat me.... I lay on the ground and they went on beating me until my mother

said she wished they would kill me instead of torturing me. I
lay down in my house. I could not move. I ate nothing for
three days. I did not expect to live. I am still a Wesleyan.[12]

On 18 April Ata held a *fono* at Kolovai to warn his people that
if they were disobedient to the king's order they would be punished.
P. S. Bloomfield was a witness to what followed:

... I was at Hihifo. I remember a number of women being
thrashed to induce them to go over to the Free Church. The
chief, Ata, flogged five or six women for refusing to go
over.... Between the floggings he asked if they would turn
over. The instrument was a long horse whip. One of them
was a grey haired old woman, I should think about sixty.[13]

Similar incidents were reported from all over Tonga. At Pea,
Lavaka held a *fono* at which Wesleyans were forced to sit for seven
hours in the sun. At Ha'akame, 'Uiliame Valu deprived all
Wesleyans of their tax-lands. Lavaka told the Wesleyans of Folaha
that 'Mr Moulton is your king' and banished them to seek refuge in
Moulton's house; their goods were plundered by the Free Church
adherents. By mid-April the Wesleyans of 'Ahau, Pea, Nukuhitolu,
Kolovai and 'Eua were all seeking sanctuary with Moulton.

Similar measures were applied to the Wesleyan remnant in
Ha'apai. Two girls of Hā'ano who refused to join the Free Church
were taken by their chief to the rocky uninhabited isle of Kao and
ordered to leap into the surf and swim to the rocks. Faced with the
prospect of almost certain drowning the girls gave way and joined
the Free Church. Shortly afterwards all the Wesleyans of Lofanga
were banished to Kao, where the only food was coconuts and wild
roots. Heamasi Fonua testified:

I was amongst those banished to an island called Kao on
account of not joining the Free Church; about eighty of us

were banished.... When I was at Kao I lived upon roots; I
was almost dying with hunger.[14]

The chiefs also turned their attention to Wesleyan property. The
seizure of the Wesleyan Church at 'Uiha for Ngū's funeral service
had established a precedent and during April 1885 dozens of
churches were confiscated by the chiefs. On 29 March Moulton
appealed to Baker against the action of Laisiki who had taken
possession of the church at 'Ahau. The following day he reported
that forcible possession had been taken of the churches at Ha'akame
and Buke. On 9 April he complained of the seizure of the churches
at Pea, Veitongo, Tofoa and Havelu. By the middle of the month
many more cases had occurred. The circumstances attending the
seizure of the Talafo'ou church on 17 April were particularly brutal.
Moulton reported the case to Tu'uhetoka, the Minister of Police:

> ... the town officer entered the church while Jiosiua Lolohea,
> the minister, was conducting the morning service.... Before
> the minister had finished praying the man laid hold of him
> and dashed him against one side and then against the other
> side while he was still praying, and then threw him outside.
> The chief of the town stood with a billet of wood and shouted
> to drag him to be beaten, and a lot of people entered the
> church and took possession and drove us out.[15]

By May 1885 every church in Vava'u, all but one in Ha'apai, and a
large number in Tongatapu had been taken over by the Free
Church.

During this time Baker had been making futile attempts to
restrain the chiefs, for reports of the persecutions, often exaggerated,
were being given wide publicity in the world press, and were
causing him acute embarrassment. When the first case of persecution
was reported by Moulton, Baker assured him that he had instructed
the Minister of Police to allow no interference with the right all
Tongans possessed of worshipping according to the dictates of their

consciences. When the dispossessed Wesleyans began moving from their villages to Nukuʻalofa Baker ordered their immediate re-patriation, and as soon as he received word of the Haʻapai Wesleyans being marooned on Kao he sent a vessel loaded with food to succour them and carry them back to their homes. In most cases, however, his protests were futile; the chiefs had received their instructions directly from the king and ignored the Premier's expostulations. The control of the movement had slipped from his grasp and events were shaping with a logic and momentum of their own. Moulton, of course, claimed that Baker encouraged the chiefs to persecute Wesleyans, but this accusation is not supported by the evidence. Baker had nothing to gain and much to lose from the unfavourable publicity that the persecutions generated. The opinion of J.B. Thurston, who visited Tonga in September 1885, that 'the Government had beyond doubt, lost control of its usual executive power and was unable to enforce proper control of the people'[16] seems to be a correct appraisal of the situation.

A chance to resolve the dispute amicably came in May 1885 with the visit of a deputation from the General Conference armed with powers to negotiate a settlement of differences. Baker's only precondition was the removal of Moulton from Tonga, but this the deputation refused to consider unless Watkin were also removed. Baker refused to sacrifice his friend and ally, and the deputation left Tonga empty-handed. Meanwhile the persecutions continued.

By the end of May the situation was becoming very tense. On the one hand Moulton had promised that the High Commissioner would come to Tonga on a man-of-war to aid the harassed Wesleyans, and was exhorting his adherents to hold on until his arrival. In one of the many Tongan language pamphlets which he issued during this time he wrote:

> Shall we deny our Lord who died to save us, yes the God who bought us with His blood? How shall we be able to stand before Him after we have denied Him? Be brave. In a short time we shall reach safety and peace. Think of the words

of Jesus, '... Trust me unto death and I shall give you the crown of Life'.[17]

On the other hand the chiefs were desperately trying to 'convert' all their followers before the king paid his promised visit to Tongatapu, for disobedience on the part of their people was felt by the chiefs to reflect on their own loyalty. Tu'ilupou expressed this feeling succinctly at his *fono,* when he scolded his people:

> Why do you persist about the Church?... Are you not fighting the King? I am living here in fear of Tupou, for it is not as if you are blamed, for who are you? Are you not about as important in the eyes of Tupou as some fowl's feathers? It is my name which is carried to Tupou.[18]

During June the persecutions continued, while Tongatapu waited for the arrival of Tupou which, it was widely rumoured, would be the signal for the wholesale slaughter of all the remaining Wesleyans. The king arrived on 4 July, accompanied by sixty boats containing some eighteen hundred warriors armed with guns, axes and clubs. All Wesleyans were ordered to attend a king's *fono* in Nuku'alofa, at which it was expected that the executions would take place. By this time the Wesleyans numbered only two thousand but they had the zeal of martyrs. Moulton reported:

> One woman, who had just given birth to a child, said to her husband, 'You go down, but promise me as soon as the hanging begins, you will come and fetch me, and let us die together'.

Another, an old man too frail to walk, came on a horse and, arriving late, told his friends, 'I was afraid I would be too late to be hanged'.[19] The *fono* was to be held early in the morning and before daylight a Wesleyan service was held in Zion Church. The congregation was still at prayer when the *lali* was beaten for the *fono* to begin, and the Wesleyans moved down to the *mala'e* in a compact body. What followed was an almost ridiculous anticlimax. There were no hangings. There were no beatings. The king addressed the gathering quietly, told them that he was displeased with them and dismissed them to their houses.

Tupou's restraint was quite unexpected. Reports had reached Tongatapu of statements made by the king in Vava'u intimating that no quarter would be offered to the Wesleyans. The circumstances of his arrival, with a large body of armed men, also suggested that his intentions were not peaceable. What then restrained him? Moulton believed that the quiet heroism of the Wesleyans moved him to compassion, and this is a possible explanation. It is more likely, however, that Baker intervened to pacify the king. The whole affair had taken a turn that he had not anticipated when he introduced the Free Church. The delegation of authority to the chiefs had given them a taste of the sort of power that they had enjoyed before the advent of the missionaries and the rise of Tupou. The taste had been much to their liking; the thin veneer of civilisation had been sloughed off and, in the anarchy that followed, the whole delicate structure of parliamentary government, which Baker had so patiently erected, and on which his own power completely depended, began to collapse. For over three months the Premier's word had counted for little in Tonga. It was therefore entirely in his interest to try to prevent further outrages, and to seek the restoration of law and order.

But, however inspired, Tupou's moderation proved most effective. Large numbers of Wesleyans, denied the glories of martyrdom, quietly defected to the Free Church – between July and September Wesleyan numbers dwindled from two thousand to seven hundred. The temperate behaviour of the king also acted as a brake on the excited passions of the chiefs, and gross persecution ceased. Baker was able to regain control of the situation, and one of his first acts was to confirm the Wesleyan Church in its rights of tenure to all property held under legally valid leases. Thus, when J. B. Thurston, the Acting High Commissioner, arrived in Tonga in September, order had been restored and the country was returning to normal. All Wesleyans, it is true, were detained in Nuku'alofa because the king, angered at Moulton's repeated assertions that a British man-of-war would come to rescue his adherents, had ordered them to wait in Nuku'alofa for the ship to come; but otherwise there was little evidence of persecution. Thurston did not come on a warship, but on an ordinary cargo vessel, and he refused to take any action on behalf of the Wesleyans or against Baker. He merely counselled moderation, and having received assurances that the Wesleyans would be gradually permitted to disperse, he returned to Fiji.

After September 1885 there was a gradual relaxing of the tensions in Tonga. On 13 October the Hahake Wesleyans were allowed to return to their homes, and by 5 December the same privilege had been extended to all the others. Persecution, at least in its more blatant forms, ceased and Baker seemed prepared to leave the Wesleyans in relative peace, probably hoping that they would wither on the vine. Nor was such a hope unjustified. The return of their church properties had saddled the Wesleyan remnant with crippling burdens: by law property holders were required to keep their lands weeded, hoed and regularly swept, and with their depleted numbers these tasks became very onerous, especially as most Wesleyans were at this time very busy rebuilding their plundered homes, cutting copra for their taxes and planting their food crops. In Vava'u, for instance, there remained only six Wesleyans, yet every week this little band was required to sweep every church allotment in the whole group. Not unnaturally, the enthusiasm of the Wesleyans began to wane.

It was Moulton who provoked fresh disturbances. In October 1885 he sent a 'missionary' to Vava'u to win back converts from the Free Church. This was a serious threat to Baker's whole project. He responded by securing from the 1885 Parliament a *Law of Six and of Thirty* making it illegal for a church to hold services in a town unless it had six adherents, who were 'rightful inhabitants', living there, and for any minister to live in a town where he had fewer than thirty adherents who were 'rightful inhabitants'. This law effectively prevented any further proselytising by Moulton. Moreover the phrase 'rightful inhabitant' was left to be interpreted by the Tongan judges, who frequently used it as a weapon against the Wesleyans. A typical situation was described by the Reverend E.E. Crosby:

> In Hofua we have a number of adherents but owing to the detention of the people in Nuku'alofa we have had no preaching there for some time. We resolved to begin with the New Year having, as we counted, six adults, rightful inhabitants. The Government Representative in the town admitted only two, counting a father, but refusing to count his two children. The Minister of Police, on being appealed to, counted the children (who were adults, one being married) and thus recognised four. The other two whom we had counted were rightful inhabitants on their mother's side, and their father had settled in the town on his marriage to their mother. Yet they were not allowed to count, and we could not have the preaching.[20]

By June 1886 there had been thirty separate prosecutions of Wesleyan native ministers for breaches of the *Law of Six and of Thirty*.

During the remainder of 1886 pressure was kept on the Wesleyans, but the religious dispute had ceased to occupy all of Baker's attention. From about September 1885, when he had regained control of events, he had begun to turn his mind once more to secular affairs, and had carried out several important projects, including an extensive program of public works, the improvement of mail and shipping services to Tonga, and the negotiation of a treaty with the United States similar to that with Britain or Germany. During this period, however, Baker continued to be the subject of unfavourable comment in the outside press, particularly in Britain and the Australian colonies, where critical letters, pamphlets and articles had appeared regularly through 1885 and 1886. So on 12 January 1887 he decided to reply to his many critics. The Free Church was an accomplished fact, the Wesleyans were a dwindling minority and peace had been restored in Tonga; it was time to put the record straight and justify his policies. He did this in a long article written for publication in the Sydney *Daily Telegraph*. Ironically, even while he was writing, five Tongans were waiting in the dark outside his house to assassinate him when he left on his customary evening visit to his office.

CHAPTER X

AN ASSASSINATION
ATTEMPT

T HE FIVE TONGANS who lay in wait for Baker on the night of 12 January were Tavake, Palu, Naisa, Fehoko and Latu. Tavake was the son of Tōpui, the old Muʻa parliament leader; the others were prisoners who had escaped from Nukuʻalofa gaol on 5 September 1886. Palu had been serving a term for adultery and theft. Naisa, Fehoko and Latu, all men of Muʻa, had originally been convicted for minor offences, but had broken custody, stolen a boat and attempted to sail to Fiji. Instead they had drifted to Haʻapai, where they had been apprehended and returned to Tongatapu. They had each been sentenced to two years work in irons for stealing a boat. Latu had been sentenced to an additional eight years, Naisa to an additional six years and Fehoko to an additional two years labour for absconding while a prisoner. Their original offences were probably merely boyish pranks, but the severity of the sentences passed on them had made them desperate. When they escaped for a second time in the company of Palu they stole four police rifles and made for the Hahake bush, whereupon they were declared outlaws and the police instructed to shoot them on sight. On two occasions several hundred men had been sent to Hahake to search for them, but their friends and relatives in Muʻa had sent the search parties off on false trails, and on each occasion the searchers had returned to

Nuku'alofa empty-handed. For four months the outlaws remained at large and, with the connivance of local officials, they often visited Mu'a at night, where they were given food, shelter and encouragement.

At about the same time Mu'a had also been receiving frequent visits from Mr Basil Thomson, a young magistrate from the Lau Islands in Fiji, who was spending his leave in Tonga. Thomson had stayed at the consulate in Nuku'alofa until Symonds left Tonga in November 1886, and had then spent most of his time with Tungi out at Mu'a. Thomson was very critical of the Baker regime in Tonga, and while it is unlikely that he purposely spread sedition, he did discuss his views very openly and they probably helped to stimulate a plot that was hatched among the chiefs of Mu'a. This original plot can only be reconstructed in shadowy outline from hints dropped by witnesses and a sifting of contemporary rumours, for those involved were men of the highest rank. The main conspirators seem to have been Tuku'aho, Tungi's eldest son, Tu'ipelehake, the governor of Ha'apai; and Laifone, the Crown Prince and governor of Vava'u. What was envisaged was a *coup d'état:* Tuku'aho was to seize Baker, ship him to Fiji on his own vessel, the *Sandfly,* and deliver him in irons to the High Commissioner. The Hahake soldiers, who were under Tuku'aho's command, would maintain order in Tongatapu during this period, while Tu'ipelehake and Laifone would prevent troops from Ha'apai and Vava'u from interfering. News of the conspiracy leaked out, however, and became common rumour in Mu'a, and the outlaws, having heard it, approached Tōpui, who was Tuku'aho's cousin, suggesting that they could settle the matter much more effectively merely by shooting Baker. Topui with Tuku'aho's approval, began holding secret meetings in Mu'a to discuss the suggestion. The meetings were attended by the four outlaws, Topui, and local firebrands and old Mu'a parliament supporters including 'Aisea Kaumoto, Penisio Hau, Lutoviko Tuhoko and possibly Leka. By the end of 1886 the group had arranged to get ammunition and additional firearms from a European and to assassinate Baker. The details were revealed later in testimony by Penisiō Hau:

> I know Filipi Taufa. I told him something about the secret meetings held by Tobui [Tōpui] at Mua. I told him that one Sunday we went to Italale and were to remain there to meet Tobui after the service of the Wesleyans was over. Tobui was there. Naisa and Latu were there. Naisa said, 'Why are the arms not here?' Tobui said, 'I have written to the European and he will have them sent'. I and Naisa went and sat by the sea, Palu came and he said that he and Naisa would go and commit the assassination.... It was the last Sunday in 1886.[1]

The European in question was Robert Hanslip. Soni Muli, who delivered Tōpui's letter, later testified:

> Tobui came to me and said could I take a letter for him to Nuku'alofa to Mr. Hanslip.... I went to Mr Hanslip's place and took the letter of Tobui to him ... and I gave it and Mr Hanslip read it: after which Mr Hanslip wrote a letter and I took it with me to Mu'a to Tobui, and as I went Mr Hanslip cautioned me for no one to know anything at all about it, and I replied to Mr Hanslip, 'I will never tell anyone'. I asked Tobui what was the meaning of the letter I took to Mr Hanslip and Tobui told me he wrote as to whether Mr Hanslip could let him have some guns and Mr Hanslip replied he could do so. Tobui told me Mr Hanslip went up to the Mu'a with a bag of bullets and Tobui took them to Naisa, and Naisa gave them to Palu and Latu and Fehoko.... Tobui commanded that no one should tell they were bullets from Mr Hanslip.[2]

Two abortive attempts were made to assassinate Baker before 12 January 1887. Tōpui had passed word of the conspiracy to his old Mu'a parliament colleague, Lavuso, who worked at Tupou College and Lavuso determined to perform the task himself. On Christmas Eve 1886, with an accomplice from the college, probably Tuitavake, he went to Baker's house, ostensibly to seek medicine, but really to club him to death when he answered the door. This plan was foiled when Lavuso found Baker's yard crowded with government college boys. Then on New Year's Eve the outlaws waited for Baker to attend a 'watch night service' at the king's chapel, but for some reason this attempt also failed. The outlaws came again to Nuku'alofa on the evening of 12 January, bringing with them Tōpui's son, Tavake, who had lived with Baker and knew his habits. They made no secret of their mission, for Sione Latuvaivai later recalled: 'I met Palu in the bush; he said he was going down to shoot Mr Baker'.[3] By nightfall the five had taken their positions by the road to wait for their quarry. But that night the moon came up before Baker emerged from his house and, fearful of being recognised, the assassins decided to postpone their attempt until the following evening. They retired to the *Mala'e Kula,* a large open square opposite Tupou College, and sent Tavake to seek a hiding place for the night. Both Hanslip and Tuitavake made excuses when Tavake asked for shelter, but eventually he gained access to Lavuso's house by threatening to shoot him if he refused.

Tavake, Fehoko, Naisa and Latu stayed that night and all the following day in Lavuso's house in the grounds of Tupou College, and word of their presence and their intentions circulated among students and staff, several of whom, including the Reverend Tēvita Finau, Fekau, Tuitavake and Nuku, came to visit them and discuss the plot. At nightfall Tavake and the three outlaws, accompanied by Lavuso, went to the Beach Road to wait for Baker. Palu, meanwhile, had returned to Mu'a on the previous evening, probably to explain the delay to Tōpui, and came back again late that afternoon with a boy, Vuni. He called at Hanslip's house at dusk to collect an extra gun, then returned to the college to find that the others had already left. Taking Fekau, a college boy, with him he arrived at the road some distance from his friends just in time to hear several shots. A few seconds later Baker galloped past. He was moving so quickly that Palu did not have time to fire.

In his official statement Baker described what had happened:

After dinner on Thursday evening at 7.10 p.m. I ordered the buggy to be ready; got into it with my son and daughter [Shirley and Beatrice] ordering at the same time my driver to follow on with a case behind. I have not been in the habit of driving of an evening, but as we had a fresh and rather restive horse in the buggy, I told my son that I would drive.

I was sitting on the front seat, my daughter being seated immediately behind me, and my son sitting beside her. The horse being fresh was travelling rather fast, and as soon as it got near Mary Halawalo's house it shied at a native who was standing directly in the road; my son Shirley called out, 'that man has a gun' and immediately jumped out of the buggy and commanded him to put his gun down, stepping towards him as he spoke. I was unable to pull up the horse, but I noticed that there was another man, also with a gun, in a stooping position looking forward, evidently to see where I was, the light of the buggy lamp shining full on his face. There were two other men a little further on also with guns; and there was also what I took to be a woman at a little distance, and a reflection like the shadow of someone else a short distance from her. The horse was still travelling and my daughter jumped up from her seat and leaning forward threw her arms around me. I must have given the horse an extra pull on the right-hand rein and he made a swerve, when immediately a gun was fired by the man first seen ... my son called out that he was shot, when my daughter immediately let go of me, and said as she jumped from the buggy 'I must go to Shirley, he is shot'. The horse being wounded, also gave a plunge which caused my daughter to be thrown on the back of her head.[4]

The boy had been shot in the shoulder while the girl had received a wound in the thigh and had also injured her spine in the fall from the buggy. The story is continued from the memoir written by Lillian and Beatrice Shirley Baker:

> The assassins turned and ran, as Dr Baker, in sickened fury, charged them unarmed. He caught the terrified horse and somehow brought it under control, leading it back to the trap. As a medical man he rendered what first aid was possible to his son and daughter then drove them quickly back to Nuku'alofa for attention, calling up the police at the same time.[5]

With the passage of time, however, the memory of the Misses Baker had evidently deteriorated, for the story of Baker's heroism did not appear in the contemporary account. According to Baker's affidavit, sworn two days after the event, as Beatrice fell to the ground:

> She ... called to me to drive on, and to my son, Shirley, to run, as I did so Shirley told me he would be all right. As the horse bolted around the corner of the King's palace, past the Watkin's house, I tried to guide him towards Tui Toka's [Tu'uhetoka's] house and succeeded in doing so ... and directed the people there to go down at once and see what assistance they could render.[6]

This impression of Baker as being somewhat less than heroic is confirmed by the description of him left by the British pro-Consul, who called on him that same evening and recorded in his diary:

> Mr Baker was half-sitting, half-lying on a chair, having just recovered from a fainting fit (I was told he had had several previous to my arrival) and two natives were fanning him, whilst Mr Campbell was supporting him also. Mr Watkin and Mrs Baker were bathing his head with cold water and eau-de-cologne.[7]

The next day, at Baker's request, Giles flew the Union Jack over Baker's house to indicate that the family was under British protection.

Tupou's reaction to the attack on Baker was characteristically vigorous. On 14 January he sent messages to Ha'apai and Vava'u informing the chiefs of the events of the day before and seeking the aid of the men of the north to secure Tongatapu for their king. On the same afternoon he called a meeting of the Tongatapu chiefs at Nuku'alofa, told them that the attack on Baker was an act of rebellion, and ordered them to gather armed men in their villages and to meet him at Vainī on the following Monday for an expedition into Hahake. Tungī, whom the king strongly suspected of being implicated in the plot, left the meeting knowing that if he did not capture and hand over the outlaws himself within two days, his district would be ravaged by the king's men. On the Saturday morning Tungī sent Tōpui with a body of soldiers to bring in the outlaws. When the soldiers approached, the outlaws came out of the bush, but no attempt was made to capture them – instead they all stood in the road discussing the situation. Meanwhile Tu'uhetoka had been sent by Tupou with a squad of police to search for the outlaws, and had been joined by the chiefs Lavaka and Fohe with some of their followers; upon reaching Tōpui's village of Holonga they had set about plundering it. Tōpui and his soldiers were still arguing with the outlaws when some women brought word that Tu'uhetoka and his party were sacking Holonga and shooting Tōpui's pigs. Thereupon Tōpui proclaimed that he would lead his soldiers and the outlaws to fight the government forces at Holonga, and sent word to Tungī of his intention. Tungī sent word back that Tōpui was to come and explain the matter and when, in obedience to his chief, Tōpui returned to Mu'a, he was seized and bound. Tuku'aho played a prominent part in his capture.

Tu'uhetoka arrived with his men about three o'clock on the Saturday afternoon and Tungī handed over Tōpui, and his old associate, Leka, to his charge. Having heard that reprisals were being made against their relatives the outlaws also gave themselves up:

Fehoko on Sunday morning, and the others the same afternoon. They were taken to Nuku'alofa, put in irons and thrown in gaol. Questioned by Tu'uhetoka, they revealed the names of all their accomplices, and over the succeeding days Tavake, Lavuso, 'Aisea Kaumoto, Fekau, Penisiō Hau, Lutoviko Tuhoko, Soni Muli, Sione Latuvaivai, Tēvita Finau, Sitiveni Finau, Nuku and several others were arrested, imprisoned and interrogated.

The trials of the prisoners began before the Chief Justice, 'Ahome'e, on 26 January. Giles, as the British pro-Consul, was one of the few Europeans allowed to attend the sessions of the court, and he recorded his impressions in his diary:

> I attended the Court this morning when five prisoners were tried, two of whom confessed to being principals in the attack on Mr Baker and his family. Everything was conducted in English style, except that it was so absolutely patent that Mr Baker was the moving spirit in the whole affair from the commencement to the end. The Registrar, Minister of Police, and even the Chief Justice were venturing hardly to speak without looking towards Mr Baker, whispering to him, or even passing notes across towards him. Even Mr Baker himself, I noticed, coloured and looked annoyed when they became too palpable in their appeals for his advice.[8]

The leading conspirators were charged with 'having borne arms in opposition to the Government of His Majesty' and with 'being an accomplice in the attempted assassination of 13 January'. On 31 January ten of the accused, Tōpui, Naisa, Fehoko, Latu, Palu, Lavuso, Tavake, 'Aisea Kaumoto, Fekau and Tuitavake, were found guilty and sentenced to death. Four others, Penisiō Hau, Latuvaivai, Soni Muli and Vuni, who had all turned king's evidence, were either pardoned or given light sentences. The Reverend Tēvita Finau, charged as an accessory, was sentenced to twenty-two years imprisonment. Several others remained in prison awaiting trial and sentence.

Baker had secured the death sentence for the leading conspirators, but he apparently did not intend it to be carried out; rather
he intended to commute the sentences to life imprisonment, and so
gain a reputation for both justice and mercy. But the king had other
ideas, and when Baker went with Tuʻuhetoka to the palace to plead
for the lives of the prisoners, Tupou refused to listen. Baker left on
the understanding that they would discuss the matter further in the
morning, but at 2 a.m. the king sent his guard to bring Tuʻuhetoka
secretly to the palace; when the Minister of Police arrived he
received orders to take six of the condemned men, Tōpui, ʻAisea
Kaumoto, Lavuso, Naisa, Latu and Fehoko, to Malinoa, a sandy
islet about eight miles off Nukuʻalofa and there execute them. The
men, still in chains, were loaded on a schooner with fifty Vavaʻu
and Haʻapai soldiers early in the morning. They were taken to
Malinoa the same afternoon.

The execution was witnessed by Von Hagen, who heard of the
matter that morning and rowed out to Malinoa with another
European, George Bindeman. He later wrote an account of the
proceedings:

> We landed at 1.0 p.m., a full hour before the schooner, and
> found Laifone, the Crown Prince, and Tuiatoka [Tuʻuhetoka]
> waiting. The graves had already been dug in the middle of
> the island. On arrival of the schooner the firing parties were
> landed and marched up. They were composed of Haapai and
> Vavau men, twenty five of each. The victims were brought
> up one at a time by police, and they were all heavily ironed
> hand and foot. Each one was made to stand facing his grave
> with his back to the firing party.... The first to be called to
> die was the youngest of all. His name was Naisa. He had been
> so brutally abused in prison that he could hardly drag his heavy
> irons through the deep sand. I kissed him as he passed me,
> poor boy. He was not twenty years of age.... They all died
> like men, standing upright with their irons on, and without a
> shiver or a flinch.... Laifone had the few coconuts that grew

on the island plucked, saying that hereafter the island would be accursed.[9]

When Tu'uhetoka reported the executions to Tupou, he was ordered to take the other four condemned men out to Malinoa and shoot them also. Baker intercepted him as he left the palace, and countermanded the order, saying that he would talk to the king and tell him that he would resign if further executions took place. Baker's protests were evidently effective on this occasion, for the executions were indefinitely postponed, and eventually the sentences were commuted to banishment.

The conspirators were not the only Tongans to suffer as a result of the attempt on Baker's life; one immediate consequence of the affair was a renewed persecution of the Wesleyans. This group, it is true, had provided several members of the conspiracy, and Tupou College boys had given their support, but the plot was in no sense a Wesleyan plot. Baker, however, possibly because the fright and strain he had suffered distorted his judgement, or possibly because he saw the opportunity to discredit Moulton completely, laid the whole responsibility for the plot on the Wesleyans. In an account of the affair which he wrote for the *New Zealand Herald* on 24 January he claimed that evidence at the trials had revealed:

> a state of things with regard to Mr Moulton's supporters which will astonish the world. Mr Moulton's bosom friend being prime mover in the case, and Mr Moulton's friends having not only devised the scheme, but laid out the plan which was to have been followed by a civil war in the land.[10]

The king also believed that the attempted assassination of Baker was part of a Wesleyan plot, and with his connivance a campaign of terror was launched against the remaining Wesleyans. It began with the arrival of the men from Ha'apai and Vava'u who had come to Tongatapu in answer to the king's appeal. They began landing on 19 January and on the following day Giles noted:

I counted twenty vessels drawn up on the beach and more coming out at sea. There are several hundreds of these armed savages now parading about the town and more coming, and I am afraid there will be a disturbance before all is over.[11]

Baulked of their expected sport by the surrender of the outlaws, the northerners vented their aroused passions in acts of violence against the Wesleyans and, probably to allay suspicion about their own part in the conspiracy, their chiefs, Laifone and Tu'ipelehake, allowed them a free hand. On 20 January one band attempted to break open the gaol and lynch the prisoners, but were ordered off by Tu'uhetoka with a squad of armed constables. On the same day another group raided Tupou College and the neighbouring Queen Salote College, and were only prevented from ransacking the buildings by the intervention of Giles, who flew the British flag over the buildings and posted up a notice on the gates declaring that the Wesleyan institutions were under British protection.

On the same day plundering began. Armed bands wandered around Hahake destroying the plantations and shooting the fowls and pigs belonging to Wesleyans. On 23 January Moulton appealed to the High Commissioner for protection, declaring:

The country during the last week has been traversed in all directions by armed bands with blackened faces and all the paraphernalia of savagery who have attacked the residences of the Wesleyans and have endeavoured to make them turn over to the Free Church by presenting their guns and threatening to shoot, by striking them with the butt ends, or in the majority of cases by threatening to shoot their pigs and carry off their property. In many cases these threats have been successful, but a large number have stood firm and have seen their property destroyed before their eyes. Many are absolutely beggared. All the reports have not come in, but I counted this morning twenty towns and villages that have been thus looted.[12]

Of the plundering of Fua'amotu on 25 January Moulton reported that not only had the Wesleyans' pigs and fowls been shot, but all their personal possessions taken, leaving the people with only the clothing they had on. By 27 January looting had begun even in the town of Nuku'alofa, and two days later had spread to 'Eua. On 3 February only the intervention of Giles, with Tu'uhetoka and a body of armed constables, prevented the sacking of Tupou College, even though it had been put under British protection. On 5 February both Tupou College and Queen Salote College were disbanded by order of the king, and the students and those Wesleyans from outlying villages who were seeking sanctuary there were dispersed to their homes.

The new British Vice-Consul, R. Beckworth Leefe, arrived in Nuku'alofa to relieve Giles on 6 February, but his arrival merely gave added impetus to the persecution campaign – on the very next day floggings began. In his instructions to the new Vice-Consul, Thurston, the acting Consul-General, had warned Leefe that it had been the habit of the missionaries in Tonga to regard their adherents as being under the special protection of Britain and to expect official intervention from the High Commissioner on their behalf. He had ordered Leefe to discountenance this attitude and to keep strictly aloof from the political and religious disputes of Tonga. Leefe called on Tupou and Baker on the day he arrived and took the opportunity to assure the king that the British government had neither wish nor intention of interfering in the internal affairs of his kingdom. He also presented the king with a goodwill letter from Queen Victoria. Until Leefe's arrival Tupou had evidently been worried that the High Commissioner would intervene and avenge insults offered to Wesleyans and he had made half-hearted efforts to restrain the plunderers, but Leefe's attitude reassured him. He told Leefe:

> ... he felt glad that the British Government had at last sent a man of years and experience ... to be Consul here; hitherto he had only had boys to deal with, who were constantly interfering and giving trouble, and who wanted to be master instead of him.[13]

Word of the interview circulated rapidly among the chiefs, becoming somewhat garbled in the process; by the next day it was widely believed in Tonga that Tupou had received a letter from Queen Victoria assuring him that he could do whatever he liked with his own subjects. At Leefe's urgent request Baker corrected this report by publishing the full text of the Queen's letter on 14 February, but by then the damage had been done.

Within a few days E. W. Parker, Thomas Parsons, P. S. Bloomfield, George Young, Thomas Payne, Philip Payne, H. M. Fisher, W. L. Foster and Frederick Langdale had all sworn affidavits before Leefe reporting the most brutal flogging of Wesleyans in all parts of the island. The evidence of Robert Hanslip is not usually very reliable, but in this case his testimony is corroborated by reports from widely separate sources:

> It was generally reported on the afternoon or evening of 6 February that Her Majesty's Consul, Beckworth Leefe Esq., who arrived on that day, had brought a letter from Her Majesty Queen Victoria to King George telling him he was at liberty to do as he liked with his own people. The chiefs, I am informed and believe the information to be correct, quoted the letter at the meetings held by them in different parts of Tonga and at which the wholesale flogging of men and women took place. I saw on 16 February a printed translation of a letter from Her Majesty the Queen to King George, the paper was dated on 14 February. A meagre issue of the printed translation had the effect of destroying the excuse given for the flogging and maltreating but not until hundreds of people, men and women, had been flogged, one so severely that he died before the publication of the letter. Semisi Ita is the man I allude to, and he was flogged by Halaholo. From 7 February to the 12 February the wholesale beating of Wesleyans continued, and the beating of individuals until 21 February, when the latest case known to me took place.[14]

One case was brought very forcibly to Leefe's attention when he found, lying under a tree in the consulate yard, a Tongan Wesleyan minister. According to Leefe:

> ... his face, breast, arms and hands were completely covered in blood which was trickling from a wound in the upper half of his face and was making a pool on the grass; his nose was knocked out of shape and he appeared almost stupefied.[15]

Another case, reported by E. W. Parker, was that of a nursing mother who had been flogged across her bare breasts until she 'swore by Jesus that the Wesleyan Church was a bloody Church'.[16] By such methods Wesleyan numbers were decimated. At the time of the assassination attempt there had been three hundred Wesleyans in Tongatapu; by 10 February Moulton estimated that he had only twenty-five adherents left and in desperation he proposed to Leefe that they be allowed to emigrate to Fiji.

The next day, 11 February, Leefe put Moulton's suggestion to Baker, who accepted it with enthusiasm. Baker was indeed in a very difficult situation. The king had sent for the Ha'apai and Vava'u men when he believed that they were required to put down widespread revolt, but when they arrived, painted for war and expecting fighting and rich plunder, the danger had passed. The fighting spirit of the northern men had been aroused, however, and was not easy to subdue. Baker held a *fono* on the day after the main body of Ha'apai men arrived and ordered them to be quiet and peaceable, but his words had no effect whatever. During the following week shots were being fired continuously in Nuku'alofa, making it impossible for Baker's children, still very ill, to get any rest, but his appeals on their behalf were disregarded. In fact Hanslip reported: 'I noticed that whenever the orders were given to stop firing the discharges were more frequent'.[17] Baker was also anxious to stop the ravages of the northerners against the Wesleyans, for he knew from past experience that such acts provoked adverse publicity in the world press, but his attempts to stop the violence were fruitless. The reason most probably lay in the attitude of Tupou, who was stubbornly determined to stamp out all opposition to his will and was using the opportunity provided by the disturbances to eliminate the Wesleyans. On one occasion a village policeman received orders from one messenger (evidently Baker's) to protect Wesleyan property from marauders, only to be told shortly afterwards by another messenger (evidently Tupou's) to ignore the orders just received and to allow the Wesleyans to be robbed. Finally Baker wrote officially to Tupou complaining that 'the land does not still listen to me'. He begged the king to put a stop to the plundering and flogging and warned: 'I shall be held responsible for these things and it will end in my being commanded to return to Papalangi'.[18] This appeal was also disregarded. Appraising the situation shortly afterwards Leefe wrote:

> There can be no doubt that just now Mr Baker has a very difficult hand to play and as little that whatever he may have been in the past he is no longer what he has been so often called, King of Tonga all but in name; the constitution nevertheless, the King has not lost that love of arbitrary power with which he was born and bred and there can be no reasonable doubt that lately he has taken the bit between his teeth, Mr Baker being in consequence, for anything but matters of detail, comparatively powerless.[19]

When Leefe approached Baker, therefore, with Moulton's request to allow the Wesleyan remnant to emigrate to Fiji, Baker grasped the proposal and persuaded Tupou to agree. At first he insisted that the emigration would only be permitted if Moulton left along with his adherents, but Moulton refused to accept this condition; he explained to Leefe, when the latter suggested that his attitude was unchristian and would cause suffering among his people, that Christ had not come to bring peace on earth but a sword. Baker then waived his condition and ordered all the Tongatapu Wesleyans to gather in Nuku'alofa. They were embarked on the schooner *Malakula,* which left Tonga for Fiji on 24 February. The

Wesleyans on board numbered a mere thirty-six, constituting the entire Tongatapu Wesleyan population; when the Vava'u and Ha'apai Wesleyans joined them in Fiji a few days later they brought the number to about ninety men, women and children. With the departure of these last survivors of the Wesleyan persuasion the violence in Tonga ended; on 7 March Leefe reported: 'the most perfect order reigns in Tonga.' But it was the peace of a desert.

The elimination of the Wesleyans and the restoration of order did not, however, conclude the episode. The High Commissioner had been very dubious about interfering in Tonga, believing that his presence would do more harm than good. But in London the British government saw the events in a different light, for a basic change in its attitude towards Tonga had taken place. In April 1886 Britain and Germany had demarcated their spheres of influence in the Western Pacific, and by agreement both parties accepted Tonga and Samoa as a neutral region. Germany, however, was not satisfied with this settlement and, in October 1886, Travers, the Imperial German Commissioner in the Pacific, sought an interview with Thurston, then British Acting High Commissioner, with a view to arranging a modification of the terms agreed upon. Travers urged upon Thurston the magnitude of German interests in Samoa, and the claim of Germany to an exclusive or predominating influence in the affairs of those islands. He intimated that if Britain would acquiesce in the establishment of a German protectorate over Samoa, as a quid pro quo Germany would probably agree to Britain having a free hand in Tonga. Thurston recommended Travers' suggestion to the Secretary of State for the Colonies; the proposal was discussed between the Colonial Office and the Foreign Office, and by January 1887 it had been accepted. On 12 January the British Ambassador in Berlin was instructed to inform the German Foreign Office that Britain was prepared to make concessions over Samoa, and in return hoped that the German government would entertain certain proposals which the British government wished to put forward in relation to Tonga.

The subsequent negotiations were protracted and eventually

RIGHT:
James Egan Moulton.
In the words of British
Consul Layard, Moulton
was 'a very different
man from Mr Baker....
He was apparently
a man of education
and a gentleman.'
Mitchell Library

BELOW:
Moulton's house.
'The folks next door
[the Bakers] have been
very kind and I hope the
gulf is getting bridged over.'

Alexander Turnbull Library, C21951

Premier Baker (centre) with Prince Wellington Ngū (far right),
J. B. Watkin (far left) and other 'Tongan notables'.
The Museum of New Zealand / Te Papa Tongarewa (Burton Bros 2687)

Wesleyan Church, Neiafu, Vava'u (*c*.1884).
The Museum of New Zealand / Te Papa Tongarewa (Burton Bros 7488)

1. Rev. Shirley Baker
2. Mr. Baker's Son and Daughter, both Shot
3. King George's Palace, Tonga, where Mr. Baker and his Family are at present taking Refuge
4. A Haapai Warrior
5. Place where the Outrage was committed
6. King George of Tonga, drawn from Life
7. Mukualofa, Tonga

THE REVOLUTION IN TONGA, SOUTH PACIFIC OCEAN

'The Revolution in Tonga'. A wood engraving.
Alexander Turnbull Library, C22002

Nuku'alofa (*c.*1880). Probably taken from Zion.
Alexander Turnbull Library, F115854 1/2

LEFT:
Tupou II
(Tāufaʻāhau).
Alexander Turnbull Library,
C21953

BELOW:
The Palace and
Royal Chapel as viewed
from Nukuʻalofa wharf.
Alexander Turnbull Library,
F154882 1/2

stalemated, but at the time when the reports of the disturbances in Tonga reached Britain Tonga was regarded in official circles as an essentially British responsibility. Thus when appeals for British action in Tonga were made by the Aborigines Protection Society, they were given an unusually sympathetic reception. On 10 March telegraphic instructions were sent to Sir Charles Mitchell, the recently arrived High Commissioner for the Western Pacific, ordering him to go to Tonga without delay to carry out a full investigation of the reported disturbances. Rear-Admiral Tryon, the Flag Officer commanding the squadron on the Australian Naval Station, who had refused an earlier request from the Premier of New Zealand to send a ship to Tonga, also received telegraphed instructions to put a ship at Mitchell's immediate disposal. With such explicit orders the High Commissioner and the Admiral demurred no further and on 27 March HMS *Diamond,* with Sir Charles Mitchell aboard, arrived off Nuku'alofa.

The High Commissioner's visit to Tonga was a humiliating experience for Baker and Tupou. Mitchell formally notified the king of his instructions and requested his good offices, but it was obvious that this was only an empty formality; the real and sufficient sanction for the High Commissioner's actions was HMS *Diamond.* On 29 March Mitchell subjected Tupou to a rigorous examination, demanding answers to fifty prepared questions, and bringing him back to the point when he tried to be evasive, like a headmaster with a delinquent boy. On 30 March he began a formal investigation into a schedule of charges against the Tongan government prepared by Moulton and including all the alleged instances of persecution of Wesleyans since 1885. Mr Justice Clarke, the Chief Justice of Fiji and Chief Judicial Commissioner of the High Commission, conducted the investigation in the consular court, and except for the king no Tongan dignity was excused; the one hundred and sixty-six witnesses called and examined included the Minister of Police, the Premier and the Chief Justice. During a break in the proceedings the charges which Baker had made against Hanslip for his part in the conspiracy were investigated, but even this provided no satisfaction for Baker. Hanslip was acquitted, not through any faith in his protestations of innocence, but because all the witnesses against him were under sentence of death, and their evidence could not be accepted. The most the Chief Judicial Commissioner could do was to put Hanslip on a bond of one hundred pounds, to be of good behaviour for six months.

Mitchell had come to Tonga with the preconception that Baker was the source of all religious trouble in Tonga, but as a result of his investigation he came to an entirely different conclusion. He reported to the Secretary of State for the Colonies that he was by no means able to concur in the widely held opinion that Tupou was a mere cipher in the hands of his adviser. On the contrary, he believed that his investigation had shown that the king had a very strong will of his own and that, having tried unsuccessfully by other means to convert all his people to the Free Church, he had seized the opportunity which the attack on Baker had presented to declare martial law and set about the forcible conversion of the remaining Wesleyans.

In another confidential report to the Colonial Office Mitchell gave his impressions of Baker. His comments, based on lengthy and careful investigations, and on personal observation, form the most valuable contemporary assessment of Baker. He wrote:

> Mr Baker is a person of great energy and of undoubted ability. He has a firm hold on the affectionate regard of King Tupou, to whom he has long rendered great and valuable services. But to say, as is commonly said in Tonga and elsewhere that he rules the King, and is, in fact, in his own person the Government of Tonga, is I believe, a great mistake. That much of his influence is due to the intimate knowledge he has of the bent of the King's mind, that much of his success may be owing to his tact and management of Tupou, is, I dare say, true; but I am much mistaken in the opinion which I have formed of the King's force and vigour of character, even in this advanced period of his life, if, having once made up his mind on a point Mr Baker, or anyone else, could move him; and I am also much mistaken if, in such a case, Mr Baker

would dare make the attempt. The fact is, as I think, that he stands in considerable awe of the King; but that he has a personal affection for him, and that he serves him, perhaps somewhat blindly, to the best of his power and ability. The European inhabitants of the Tongan Islands, almost without exception, dislike Mr Baker. Some detest him cordially. The reasons for this are not far to seek. In doing, since he became Premier, what he conceived to be best for the interests of the King and of Tonga he has, in various ways, interfered with the absolute freedom – I will not say license – enjoyed by the European inhabitants of Tonga. He has imposed customs dues, harbour dues, and various other taxes; he has been more than suspected of bringing his influence and framing his laws so as to favour the Germans; and he has, I understand, held himself very much aloof from his countrymen of the islands, whether as regards to their business or their amusements. By many of the Chiefs also Mr Baker is, for different reasons, regarded with suspicion. Indeed he would have been more than human had he been able to escape the jealousy and apprehension which his intimacy with the King must have tended to create in the minds of a people so watchful and suspicious as are the Tongans of a higher class. If, to what I have already said of Mr Baker, I add that I think he is very ambitious, and anxious to make a name for himself in the world – if only in the limited world of the South Seas – I think I have said enough to throw light on many of his actions during recent events. Thwarted by his superiors in the Wesleyan Church in his endeavours to extend his political influence, while at the same time holding his Church position, he showed little hesitation in abandoning the latter and as little in consolidating the former. Astute though he is I believe he has been run away with by the course of events.... The attack on himself, and the grievous injury done to his son and daughter, without doubt, affected his judgment at the time they occurred and when he recovered it, it was too late to change the course of events.[20]

Mitchell decided not to deport Baker. Instead he wrote to Tupou advising him to declare a general amnesty for all connected with the recent disturbances, to issue a proclamation restoring religious liberty, and to repeal the *Law of Six and of Thirty*. He also suggested that his good offices should be used to seek a reconciliation between the Wesleyan Church and the Free Church. He called the king's attention to the power possessed by the High Commissioner to deport any British subject whom he considered to be prejudicial to the peace and good order of the Western Pacific, and pointed out that the situation would justify the exercise of this power against Baker. Because of the friendship and esteem the king felt for his Premier, however, he was reluctant to take such arbitrary action, and he intimated that provided Tupou accepted the advice he had offered he would refrain from exercising the powers vested in his office. Under the circumstances Tupou could scarcely refuse these terms and on 26 April he gave a written undertaking to accept the High Commissioner's recommendations. Mitchell returned to Fiji on 28 April.

After the departure of the High Commissioner Baker and Tupou resumed the business of government almost as if nothing had happened. The episode had been humiliating, but they had weathered the storm and their partnership remained intact. They would have been more concerned had they known of the change which had occurred in the policy of the British government with regard to Tonga, or of the confidential report which Mitchell had sent to the Secretary of State for the Colonies advising that the time was ripe for Britain to exercise a more direct control over the destiny of Tonga. The king, he reported, was nearly ninety years old and could not live much longer, and his successor, Laifone, would concur in any move made by Britain. Therefore, he ventured to suggest, Britain should seek an understanding with France and Germany as to the exercise by each of a protectorate over the group in which it had its main interest, and that this having been achieved, the High Commissioner should be empowered to declare a protectorate over Tonga as soon as news was received that Tupou had died.[21] Naturally, Baker and the king knew nothing of this.

CHAPTER XI

~~~~~

THE HIGH COMMISSIONER'S COUP D'ÉTAT

D URING THE EARLY months of 1887 negotiations continued
between Britain and Germany over their respective spheres
of influence in the Pacific, and, after a lot of hard bargaining,
agreement was tentatively reached in April that Germany should
recognise the priority of British interests in Tonga in return for
British acceptance of German hegemony in Samoa. At this stage the
two powers left the details to be negotiated at the conference on
colonial problems which was to be held in Washington in mid-
1887. But at Washington the British and German proposals for
settlement of the Samoan problem were strongly opposed by the
representative of the United States, and the conference adjourned
without reaching any decision. Germany then resorted to direct
action. In March 1887 several German subjects in Samoa had been
ill-treated by the followers of Malieto'a on the occasion of the
German Emperor's birthday and, using this insult to national honour
as a pretext, Germany declared war on Malieto'a in August 1887.
Marines from a German naval squadron occupied Apia, subdued
Malieto'a's supporters and deposed him. A rival chief, Tamasese,
who was considered to be friendly towards Germany, was proclaimed king of Samoa in Malieto'a's place.

Germany's strong measures assured her primacy in Samoa; the British were determined to stake a firm claim for compensatory advantages in Tonga. Instructions were therefore telegraphed to Mitchell giving him wide latitude to declare a protectorate over Tonga on the first indication of German interference there, and at the same time orders were given for the immediate dispatch of a man-of-war to the area. HMS *Opal* was accordingly detached from the Australian squadron and sailed to Tonga at full speed, only just anticipating the arrival of a German warship, the *Adler*. When the *Adler* found the *Opal* already in position, it withdrew. From September 1887 until January 1888, HMS *Opal* lay off Nuku'alofa without giving any explanation of its purposes to the Tongan government. The local Europeans, however, were quick to assume that British annexation of the group was imminent, and in October E. W. Parker wrote to the High Commissioner seeking appointment as an official in the new administration when the takeover occurred. There can be little doubt that it was the threatening presence of HMS *Opal* which goaded Baker into making his last defiant stand against British encroachment.

Until the arrival of the *Opal*, Baker had been trying to fulfil the undertaking which Mitchell had imposed as the condition of his continued residence in Tonga. There were, of course, minor incidents and a certain amount of unseemly recrimination when Wesleyans who had joined the Free Church under duress began to drift back to their older allegiance, but after reviewing all the complaints which he had received from Moulton over the preceding seven months, Mitchell reported to the Colonial Office in November 1887 that they were for the most part trivial and that Baker and Tupou were keeping to the letter, if not entirely to the spirit, of the promises they had made.[1]

During the same period, moreover, promising moves had been made to bring about a reconciliation between the rival churches. In May 1887 Mitchell had written to the Committee of Privileges of the Wesleyan Church in New South Wales, informing its President that Tupou had requested him to use his good offices to initiate reunion negotiations; he advised that the opportunity should be grasped, as it might be the best offering for many years. The response in Sydney was very guarded, but the Committee decided to appoint three 'commissioners', the Reverend W. G. R. Stephinson, the Reverend George Brown, and a layman, Mr P. P. Fletcher, to visit Tonga and investigate the prospects for reunion. The commission arrived in Tonga in July 1887. Its beginning was most inauspicious. Tupou clearly remembered that seventeen years earlier, when he had supported Baker in the dispute with Stephinson, the latter had written to the press declaring that Tupou was in his second childhood; so when Stephinson sought an interview with him he was brusquely told to put his requests through Baker or Watkin, and not to bother an old man in his dotage. Stephinson left Tonga the next day, on the same vessel which had brought him, but Brown and Fletcher remained and, through their tactful treatment of Baker, they were able to make considerable progress. They held what they described as 'most frank and open' discussions with Baker, Watkin and the king which convinced them that a reconciliation was possible, but only if Moulton were removed – in fact, Tupou assured them: 'Let Mr Moulton go, and everything will be all right'. Before they left Brown and Fletcher had a private interview with Leefe and told him that no doubt remained in their minds of the necessity of withdrawing Moulton and Crosby and that they would recommend this move to the Conference. It was thus with considerable satisfaction that Mitchell reported to the Secretary of State for the Colonies in September 1887:

> There appears ... to be some grounds for hoping that the long outstanding religious difficulties may at last be amicably settled; and if this is done there will be no need to fear any further trouble, such as has lately occurred, during Tupou's lifetime.[2]

During this whole period Baker was subjected to many anxieties. In the first place, his children were still very ill from the injuries they had suffered at the time of the assassination attempt. Shirley had lost the use of his arm, and Beatrice was completely paralysed. In the second place, Baker went in constant fear of his life, allowing no one but his daughter Alice to prepare his food for fear of poisoning, and not venturing out of the palace without an armed guard. He was also apprehensive that any outburst among the people would result in the intervention of the High Commissioner and his own summary deportation. When HMS *Opal* arrived at Nuku'alofa in September 1887 Baker illuminated the town in her honour, and arranged entertainments for her officers and men, but when the weeks and months passed, with the *Opal* still at anchor and the rumours of British annexation multiplying, he became by turn apprehensive, resentful, and finally recklessly defiant. The first sign of his changing attitude appeared in an article which he wrote for the Auckland *Evening Bell*, a newspaper in which he had an interest, in October 1887:

> ... some folks think that the Opal is here to watch proceedings but the Rev. Mr Baker has nothing to fear, and the closer his actions are watched the more proof will be obtained to prove the great work he has done for Tonga ... and the more convincing will be the proof of the wicked calumnies which have been so industriously circulated by his enemies.[3]

Later the same month Leefe conveyed a warning to Baker from Mitchell (who had in turn been instructed to administer it by the Secretary of State for the Colonies) that, if any further persecution occurred in Tonga which could be traced to his influence, he would be prohibited from remaining in the Western Pacific. This warning was a response to Mitchell's report of his investigations in the previous April, and had taken five months to pass through the official channels – by coincidence it reached Baker at this critical time and merely confirmed him in the belief that he was the special target of a British plot seeking his removal and the annexation of Tonga. Almost immediately he began making moves which individually seemed to have little significance, but which collectively demonstrated the new 'hard line' which he was taking towards all things British. Thus in November 1887 when the Parker brothers applied to Baker for an extension of the lease on their sheep run at 'Eua, their request was refused. After their lease expired and before they had been able to sell more than a fraction of their flock, they drove the remaining animals over the cliffs into the sea rather than allow them to fall into the government's hands. In February 1888 Baker began pressing Europeans for poll tax, back-dating the claims to January 1881 when the *Poll Tax Act* was passed, although no demands had previously been made upon Europeans to pay this tax. In the same month another blow was struck at the traders (the great majority of whom were British subjects), by requiring them to pay all customs duties, postal fees, wharfage, pilotage and shipping dues in English currency, although they were required to accept the debased Chilean currency from their Tongan customers. At the same time Baker began adopting a very peremptory tone in his correspondence with Leefe, the British Vice-Consul. For instance, in January 1888 he wrote:

> It is simply ridiculous that the Tongan Government and the Tongan chiefs should be put to such annoyance and such expense as they have been and are in consequence of the gross falsehoods which are constantly being made the subject of consular correspondence.[4]

The most convincing indication of the new trend in Baker's thinking, and of the lengths to which he was prepared to go to discredit Britain was, however, an extraordinary report which he released to the Auckland *Evening Bell* in January 1888:

> It will doubtless surprise some of your readers that an Enfield Rifle used by one of the assassins who attempted the life of the Premier has been found in the British Consulate here, and is in the possession of the Tongan Government. It is supposed that some person in connection with the Consulate con-

cealed it there – the rifle has the assassin's name carved on it![5]

This story was a grotesque distortion of the real facts. After the assassination attempt the Tongan government had passed an *Arms Act* requiring all firearms to be registered, and at a dinner party shortly afterwards Leefe had mentioned to Baker that there was an old musket in the consulate which he would be glad if the police would collect. The musket had been brought to Nuku'alofa from Fiji by one of the men who had come from Lau with the reeds to thatch Maudslay's home in 1878, and had lain in the consulate ever since. It could not be fired for it was badly corroded and had parts of the firing mechanism missing. Carved on the stock and barrel-rest were the names of two chiefs of Lau who had previously owned the musket, Raturanga and Ratuivuna. By a phonetic coincidence the first syllables of each of these names was pronounced *Latu* in Tongan, because Rs are pronounced as Ls in the Tongan language. This was the supposed Enfield rifle and the basis of the assertion that the name of the outlaw, Latu, was carved on the stock.

Had Baker been satisfied to circulate the story only through the *Evening Bell* little harm would have been done, for the *Bell* had a limited circulation and the article apparently escaped the notice of the High Commissioner; but in May 1888 he repeated the charges in more elaborate form in a Tongan Government Blue Book. The occasion was the General Conference of the Australasian Wesleyan-Methodist Church which met in Melbourne to debate the Tonga question. The New South Wales and Queensland Conference had been held in January 1888, had received the report of Brown and Fletcher and had heard an address by Sir Charles Mitchell earnestly advocating the reunion of the Tongan Methodists, but had refused to withdraw Moulton. As this was tantamount to a rejection of the king's proposal for a settlement, and as the Tongan question was a matter of importance for all Australian Methodists, the handling of the affair by the New South Wales and Queensland Conference was referred to the General Conference. Baker prepared and printed his Blue Book and privately circulated it among the delegates to the

Conference. It purported to be a report from the Minister of Police to Tupou outlining the evidence collected by the police against those who had participated in the assassination attempt, but in fact, although it was based on the real and much shorter report of Tuʻuhetoka of February 1887, it was written and composed entirely by Baker, and was only later translated into Tongan and signed by Tuʻuhetoka. The main object of the Blue Book was to create the impression that Moulton was privy to, and to a large extent responsible for, the plot against the Tongan Premier, but Baker also used the opportunity to vent his grievances against the British by repeating the story of the 'discovery' of the 'Enfield Rifle' with the outlaw's name carved on it, thus implying the complicity of the British officials in the assassination attempt.

The Blue Book achieved its immediate purpose for, although Moulton wrote and distributed a pamphlet to the delegates countering the allegations against him, the General Conference decided to remove him from Tonga. The Reverend George Brown was elected to replace him as the Special Commissioner to Tonga of the General Conference with authority and instructions to inquire into the best means of securing reunion of the two churches, and to draw up a scheme for a permanent settlement. This decision meant the final victory for Baker over his opponent of eighteen years' standing, but the cost was high. In the first place the new Special Commissioner, George Brown, who was described by a contemporary observer as having 'a sharp rat-terrier look', was a much more formidable opponent than the scholarly and ingenuous Moulton. Secondly, the allegations against British officials made in the Blue Book were brought to the notice of the High Commissioner and were largely responsible for bringing about Baker's undoing.

The High Commissioner at this time was Thurston, now Sir John Thurston, who had been appointed to the office on the transfer of Mitchell in February 1888. Until August 1888 Thurston was most sympathetic towards Baker for, having himself once been adviser to a native king, Cakobau of Fiji, he knew from personal experience the difficulties inherent in such a position. He adopted a more

indulgent attitude to Baker than any of his predecessors, and in his
official reports to the Secretary of State for the Colonies of 28 May
and 4 June 1888 he expressed satisfaction at the state of affairs in
Tonga, and blamed Moulton for the minor difficulties which still
existed.

As Baker became increasingly suspicious of British motives, however, and more openly hostile towards the High Commissioner,
Thurston's sympathy began to evaporate. By August 1888 he had
completely lost all patience. The turning point was Baker's defiant
stand on the currency question. When Thurston had received word
of Baker's decree requiring all government dues to be paid in sterling
currency, he had advised Leefe that it was an injustice to British
subjects that could not be permitted, and that the Tongan government should be informed that British subjects must be permitted to
pay their dues in any currency they wished. Baker was absent in
Auckland at the time and Leefe was not able to deliver Thurston's
warning message until he returned to Tonga late in July 1888. It
was a most inappropriate time to deliver such a peremptory message
for on 1 August Baker exchanged ratifications of the treaty between
the United States and Tonga and was in consequence feeling very
confident, while at the same time he had just heard news from
Australia that Moulton was to be removed, which further increased
his self-assurance. Accordingly on 6 August he wrote to Leefe
denying the right of British officials to interfere in Tongan affairs
and threatening that if the British government upheld Thurston's
stand on the question of the currency, Tupou would appeal to the
German Emperor and the President of the United States to arbitrate
on the matter. Such an action would have been tantamount to an
appeal to Germany and the United States to protect Tonga against
British encroachment, an appeal which the United States, at least,
might have been willing to entertain. Such an appeal would have
been very embarrassing for the British government, but even more
embarrassing for Thurston, who would be blamed for precipitating
an international incident. Therefore, when Baker's answer was
conveyed to the High Commissioner, his attitude towards Baker

underwent a sudden change. On 28 August he wrote to the Secretary of State for the Colonies listing a number of grievances against Baker, none of which were in any way new, but drawing an entirely new conclusion:

> The engagements of the king of Tonga set forth in this letter to Sir Charles Mitchell ... have not been kept, nor do I think they will be so long as Mr Baker remains in Tonga to direct the course of affairs. To this conclusion I have arrived slowly and with reluctance under a sense of violent and often unwarranted hostility with which Mr Baker has been pursued by his opponents both clerical and lay. But the condition of things is now changed, and any neglect or refusal on the part of Mr Baker to do justice to the people and conform to the king's engagements can only be construed in a manner most unfavourable to himself, and point to the necessity of his being prohibited under the provisions of the Western Pacific Order in Council from longer remaining in Tonga.[6]

Thurston intended to go to Tonga at once, evidently to demand Baker's dismissal and to prohibit him from remaining in Tonga, but Admiral Fairfax could not spare him a warship for the purpose, and before one was available the Secretary of State for the Colonies had stayed his hand. Thurston's report recommending Baker's deportation had been referred to Sir Charles Mitchell for comment and Mitchell had found no valid reason for altering his earlier opinion on the subject. He wrote:

> The banishment of Baker ... would lead to no improvement in the state of affairs in Tonga and might, and probably would entail a condition of things that would compel the armed intervention of Her Majesty's Government, a result I should earnestly deprecate leading up to, but which I have sometimes felt would not be unwelcome to the Wesleyan community of New South Wales, or to their supporters at home.[7]

Consequently Thurston was warned not to deport Baker without prior instructions from London. This warning only temporarily diverted him and he began to seek other, more indirect, means of bringing about Baker's removal. Baker was given a respite, however.

After February 1888 Baker spent most of his time in Auckland, where he had taken his daughter, Beatrice, for medical attention, and only visited Tonga for a few weeks at a time when urgent business required his attention. He was in Tonga, however, when George Brown arrived as the Special Commissioner of the General Conference in August 1888. At first Brown and Baker got along very well and the ostentatious friendliness which they showed each other noticeably eased the tensions between the rival religious factions. But in October Brown held his missionary meeting for the Wesleyans in Tongatapu and in his speech to his congregation he assured them that his purpose was not to allow the Wesleyans to be absorbed into the Free Church. He declared that the Wesleyan Church in Tonga would last *'e taegata bea taegata'* ('for ever and ever'); he claimed that the division of the church in Tonga was the work of the devil (which the Wesleyans construed to mean that Baker was the devil); he also let drop the information that the Free Church, which had always taunted the Wesleyans with having to send money to Australia, had sent away $1,000 (£200) to assist the work of foreign missions. Within days of this meeting Tonga was seething with religious dissension and the fragile *détente* between Brown and Baker was destroyed. Furthermore, when in December Brown left Tonga for Australia to report his progress to the Standing Committee of the General Conference, he took with him the Reverend Tēvita Tonga and his wife, Rachel, who were living with the Wesleyan 'exiles' in Fiji. After presenting his report Brown visited Adelaide and Melbourne to collect funds for the cause in Tonga and the main speakers at the meetings were Tēvita and Rachel. Their testimony was moving. After their South Australian meeting the Adelaide *Advertiser* commented:

> Of this we are sure: should the Revd George Brown tell the
> tale in London which he has told in Adelaide and produce as

his witnesses Mr and Mrs Tonga, such a storm of feeling might speedily be raised as would not only render Mr Baker's residence in Tonga impossible, but drive him to seek shelter for his dishonoured head in some corner of the planet where his name has never been heard.[8]

After his Victorian meetings the Melbourne *Daily Telegraph* carried two articles in a similar vein entitled 'Exiles for Conscience Sake' and 'An Unworthy Englishman'.[9]

Baker received copies of these articles in Auckland early in May 1889 and was furious. He wrote to Brown indignantly refuting the assertions made against him and describing Brown's conduct as 'most base, mean and dishonourable'. He concluded his letter with a reference to a raid which Brown had led against natives of New Britain who were threatening his mission station in 1879. At the time Chief Justice Gorrie of Fiji had been determined to put Brown on trial for murder but was overruled by Gordon. Baker believed that, as the price for not indicting Brown, Gordon had demanded his (Baker's) recall from Tonga, and in his letter to Brown he said so:

> I should certainly have thought that you, who escaped a felon's cell at Suva because I was made your scapegoat – for it is well known the understanding between the officials of the British Government and Messrs Chapman and Hurst 'that if I were not sacrificed and recalled you would not escape, but if I were recalled you should be let go free on the charge of having murdered the innocent women and children of New Ireland [*sic*] in your murderous raid you made upon them' – would have acted more honourably to an absent friend.[10]

Brown was back in Tonga when he received this letter and, realising that there was no longer any possibility of working with Baker, he made a direct approach to Tupou. On 6 June he wrote to the king proposing that together they should work out the details of a reunion. It was no use trying to work through Baker, he declared:

... he is not seeking the things which will benefit the Lord's
work, but his own only. If anything bad has been done in
Tonga which is hateful to the world, he shirks it and uses
your name saying – 'The King did that'; yet it is well known
by everybody that he did it. Any good done he takes the
credit for it and says, 'I did it'. I used to love him a great deal
but at the present time I weep for shame at his conduct.[11]

Tupou did not answer Brown's letter until Baker returned to
Tonga, and Baker probably drafted the reply. There is no reason,
however, to suppose that the king did not agree with the vindication
of Baker's conduct which it contained:

Who prepared the Constitution and Laws of Tonga but him?
Who succeeded in relieving Tonga from the heavy debts
which well-nigh swamped us; was it not him? Who has
erected our buildings and laid out our roads; was it not him?
Who set up Tonga to be a Kingdom; was it not him? Who
assisted me in giving liberty to Tonga and setting them free;
was it not him? Who set up the courts in Tonga? Fie, your
language is that of jealousy. If he boasts, let him do so, for he
has accomplished something.

The letter concluded by dismissing out of hand Brown's proposal
for direct negotiations with the king:

Now Mr Brown I did not expect that I should again be thus
threatened and I have no more to say to you or your Church.
It is with Mr Watkin and the Conference what is to be done;
I have nothing more to do with it. I am annoyed.[12]

With this letter the last hope of effecting a reconciliation between the churches was extinguished. Brown therefore turned to
the High Commissioner for assistance, and on 11 July 1889 he
forwarded to Thurston a copy of Baker's letter alleging collusion

between British officials and the Wesleyan hierarchy over the New Britain affair. This incriminating letter provided another piece of evidence for Thurston to use against Baker. He had already received a copy of the Blue Book. On or about 14 September 1888 Brown had given a copy of this document to Leefe, and Leefe forwarded it to Thurston, together with an explanation of the true facts about the gun in question. In April 1889 Thurston had written to Tupou demanding a full explanation and apology for the publication of what he described as a 'false story ... fabricated and circulated in order to injure the good name of England and the reputation of the Queen's officers residing in Tonga', and threatening that unless the allegations were publicly withdrawn he would print and publish the truth of the matter in the Tongan language.[13] To give his warning more point he sent Leefe a hundred copies of Tupou's letter to Sir Charles Mitchell promising to allow freedom of conscience in Tonga, printed in Tongan, with instructions to Leefe to distribute them to people he thought they might interest. Baker was informed of these moves when he visited Tonga in June 1889, and he blustered to Leefe that he was 'not a man to be frightened'. Soon afterwards a strong answer was sent to Thurston, signed by Tupou but almost certainly written by Baker, declaring that any injury done to the British name and fame in Tonga was 'solely through the doings of Mr Symonds, Mr Moulton and their friend Mr Hanslip'. The letter concluded: 'How would you like it if I printed and distributed here and amongst my friends in Fiji what is going on in Fiji? I think not!'[14] When this letter was received in the High Commissioner's office Collet, the Secretary to the High Commissioner, minuted on the cover: 'I cannot see that any good can come of allowing Mr Baker to remain longer in Tonga'. Thurston no doubt agreed, but he had to move with caution, for he had just received a further warning from London not to deport Baker without specific instructions. He, therefore, merely wrote to Leefe instructing him to seek an interview with Tupou and to inform him privately that while the High Commissioner continued to hold the king in high esteem, he had lost all faith in his Premier, who seemed lost to the commonest dictates of honour, and who would be called upon to answer for his iniquities before very long.

At this time Baker was facing problems from other quarters. During 1889 the growers' price of copra had dropped from £5 12s per ton to £4 9s 7d per ton and this, combined with the chaos in the Treasury Department caused by Baker's prolonged absences, had decreased the tax revenue by £1,600. With government debts to traders amounting to £2,000 and with salaries already in arrears, Baker had sensed impending disaster and in July 1889 he had sought to resign. Tupou, however, had persuaded him to stay on. He had then sought to appoint a young German named Leinstein, an employee of the German firm in Samoa, to the office of Assistant Premier, with responsibility for the finances, but had been forced to abandon this project when the British residents in Tonga set up a clamour of indignant opposition. So when it became evident that Thurston was in deadly earnest Baker's ebullient self-confidence began to evaporate and he began trying to make his peace with the High Commissioner. But by this time Thurston had obtained copies of both the offensive Blue Book and the letter to Brown and was ready to move.

In September Baker received a letter from Collet informing him that unless a full and public apology were made for the slanders he had issued against British officials he would face a civil action. Baker replied, apologising for the statements made in the letter to Brown, declaring that he had had nothing to do with Tu'uhetoka's report and adding: 'It must have been absurd for anyone to suppose Mr Symonds had anything to do with the gun'.[15] But in November he was informed that while his apologies were accepted concerning the allegations made in the letter to Brown, nothing less than an unreserved and public withdrawal of all the charges which had been made against Symonds in the Blue Book would satisfy the High Commissioner. So Baker had printed a five-line supplement to the Blue Book proclaiming that the statement concerning the gun in the original document had been found, on further investigation, to be incorrect. This was forwarded to Thurston in January 1890 while he was visiting Auckland. Thurston, however, refused to accept it as a sufficient retraction. When Baker made a personal call on Thurston to explain the matter the High Commissioner refused to see him. Baker was beaten; the next day he wrote to Thurston abjectly apologising for the Blue Book, and withdrawing all the charges and insinuations against British officials contained in it. Thurston then had all the correspondence on the subject translated into Tongan, and together with a memorandum outlining the true facts about the gun, had it printed as a pamphlet. This pamphlet was circulated in Tonga between March and June 1890, and destroyed what little prestige Baker retained among the Tongans.

Baker had once enjoyed considerable popularity in Tonga and, until the assassination attempt of February 1887, the majority of the people had accepted his authority. The execution of Tōpui and his associates, however, and the elaborate precautions which Baker took to guard against further attempts on his life had alienated Tongan sympathies, while his prolonged absences in Auckland and the financial problems resulting from the drop in the price of copra had further contributed to a swing of popular opinion against him. By the beginning of 1890 Baker's position had become precarious; the people were openly opposing him by refusing to pay their taxes, thus making it impossible for the government to pay the salaries of their officials, which in turn further increased Tongan resentment. The publication and distribution of the Thurston–Baker correspondence at this stage was therefore very damaging to Baker and strengthened a movement of opposition which was already assuming formidable proportions. Even so, Baker still enjoyed the support of the king and might have survived this crisis, as he had many earlier ones, had he been left to deal with the situation without outside intervention; but at this critical juncture Thurston paid his long-promised visit to Tonga.

Thurston arrived on 25 June aboard HMS *Rapid* and spent the first two days in discussions with Leefe. On 27 June he interviewed the king, taking with him Captain Castle of the *Rapid*, Collet, and George Moss (the son of Tupou's earliest European adviser and adopted son, Tupou Haʻapai) to act as interpreter. Baker attended the interview but was allowed to take no part in it — Moss told Moulton's daughter that 'he sat in a corner of the room, his lips drawn and his face blanched with fear and excitement, completely ignored and not vouchsafing a single utterance'.[16] Thurston told Tupou:

> I have come down here on important business, and out of consideration for your great age and feebleness I ask you to appoint three chiefs, which I shall choose, as your representatives to deliberate with me on these matters.[17]

The king tried to procrastinate by asking Thurston to submit his request in writing, but Thurston ignored him and terminated the interview. As the British party was leaving Collet acknowledged Baker with the peremptory demand: 'You will be on board at two o'clock this afternoon'.

That afternoon Baker visited the *Rapid*. He was received by no one, a junior officer merely directing him to the High Commissioner's cabin. During the ensuing interview Baker was asked whether or not he would support Thurston's request for the appointment of a Council of Chiefs. When he declined and refused to attend the meetings of such a council he was dismissed with the curt command: 'Order your boat and go on shore'. During the subsequent proceedings Baker was completely ignored.

Thurston invited the chiefs to meet him without waiting for the king's permission, and from 28 June to 5 July he held daily discussions with the chiefs — Tungī, Tuʻipelehake, Tukuʻaho, Ata, Sunia and Kupu. When he had assured them that his intention was not to annex Tonga and guaranteed them his personal protection against reprisals, they became very co-operative and each made a written affidavit asserting that Baker was solely responsible for all the troubles of Tonga. On 5 July Thurston called the chiefs together and told them that, as a result of the information which they had given, he had decided to exercise the powers which he held over

British subjects in the Western Pacific whose presence was dangerous to peace and order. He then read to them the Order of Prohibition which he had drawn up against Baker, ordering him to leave Tonga by 17 July (the departure date of the next mail steamer) or face prosecution before the High Commissioner's Court and the liability of a gaol sentence not exceeding two years. He told the chiefs to tell the king of his decision, and then to elect a new Premier from among themselves.

The chiefs retired to Tungī's house to discuss the best manner of approaching the King, and then went in a body to the palace. Kupu gave Mrs Symonds a full account of their interview with Tupou:

> The King was sitting on the verandah. Kubu [Kupu] and Tuibelehake [Tuʻipelehake] sat at his back to prevent him if he attempted to resist any of the chiefs by physical force. Tungi and Ata sat facing him and Tuibelehake sat between the King and Mr Baker, who had come out and was sitting on a chair. Tuibelehake began, 'Tupou, your reputation is bad throughout the world; your name stinks; another wrote the letter, your name appeared on it sent to Victoria; the letter was very bad; much is done about which you do not know, etc. etc.' Then Tungi went out and Ata took it up and told the whole thing. Mr Baker sat there speechless – never uttering a word, and Alice and Shirley sat listening on the other side. The Chiefs told the King that the Governor had done what they asked him and that they must choose another Premier – whereupon the old King said, 'That is all right', then turning to Tuibelehake asked, 'Could you be the Premier?' and he said, 'I could'. (I must tell you that they had faufau fone [agreed] before to answer so whoever was asked because the King had always before made the excuse when they wanted him to send Mr B. away that no-one would undertake his work). He then turned to Tungi and said, 'Could you do it?', to which, of course, Tungi replied, 'Yes,

I could'. The King said, 'Please yourselves who it will be but you are not educated; the two young ones, they could do the work, but please yourselves'.

The chiefs then adjourned to the Government building on the other side and discussed matters. Suddenly Kubu's attention was attracted by the sight of the Premier's flag floating in the breeze over his office. He got up and without disclosing his purpose made for the flag staff, hauled the flag down, threw it on the ground, stamped on it and said, 'Your rule now ends. You are discredited for bringing Tonga to evil, and never never again shall you stand here!'[18]

That night it was formally announced that Baker had been dismissed from office and that Tuku'aho was the new Premier. Baker left the palace and sought refuge in Watkin's house. On the follow-ing morning a guard of marines was landed from the *Rapid* to prevent Baker returning to the palace, or having any intercourse with the king. He was not permitted even to visit his office to collect private letters and papers. On 15 July it was reported that he had attempted suicide, but had been prevented by Watkin.

On 17 July Baker boarded the mail steamer, *Wainui*, before day-light to avoid running the gauntlet which the triumphant European residents had prepared for him. During the morning the official order was served on him prohibiting him from returning to Tonga for a period of two years. That afternoon he was subjected to a final ignominy. Thurston reported in his official dispatch to the Colonial Secretary:

On the 17th July I attended, with Captain Castle and a large number of officers and men of Her Majesty's ships present [HMS *Egeria* was also in the harbour] and nearly the whole of the European inhabitants of Tonga, to receive the thanks of the united population of the island. This gathering, called a 'Kawa' was attended by upwards of 4000 people, all of whom in passing me said 'Thanks' or some similar expression of gratitude and laid at my feet some small offering which generally consisted of a fan, a little ornamental basket or, as in many cases, a few roses. After the people had all passed and re-formed in a semi-circle, the King's Chief Matapule, by command of the King, stood up and addressed me in a speech of eloquent thanks on behalf of the king and the people of Tonga for enabling them, by my presence and some assistance, to free themselves from a British subject who was described as a dangerous and malevolent tyrant.... The whole of this un-precedented and interesting ceremony took place in the presence of a large number of passengers of the steamships Lubeck and Wainui, and was watched by Mr Baker from the cabin window of the latter vessel.[19]

The festivities were still proceeding when, at 3 p.m., the *Wainui* got under way for New Zealand, bearing Baker into exile.

CHAPTER XII

A RATHER FEEBLE LITTLE GENTLEMAN IN BLACK

W HEN THE NEWS of Shirley Baker's fall reached Australia it caused great jubilation among the Wesleyans. A public meeting was held in Sydney to move a vote of thanks to Thurston, whose actions, the meeting declared:

> ... will long be remembered to his honour, and are in keeping with the traditions of that great Empire of which we are proud to form a part. We are of the opinion that Sir John Thurston has acted with the impartiality demanded by his high and responsible position, and that throughout the progress of events which culminated in the departure of Mr Baker from Tonga and in the reorganisation of the Tongan Government, his advice and action exhibited all the prudence, considerateness, and strength which should characterise the counsels and conduct of a servant of Her Majesty's Government.[1]

Editorial opinion in Australia and New Zealand was of the same mind, for Thurston had made sure that his version of the events in Tonga in June and July 1890 reached the press before Baker's. Only

the New Zealand *Herald* and the Auckland *Evening Star* expressed
doubts whether the deportation of Baker, which they feared would
lead to the collapse of Tongan independence, was in the best interests of the Tongan people, but as these papers were known to
have profited from the printing of Tongan government documents
for Baker, their opinions carried little weight. The general approval
of Thurston's actions expressed in the colonies had its effect in
London, and as Thurston had anticipated, the British government
overlooked his disobedience of orders and approved his conduct.

In Tonga, however, the elation and high glee which was generally felt over the fall of the *Ta'emangoi* soon faded. Thurston had
promised Tuku'aho that he would send a British officer to Tonga
to be the *tangata fakahinohino*, or expounder of civilised ways, and
Basil Thomson, Thurston's chosen vessel, sailed to Tonga with the
returning Wesleyan exiles in August 1890. By the time he arrived a
reaction had set in: the king had moved to Ha'apai as a gesture of
rebuke to his self-appointed government; the traders had extracted
ruinous concessions from the fledgling administration; Tongan
confidence in the new regime was rapidly dissipating; and Tungī
and Tuku'aho, who held the most important portfolios in the new
cabinet, were threatening to resign. Thomson was made Deputy-
Premier, and under his guidance the government was rehabilitated
and its finances stabilised. Tupou even returned to Nuku'alofa. But,
while in theory the independence and sovereignty of Tonga were
scrupulously maintained, in practice the Tongan government came
to rely heavily on the support and advice of the High Commissioner:
when Thomson left Tonga in August 1891 he reported in a confidential memorandum to the Colonial Office that British influence
in Tonga had become completely predominant.

Tupou died in February 1893 from a chill caught after an early
morning bathe in the sea. He was succeeded by his great grandson,
Tāufa'āhau, the son of Tu'ipelehake and 'Unga's daughter, Fusipala.
Tāufa'āhau was the legitimate successor according to the Constitution, but it had been confidently expected in High Commission
circles in Fiji that Tuku'aho, who was Thomson's protégé and very

pro-British, would succeed. The accession of Tāufa'āhau Tupou II
was therefore something of a setback for British policy, especially as
the young King was determined to assert his independence. When
Leefe wrote to him soon after his accession explaining why he
should appoint no Europeans other than British subjects to government positions, he was informed very sharply that the king would
appoint whomever he liked. Tuku'aho, who had administered
Baker's quarantine regulations with such laxity that a measles
epidemic had carried off one in twenty of the Tongan population,
was dismissed from office altogether, and the king appointed a new
cabinet made up largely of Baker's old supporters. But the setback
was only temporary. In 1899 Britain, Germany and the United States
finally came to an agreement over their respective positions in
Samoa, which was divided into two spheres of influence dominated
respectively by Germany and the United States; in return for
surrendering her treaty rights in Samoa the other Great Powers
surrendered to Britain their treaty rights in Tonga. The natural
consequence of this deal followed soon afterwards: in 1900 Germany
formally annexed Western Samoa, the United States assumed sovereignty over Pago Pago, and in March 1900 HMS *Porpoise* arrived
at Nuku'alofa to negotiate a treaty defining a new relationship
between Britain and Tonga. The British plenipotentiary was, not
surprisingly, Basil Thomson.

Thomson spent six weeks in Tonga trying to persuade the
reluctant King to accept British protection, and only succeeded by
threatening to depose him if he refused. The treaty was signed on
18 May 1900, and the next morning Thomson proclaimed Tonga a
British protectorate. He described the scene in his own words:

> The entire population, white and brown, were assembled on
> the beach, and I heard afterwards that the Tongans were
> saying, 'There they go, beaten; they fought our chiefs for our
> country and got the worst of it.'... I read the English version
> announcing that the country was a British Protectorate. The
> natives made no sign, but when I read the proclamation in

Tongan and came to the words *'buleanga malui'* (protectorate)
there was a kind of sob.[2]

Thomson later admitted that at the time the whole affair made
him feel 'rather cheap', but the knighthood he received for his part
in it no doubt restored his self-esteem.

Ironically it was Shirley Baker who translated the Treaty of
Protection into Tongan for Tupou II. After his deportation Baker
had tried unsuccessfully to find powerful supporters to demand his
reinstatement, and had visited America in the hope of persuading
the United States government to invoke its treaty rights in Tonga
and intervene on his behalf. But in November 1890 Thomson had
published a report on the finances of Tonga which drew attention
to the irregularities in the Treasury department during Baker's later
administration and revealed numerous minor peculations of public
funds which Baker had committed, including charging his groceries
and liquor to the public account and allowing the Tongan taxpayers
to meet his subscription to the Auckland Club. These disclosures
had tarnished Baker's reputation and his interviews with the United
States senators proved fruitless. He had then settled down in
Auckland, where he owned a large house in a select part of the
town and where, according to popular rumour, he had extensive
investments. His status was considerably enhanced in 1895 when he
announced to the Auckland press that the University of Chicago
had recognised his services to education, law and government in
Tonga by awarding him the honorary degree of Doctor of Laws –
strangely, the university has no record of making such an award.

Baker lost heavily during the severe economic depression which
overtook New Zealand in the mid-nineties, and he was reduced to
comparative penury. Consequently, in February 1897, a short time
after the death of Thurston, he went back to Tonga seeking
appointment as Government Medical Officer. Through the intervention of the British Vice-Consul his application was refused, and
he returned to New Zealand. But in October 1897 he went back
again, this time to apply to the Free Church Conference, then

meeting, for appointment as a minister. This application was also rejected. During this visit his wife died in Ha'apai.

In May 1898 Baker moved permanently from New Zealand to Ha'apai, where he had built a small house. His three unmarried daughters, who had returned to Tonga with him, opened a school, and their father supplemented the family income by dispensing medicines. In August he attended the Annual Conference of the Free Church in Vava'u to demand back payment of his supernumerary allowance of £100 per annum, with interest at ten per cent, from the time of his dismissal from Tonga. When Watkin and the Conference declined to meet this charge Baker left Vava'u threatening to start a Church of England mission in Ha'apai. He was as good as his word, and on 17 September he inaugurated the *Siasi a Vikia* (Queen Victoria's Church) in Ha'apai, and soon gained a following of upwards of two hundred people. In November he carried the mission to Tongatapu, where a political dispute had prepared the way for a division in the Free Church. Tupou II had been affianced from childhood to Ofa, a near relative of Tungī, and it was probably owing to this prospective alliance of the two families that Tungī had not opposed the succession of Tāufa'āhau to the throne. In 1899, however, the king had renounced Ofa and married instead Lavinia, the daughter of Kupu. Tungī was incensed at this insult and members of his lineage began burning the houses of Lavinia's supporters. In Tonga church membership was ever a political question, and so, when Baker announced the formation of the *Siasi a Vikia* in Nuku'alofa, with splendid irony, Tungī and his family, expressing opposition to the government in the traditional way, all joined!

Baker's success was short-lived. The king, seeing that Baker was becoming a focus of opposition, made inquiries of the Right Reverend Alfred Willis, the Bishop of Honolulu, concerning the validity of Baker's holy orders and when he was informed that Baker had no right to wear the Anglican surplice, he publicly denounced him. Baker thereupon hastened to regularise his position by obtaining a lay reader's licence from the Bishop of Dunedin, who had long been his supporter; but it was too late. His disillusioned congregation deserted him and sought the assistance of the Bishop of Honolulu, and Willis, who had been left without a living when the Church of England in Hawaii was handed over to the American Protestant Episcopal Church, agreed to come to Tonga to super-intend the infant congregation.

After this reverse Baker sank rapidly into decrepitude. In May 1900 Basil Thomson, in Nukuʻalofa to negotiate the new treaty, held an 'at home' at the British consulate for the local Europeans; he recorded:

> ... while I was talking to two new arrivals an elderly and rather feeble little gentleman in black entered the room, and my two visitors hastily seized their hats and took their leave before I had had time to exchange a word with them. The features of my new visitor seemed familiar, but the suspicion that crossed my mind while he was talking affably of the weather and the earthquake and other general topics died away as I noticed how decrepit and broken he seemed. Suddenly through the open window I saw a party of new arrivals stop short, hesitate for a moment, and then turn tail, and knowing that there was but one man in all Tonga who could produce this effect, I recognised my visitor. It was Mr Shirley Waldemar Baker himself. He was greatly changed from the masterful and prosperous minister of King George, whose name had been a byword through the Pacific and Australasia. His gains were all gone; years of hard living had played havoc with his health and prematurely aged him; he seemed even to have lost the self-confidence behind which he had concealed his lack of education. And yet even in this broken state he was able to make himself feared.[3]

Soon after the failure of his plan to establish himself as the head of the Church of England in Tonga, Baker returned to Haʻapai where his congregation remained faithful. Here a blow was delivered from within his own family. His daughter Laura, who was beginning to lose the bloom of youth with no marriage prospects in sight, succumbed to the blandishments of a young Tongan and bore him an illegitimate son. Baker expelled his daughter from the family to make her own future in New Zealand, and handed the child, Fetu'u, to the father's parents to be reared as a Tongan. But shortly after this, on 16 November 1903, Baker died of a heart attack. According to the local tradition he was found dead with his tongue protruding, by which the Tongans knew that the devil had got him at the end. He suffered one last humiliation. His daughters applied successively to the local representatives of the Church of England, the Free Church, the Wesleyan Church, and in desperation the Catholic Church, but no one would bury him. He was finally laid to rest in the cemetery at Lifuka, Ha'apai, by an itinerant Seventh-Day Adventist preacher who happened to call at Ha'apai in search of converts. But the king at least had sufficient sense of propriety to fly the Tongan flag at half-mast on the day of the funeral.

EPILOGUE

THE JUDGEMENT OF history had been passed on Shirley Baker before he died. In 1897 Basil Thomson published *The Diversions of a Prime Minister*, a devastating satire on Baker's Tonga which was written so wittily and in such elegant prose that it was widely read and accepted; it set the tone for everything that has since been written about Tonga under Baker's administration, and indeed so far pre-empted the field that no further or fuller investigation has, until now, been attempted. This essay is an attempt to fill the gap by tracing, in sequence and in context, the events and developments of the period, and thus to provide the basis for a re-evaluation.

From the evidence adduced it would seem that the accepted estimate of Baker's character is inadequate. According to Thomson, Baker was a remarkably unpleasant person – ignorant, pompous, bigoted, and venal. This, as far as it goes, is probably true, for Baker did have rather more than his share of unattractive characteristics. He also had a number of more estimable traits, however, which Thomson failed to mention. Some of these were noted by Thomas Trood, a British resident in Tonga with no particular axe to grind, who wrote of Baker:

> However bitter might be the attacks of his enemies, he ever, in times of their sickness or that of their families, gave his medical advice, always most valuable, freely, and did his best for the sick persons; nothing true, in my knowledge can be

urged against his moral character. He was also, without being
a total abstainer, strictly temperate. Neither was he revengeful;
no man can attack him justly on that score.... He was also a
very kind hearted man, much more so than some of his
opponents.... He was a worker in the hive of men, and no
drone, rising long before daylight and continuing work in his
study till eight or nine o'clock. Probably if judged by the rule
of 'charity' he may in the unseen world find a better record
than that which men have assigned to him here.... 'The
greatest of all virtues is charity', and that Baker, with all his
faults, possessed to a greater extent than his enemies.[1]

The final judgement on the matter must be left to the recording
angel, but it seems clear that Baker was neither so deficient in virtues
nor so replete with vices as is commonly alleged.

It is equally difficult to make an unequivocal assessment of
Baker's work as a missionary. On the one hand, he made the Tongan
mission self-supporting and brought solvency to the Australasian
Wesleyan Missionary Society; on the other, his methods of achieving
this worthy objective caused a scandal that still embarrasses the
Methodist Church and provides ammunition for its critics. Again,
Baker gave Tonga its own self-governing church, but in doing so
he provoked bitter internal conflicts and brutal religious persecution.
But perhaps, in the long view, Baker has been vindicated. Today
Tongans are among the most devout people on earth, a state of
affairs for which the Free Wesleyan Church of Tonga is largely
responsible. Liberated from outside control, and closely in touch
with the needs of the people, the Free Church has kept the loyalty
of the Tongans as no *fakaongo* (dependent) church could.

But, in the final analysis, it is as a statesman and politician that
Baker must be judged, and it is in the verdict of Thomson and later
writers on this question that the greatest miscarriage of justice lies.
Baker wrought a revolution of tremendous significance in Tonga.
Under his guidance a tribal, quasi-feudal society was transformed
into a modern constitutional state; government by the whim of the

powerful was replaced by the rule of law; and from dependence on subsistence agriculture the country was enabled to progress to a money economy based on trade. At the same time the kingdom's independence was maintained against powerful adversaries and the alienation of native lands effectively and permanently prevented. Changes as profound as these have seldom occurred in other societies within so short a space of time, and when they have taken place they have usually been accomplished by violence or accompanied by widespread distress. But in Tonga a combined social, economic and political revolution was accomplished swiftly and smoothly, with a minimum of distress and with the loss of only six lives, those of Baker's would-be assassins.

The magnitude of this achievement has been obscured by the writings of one man, at least for Europeans. Polynesians perhaps know better: in 1946 the New Zealand Premier visited Samoa to begin the discussions that led, several years later, to the granting of independence to the state of Western Samoa. In his speech of welcome on that important occasion the Samoan Head of State, Tamasese, paid the New Zealand Premier the highest compliment he could think of — he compared him to the Reverend Shirley Baker.[2]

POSTSCRIPT

I T IS IN THE nature of historical writing, that once a thing is published it is open for criticism and reassessment. That has happened to this little book. On the whole I think that my original assessment of Baker and his work in Tonga has weathered the quarter century fairly well, which suggests that I probably got it about right. However, getting it right in an overall sense does not preclude a realisation that in some matters of detail I may have got it quite wrong. Often these matters of detail have no effect on the general scheme of things, but sometimes the detail is crucial and may alter an interpretation entirely. Since 1971 new evidence has come to light on some aspects of this story which, in three specific areas, require a reassessment.

The first and major area where a reassessment seems necessary concerns Baker's origin, social class and education. Baker's story was that he was the son of the Rev. George Baker, an Anglican clergyman, and a person of some standing in mid-nineteenth century England; that he had a formal classical education; and that he left England to visit an uncle in Australia and to seek his fortune in the colonies. This account was accepted in Wesleyan circles in the Antipodes for twenty years, and no doubt gave him some social standing in that community. But from the arrival of an official British presence in Fiji after the 1874 cession, and especially after Sir Arthur Gordon's celebrated clash with Baker in 1878, there was a constant undercurrent of suggestion from British officials that Baker was not as he had presented himself. It was put about that he was uncouth, ill-educated and only semi-literate. Worst of all it was said that he spoke with a cockney accent, that least respectable and most denigrated of all the regional variants of the mother tongue, regarded in genteel quarters as the dialect of spivs, costermongers, pickpockets and prostitutes.

When I came to examine the evidence, I found great difficulty in substantiating Baker's story. I did establish that the Rev. James Calvert from Fiji, who met Baker soon after his arrival in the mission field, had noted in his diary that Baker was the son of an Anglican cleric, but surely he only had Baker's word for this. Moreover, when I came to look for the Rev. George Baker, he failed to appear in any of the directories. Nor did the school, the Oxford Home Grammar School, where he was supposed to be Headmaster, appear in any of the school directories. Faced with the lack of any reliable evidence to support Shirley Baker's story, and based on the conclusions I had come to concerning his character, I concluded that the Rev. George Baker was a figment of his imagination, devised to improve his own prospects and social standing in Australia.

Dr Geoffrey Cummins, in his research into the life of James Egan Moulton pursued further leads on the life of the elusive George Baker. He discovered, firstly, that James Calvert, noted earlier, had been a life-long friend of the Rev. Theophilus Woolmer, Shirley Baker's maternal uncle. This was an important link, because Calvert accepted Baker's story and as he knew the family it seemed likely that the story was true. Cummins also sieved through the death notices in *The Times* around the presumed date of George Baker's death and having found the notice went on to unearth the death certificate. This showed that the Rev. George Baker died in the Marylebone workhouse on 28 December 1869 of 'chronic cerebral disease and paralysis', which was the nineteenth century euphemism for the symptoms of either tertiary syphilis or alcoholism.

More recently further evidence has come to light. Mrs Joan Ellis of Nottingham, U. K., a descendent of George Baker through his second wife, Caroline Sarah Mallam, began compiling a family history. She found, firstly, the record of the marriage of George Baker to Caroline Mallam in 1846. The address of the groom was given as 'Oxford House'. Perhaps this was the missing 'Oxford Home Grammar School', which had become defunct by the time the 1851 census was taken. She also discovered that a member of the family had a copy of a letter sent by George Baker to his wayward son, Shirley, then in Australia. It is a very long letter, but as it is the only extant evidence concerning the character of Baker's father and the nature of the family relationship it is worth quoting fairly extensively. It was written from Lincoln's Inn, London, on 27 December 1854. George Baker wrote:

> My Dear Shirley,
>
> Your letters reached us safely and welcome indeed they were. We had for some time entertained fears for your safety. The uncertainty with us of your being able to endure the difficulties and fatigues of the journey ... and troubles of attempting some occupation among strangers made us at times very wretched and miserable, yet under all circumstances I never failed day by day and several times during the day by prayer to commit you to the tender mercies and protection of your Father...
>
> Your present state of mind ... to continue your studies for the ministry is most gratifying to us and your intended course for the future has my hearty approval, but with this provision, that you will meet my wishes in continuing your studies in Latin and Greek...
>
> I have not entertained any angry feelings towards you on account of your leaving home so abruptly, always trusting that Almighty God would overule [sic] it for good. Be assured of my full pardon for any offence against me with which you may charge yourself...
>
> I must lament your loss in business and trust you did not suffer any want of the necessities of life during your misfortune ... I myself took a country engagement shortly after you left to assist a clergyman in the duties of an extensive

parish. Having concluded that engagement I am anxiously awaiting some negotiations in progress and should the result prove favourable we shall do well.... Had you been successful in your undertakings I should have been glad for you to have joined me in the purchase of some premises in the country which I have lately occupied, we will however hope for better times and tidings...

We all join in love. We pray to God to bless you, to pour out his spirit upon you and keep you in all your ways.... I am my dear son, your affectionate father,

George Baker.

So it seems that the Rev. George Baker was precisely what Shirley Baker said he was. Reading between the lines, however, we can deduce that he was less than successful in his vocation. It is clear that he had no benefice and had recently been acting as a curate in the country. In fact it seems possible that Baker Snr had spent much of his life 'anxiously awaiting some negotiations' through which he could 'hope to do well', in the manner of his fictional contemporary, Mr Micawber. If he was an inveterate alcoholic it would explain why such negotiations were always unproductive, and why he should have had to spend his last days in the workhouse; it could also explain why Shirley Baker ran away to Australia, and why he was always so vague and guarded when referring to his father.

Another fascinating scrap of information in George Baker's letter is his exhortation to his son to continue his study in Latin and Greek. This argues rather strongly that the young Shirley had already studied the Classics at school, almost certainly at a grammar school, and probably at the school where his father was headmaster. A picture of Shirley Baker's background thus begins to emerge which is at odds with the one sedulously promulgated by British official-dom and which I had accepted at face value. This alternative picture led me to look again at Baker's prose style to see whether, in fact, he wrote in what Basil Thomson described as 'English that would have disgraced a housemaid', and whether his letters and other writings gave evidence of his being, as Sir Arthur Gordon described him, 'narrow minded and ignorant' or as Sir John Thurston said, 'illiterate'. One of the problems was that everything I had been able to find written by Baker was very formal stuff – either reports to his missionary superiors, formal government letters or official papers. These were stilted and often a bit pompous, but that is the nature of such materials. What one needed was some private, unguarded, personal correspondence, but none of this seemed to have survived.

Recently, however, some of just this sort of material has come to light. It seems that Baker's daughters lived on in Ha'apai in some penury after their father's death and, to raise cash, they occasionally sold some of their father's correspondence to Sir John Ferguson, a wealthy Australian jurist and bibliophile. When Ferguson died he left his library and papers to the Australian National Library. The Librarian there drew my attention to some Tongan materials listed among his papers and I looked them out – and there was the cache of much of the material I had sought in vain in the sixties. Some of the most interesting are letters from Baker to his friend and ally, the Reverend Jabez Watkin. One written on 12 November 1884 is typical:

My Dear Bro Watkin,

Your letter of Wednesday last duly to hand. On the receipt of your letter and also the King's, and after a little thought on the matter I determined to send the 'Sandfly' at once to New Zealand with the telegram, a copy of which is now enclosed, and she left here on Sunday morning and until today she has had a favourable and good breeze, so I expect she is far on her course.

I somehow or other think that such an influence will be brought to bear on the General Conference that they will be compelled to grant the King's request. Somehow or other I have a presentiment that it will be so, and if such be the case

I think we may say that our troubles are at an end.

However he could make the statement he made at the District Meeting I cannot conceive. And I have just received news from Niuafo'ou, by a German barque, that Joeli Nau stated in some meetings he has held there that Tonga has gone 'Kuo mole e Toga'; really Moulton must be a lunatic, and all agree here that his actions are more like a madman than anything else. What he did at the District Meeting – allow Nebote Fale to vote – I consider most scandalous in the extreme. I should like to hear what excuse even his Sydney friends will be able to make for him.

I think your brother at last decided to attend Conference, and I see he was advertised to give a speech at the Gen. Miss. Mtg. so I am in hopes that he will be there after all.

Mr Buddle told me that you would be there too, how he got his information I can't say. I half expected when I arrived to find that you had gone up.

However should the telegram arrive in time I think it will be a settler for them. If the Gen. Confce. should not grant the King's request, I shall go hand in glove with him in carrying out his purpose.

I too have received a letter from Mr Brown, but it was written in May last. The Consul seems to have detained it with many other important letters, although marked 'urgent', and I am sorry for Brown might think I wanted to slight him. But however grieved I may be with him about his articles in re Mr Moulton's revision, yet I do not wish to do that.

I heartily sympathise with you in what you had to endure at the D.M.. I must confess I am somewhat surprised at Phillip Taufa, but he has tried to explain the matter away and he says he firmly believed what Mr Moulton said.

That a drunken fellow like Maealiuaki should be permitted to attend the District Mtg., and to be a steward of the Church, is decidedly a disgrace to Christianity and a mockery to religion.

I could not help smiling when I received your letter about Mr Crosby's remark to you in Vavau, and was thoroughly prepared on my arrival to find that he had got some hashed up case or other, and was therefore not much surprised when he demanded an interview, but certainly was surprised when we met to find that they were some ridiculous stories about land, and if I ever saw a man collapse in my life it was Crosby. It is certainly grievous to think that Moulton should have ruined another life, as though he had not ruined sufficient before. I look upon Crosby as a ruined man, he is neither mentally, physically or morally the same man he was twelve months ago, and he certainly can have very little mind of his own to be tomfooled as he is by Moulton. It appears they had to detain the 'Myrtle' for three days on a/c of Mr Moulton for he was so ill that they did not expect him to live. I truly believe in your words, that if the Conference does not act in the matter, the Lord will.

We are going to have a grand affair at the opening of the King's Church, and also a great Katoaga [festival], which we are going to call Katoaga Kula [red festival], in commemoration of King George having reigned 40 years over Tonga.

(The remainder of the letter is missing.)

I believe that this letter, like others in the collection, represents vigorous and highly effective communication. The prejudices are obvious and there is much that is vindictive, but he expresses his views clearly and unambiguously. Moreover, considering that this is a first draft of the letter (as scratchings out and corrections in it indicate) the syntax is on the whole pretty good. In fact, to a modern reader, the clarity and vigour of Baker's prose makes a very favourable impression. A balanced view today would probably accept that Baker was highly intelligent and that he had a good educational grounding at a minor grammar school, to about the equivalent standard of modern English "O levels" or the Australian School Certificate. This is exactly what Baker himself claimed.

On the question of Baker's spoken English the evidence does, however, seem to support a conclusion that he possessed at least the hint of a Cockney accent. This is not surprising considering the address on his mother's death certificate, which is given as Whitechapel, in the heart of the East End and the scene of the 'Ripper' murders towards the end of the century. Even a vicar's son and grammar school scholar could not but absorb some of the local patois, and it was probably this damning class identifier that inspired those detractors who were at such pains to paint him as an ignorant vulgarian.

The question remains as to why Baker's detractors should have so assiduously propagated such a prejudiced view. Perhaps there was a political purpose behind it all. The comments all came from British officialdom, from men who were busy running the British Empire in a remote corner of the world. They were not, however, merely maintaining it, but were busily trying to extend it. As far as the British Government was concerned the Empire may have been collected 'in a fit of absence of Mind', but for officials on the frontier there was nothing absent-minded about it. The Empire was, as one historian has written, 'a vast system of outdoor relief for the British upper classes' and the wider its bounds could be set, the better the career prospects for those at the cutting edge. Tonga was the natural extension of Fiji, as Sir Arthur Gordon had so clearly described to his superiors in 1878. The lion in the path preventing this natural extension was Shirley Baker. So the propaganda campaign to belittle and diminish him was a natural tactic in a concerted effort to get rid of him. The campaign took fourteen years, but eventually succeeded in 1890. It was followed, a decade later, by the absorption of Tonga into the British Empire.

The second area where new material throws light on events in Tonga in the 1880s concerns the tensions and motivations of the leading characters playing a role during this crucial decade of modern Tongan history. These new insights do not call for a reappraisal, but they do tie up some loose ends and provide answers to some puzzling questions.

For instance, one letter in the Ferguson collection helps explain the decision of the Reverence Jabez Watkin to throw in his lot with Baker over the Free Church secession. This seemed a surprising decision. Watkin had an impeccable Methodist background, being the son of the Reverend James Watkin, a pioneer missionary in Tonga and a recognised 'father' in the missionary community. Until 1881, Jabez Watkin's relationship with Baker had been somewhat equivocal. He had been an outspoken critic of Baker's role in the 1875 Constitution, though he had supported Baker in his conflict with Sir Arthur Gordon in 1879. When as a result of that conflict Baker had been withdrawn from Tonga, Watkin had been appointed Chairman of the Friendly Islands Mission in his place.

The years 1880 and 1881 were difficult years for Watkin because of the opposition of the King. Tupou had been angered by the treatment of Baker by the Missionary Society and had withdrawn his support for the missionaries and Baker, who had become Premier in 1880, had done nothing to pacify the King or moderate his displeasure. In fact he had probably added fuel to the fire. Watkin, however, seems to have been convinced that the fault lay with the Missionary Committee, not with Baker or Tupou. It was Watkin's perceived indulgence towards Baker and the King that led the Missionary Committee to recommend to the 1881 Conference that Watkin, too, be withdrawn from Tonga. This decision represented a crucial turning point in the relationship between Australian Methodism and Tonga, for Tupou and Baker threw their weight behind Watkin, and this was the first step in the process that led to the secession of the Free Church. The niggling question remained, however: was Watkin's pique over being transferred from Tonga to an Australian circuit a sufficient cause for his sudden conversion to the Baker camp, with the obloquy and condemnation from contemporary and subsequent Methodists which this move entailed? Would a man abandon his whole religious connection over what appears to be so small a matter? For lack of any other evidence, I had to accept that he would and did.

However, among the letters of the Ferguson collection is a copy of a letter from Watkin's brother, the Reverend E.J. Watkin, to the

Reverend G. Woolnough, Secretary of the Board of Missions dated 9 February 1882, remonstrating with the Board for its unfair treatment of his brother. He wrote concerning a resolution of the Board of November 18, 1881:

> The resolution of Nov. 18 singles the Rev. J.B.W. out from the other missionaries, treats him in a different way from them. If I read the resolution aright it means this: that if necessary the Chairman of the District may pay his own and the other missionaries' claims, but that the Rev. J.B.W. could only be paid for the first quarter of the year without further reference to the Board. The resolution of the Board was calculated to have, and I presume was intended to have, a punitive effect upon the Rev. J.B.W. The Board could not fail to see when it passed the resolution that its effect might be to deprive the Rev. J.B.W. of his salary for nine months of 1881...
>
> The Board of Missions has no right to punish a missionary by withholding from him his salary, without formulating charges against him, and calling him to answer those charges before the Church courts to which he is responsible...
>
> My brother has had meted out to him treatment which is much more severe than would be given to a minister suspended on a charge of moral delinquency.

Here then, is the missing link. The action taken by the Board of Missions against Watkin in November 1881 was not a mere transfer, but a very severe punitive measure, and one that was to drive Watkin into the arms of Baker. Watkin thus became the third member of a triumvirate that was to reconstruct the political, religious and educational environment of Tonga.

Once the alliance was forged, Baker's support for Watkin was unstinting. In fact it was Baker's absolute support for Watkin that prevented the healing of the religious breach soon after the secession. In a letter from Baker to the Reverend George Brown, dated 4 May 1885, also in the Ferguson collection, Baker made it clear that he would accept all other conditions laid down by the deputation sent to Tonga to promote reunion of the Free Church with the Australian Wesleyans, except the removal of Watkin. Such a proposal he wrote,

> ... we were not willing to accede to, knowing that the King and chiefs would never agree to it, that they look upon it as a kind of punishment on Mr Watkin and censure upon the King.... If the Free Church is to be taken back to Methodism, then Watkin must take it back.

If the relationship between Baker and Watkin was of great importance in moulding the events of the 1880s, the relationship between Baker and Moulton was of even greater significance, but while little has been said or written about the Baker-Watkin friendship, a great deal has been made of the Baker-Moulton antipathy. Moulton, of course, has always had a good press because he was supported by a very effective propaganda machine, that of the Australian Wesleyan Church. So while it is clear that the antagonism between Moulton and Baker was the pivot around which much of the turmoil of nineteenth century Tongan history revolved, yet this was almost always viewed from the standpoint of Moulton, the Sydney Wesleyans and the British connection in Fiji. My own contribution to this debate was, I think, to demonstrate that there were two sides to this argument and that Baker had a point of view that was capable of being sustained.

There is nothing in the Ferguson papers that adds anything very new on this question but there are letters that do help flesh out the Baker side of the story. For example, there is the letter from Baker to the Reverend G. Woolnough written in October 1881 referring to the rift between the king and Moulton over Watkin being relegated to Ha'apai in that year. This letter presents a reasoned and moderate account of the affair and makes a fair case that the problems were caused by Moulton's arrogance and lack of tact, rather than by Baker's interference. Baker wrote:

> I am happy to say that Mr Watkin has gone to Ha'apai. I used my influence with the King to let him go pointing out to the King you had endeavoured to meet his wishes by using your prerogative in allowing him to remain in the Islands and that Mr Moulton had informed you that it was His Majesty's wish for Mr Watkin to go to Ha'apai, and in accordance with the information you had then received, you had sent [him]... I pointed out that it would materially help the granting of his wishes and prove that he did not wish to come unnecessarily into collision with the Church or to dispute the power of the Conference...
>
> As regards Mr Moulton misunderstanding the King it is only another proof of Mr Moulton's ignorance of Tongan customs, as I have often said before I say again, Mr Moulton does not understand Tongan customs – no one in Tonga would have so misunderstood the King as Mr Moulton seems to have done. Mr Moulton suggested Mr Watkin should go to Ha'apai, the King makes no reply [;] no one else would have ever dreamed or thought of saying the King was agreeable to it [;] the same with the letter [;] his receiving no reply would have been quite enough for anyone acquainted with Tongan customs. This affair has greatly widened the breach and the King's word being questioned will bear unhappy fruit.

Three years later, Baker's hostility to Moulton had become something of an obsession. In the intervening years Moulton had become more and more closely linked with the opposition to Baker through close association with the focus of Tongan opposition at Mu'a, and with British officialdom (his daughter had become engaged to be married to the British Consul). The removal of Moulton from Tonga had become, by this time, one of Baker's primary objectives, and his letters display an increasing rancour. A letter to the Reverend George Brown of 31 May 1884, also from the Ferguson collection, reveals this clearly:

> My Dear Bro,
>
> I have only time to drop a line or two, but I thought you would like to know how things are going on. I don't know whether you will have heard or not that when Mr Moulton went on to Vavau to see His Majesty, it appears that the King would neither see Mr Moulton nor speak to him nor shake hands with him. I hope this will convince the Sydney Ministers of the falsity of Mr Moulton's statement 'it was not the King's wish that the charges should be brought against Mr Moulton'.
>
> Mr Moulton has lately sent two of his Tutors to collect the College lads from Ha'apai and Vavau to go on to the great Katoaga which he is preparing in connection with his college, not one in Ha'apai has paid any attention to his command, and the same in Vavau with regard to those who hold Government places or are employed in Government schools. This will give you some idea of the boasted influence of Mr Moulton.
>
> When I arrived in Tonga most of the chiefs of Tonga where [sic] in Vavau and they have said on their arrival in Tonga that they too will not go to hear Mr Moulton preach or have anything to do with him. The King also has wished me to command that until the removal of Mr Moulton no Bule Kolo [village chief] or Ofisa Kolo [village officer] nor anyone connected with the Government shall be a Trustee or take the Chair or speak at any Missionary Meeting. You may rely upon it that the New South Wales Conference will bitterly repent not having accepted the compromise that I authorised you to offer them.... However I think that nothing but secession will bring the Sydney Conference to its senses and should the General Conference not yield to the wishes of their

Melbourne brethren I will go in for it with all my might and
that means something.

From this letter the hostility of Baker towards Moulton is very
plain, but it is also clear that the king was no longer on speaking
terms with Moulton, and that Baker was also considering the idea
of secession. None of this is really new, but it does confirm the
general hypothesis that the bitter rivalry and poisonous relationship
between Baker and Moulton was at the root of the problems that
were to beset Tonga for a generation. It was to embroil Tongans in
many hardships and to lead six of them to their death on Malinoa
in 1887 – for Moulton was as deeply involved as Baker in this
tragedy.

It is concerning this affair, the execution of Tōpui and his
associates, that new evidence has also come to light. Most of the
details concerning the trial and execution of the conspirators involved in the attempt on Baker's life in January 1887 are well
documented. As a result of the trials conducted by Chief Justice
Ahome'e ten men were convicted and condemned to death, the
Reverend Tēvita Finau was found guilty of being an accessory and
was sentenced to 22 years imprisonment and four men, who had
turned king's evidence, were pardoned.

The details of what followed, however, are somewhat obscure.
The story that I pieced together was based largely on the sworn
statement of Tu'uhetoka, Minister of Police, to Sir Charles Mitchell.
From this evidence it seemed clear that Baker, having gained a
conviction, sought commutation of the death sentences, and that he
went to the palace with Tu'uhetoka to plead with the king to
reprieve those under sentence of death. The king was non-com-
mittal. Baker and Tu'uhetoka left the palace on the understanding
that they would return the next morning to discuss the matter
further. But at 2.00 a.m. the king sent for Tu'uhetoka and ordered
him to take six of the conspirators to Malinoa and execute them
immediately. When Tu'uhetoka reported to the king that this had

been done, he was ordered to go again and execute the other four. One the way Tuʻuhetoka met Baker and told him what had happened. Baker revoked the king's order and told Tuʻuhetoka he would take the matter up with the king, and resign if further executions took place.

That outline of events satisfied me at the time as being consistent with all the available evidence, as well as with the characters of the dramatis personae. However among the Ferguson papers I found a bulky typescript document, undated, but bearing the name of A. W. Mackay, who became the son-in-law of Moulton after the death of his daughter's first husband, Henry Symonds. This document comprised a narrative, written in the most florid prose, and purporting to be an eye witness account of the events surrounding the executions on Malinoa. There were several discrepancies between this account and the one I had assembled.

For example, Mackay claimed that a further twelve prisoners, not four, were scheduled for execution on the day following the events on Malinoa. However, the evidence of Chief Justice Ahomeʻe, given to Sir Charles Mitchell, and included in the papers accompanying his report, list those condemned as: Tōpui, Naisa, Fehoko, Latu, Palu, Lavuso, Tavake, Aisea Kaumoto, Fekau and Tuitavake. That makes ten, and all agree that six of these were shot. Six from ten leaves four, not the twelve claimed by Mackay.

There is also in the narrative an extraordinary story that could have found a place in *Boy's Own Annual*. Mackay recounted how he witnessed the executions on Malinoa from the deck of the German barque *Cardinal* on which he was a passenger, and that when he arrived at Nukuʻalofa he tried to rally the European community to rescue the 'twelve' who were to be executed the next morning, but:

> … they were not enthusiastic about further interference, for the reason that Baker had threatened a general massacre of all whites if any interference took place. I soon formed the conclusion that if anything was to be done, I would have to do it myself.

Mackay then, according to his story, persuaded a chief to let him secretly into the palace:

> He led me by a circuitous route landing me eventually where I wished to be, viz. on the upstairs landing in the Palace, and indicating a door, he vanished. In another instant I was inside the door, and had it locked and the great autocrat of Tonga was at my mercy. It was all very quietly done, Baker made one abortive attempt to snatch at his drawer, but I ordered him to do something else, and he thought it wise to obey. I informed him that I held him responsible for the lives of all the Tongans, and that if there were any more shooting I intended to shoot him. And what is more to the point I succeeded in convincing him that I meant what I said. He begged his life at my hands and I granted it on certain conditions...
>
> I reminded him of the petition for the reprieve of the condemned men – which he had refused to place before the King. He tried to make excuses, but at last said that if it had been presented in a proper manner he would have signed it and presented it himself. I thereupon produced a copy, and he signed it. He promised me that the orders to ship the condemned men would be countermanded within fifteen minutes after I left the Palace, and he also promised good behaviour to me for the rest of his natural life. The reign of terror was at an end.

This is all very exciting stuff, but it seems unlikely to be true. Sir Charles Mitchell dismissed Mackay as an unreliable witness. He included in his official report a newspaper clipping from the *Sydney Morning Herald* of 3 March 1887, which gave Mackay's account of the disturbances in Tonga. Mitchell noted that although Mackay's account purported to be that of an eye witness, in fact he was not, and the details of the events on Malinoa were provided by Von Hagen. Mitchell also drew attention to a supposed conversation between Mackay, the British Consul, R.B. Leefe and

the Catholic missionary, Father O'Dwyer, which was reported in
the same article. He wrote:

> I hold in my hand a letter from the latter gentleman (Father
> O'Dwyer) in which he says, referring to these accounts, 'they
> are painfully inexact. Many statements are absolutely false and
> of the remainder there is much that is offensively exaggerated,
> so that it is unjustly annoying to us to have our names
> mentioned in connection with his incorrect effusions'. I attach
> to this newspaper report a copy of a further statement by Mr
> Mackay which was sent to me by the Rev. Mr Langham but
> whether published or not I am unable to say. It would occupy
> too much time were I to go through the various statements
> and sift the modicum of truth from the mass of exaggeration
> contained in them.

Mackay's account of his act of derring-do should probably,
therefore, be taken with a large pinch of salt. This need for caution
is confirmed by Mackay himself. Mackay's papers are in the
Australian National University Library and they include a MS
journal. This was not intended for publication and is inherently
more reliable than the typescript referred to above, which bears all
the signs of being written for the general public. This journal reveals
that although Mackay saw a cutter moored off Malinoa on the
morning of the executions, he was totally unaware of the events
that were taking place there. Moreover, there is no mention in the
journal of the midnight foray to the palace and the dramatic rescue
of the condemned.

On balance, therefore, I prefer Tu'uhetoka's version of events,
and will stand by my original account. This is an important issue,
because if Mackay's account were true it would signify that the real
prime mover in the political events in Tonga was Baker, and that
Tupou was a mere cipher, a puppet manipulated by a missionary
mountebank, which was essentially the view consistently propagated
by the British establishment. However, if Tu'uhetoka's account is
accurate it becomes clear that it was decidedly Tupou who was

calling the shots, that when Baker would not support him, he would go it alone, and when he was bent on something, neither Baker nor anyone else could influence him. This was, I believe, the true position. It is the interpretation implicit throughout *Shirley Baker and the King of Tonga,* and stated explicitly in my chapter on Tupou and Shirley Baker in *Friendly Islands, a History of Tonga.* This little exercise helps confirm my belief that that is the way it was.

Noel Rutherford
September 1995

Abbreviations used

in the Notes

F.O. 58   ❦ British Foreign Office records relating to the Pacific Islands, 1822-1905

F.O.C.P.   ❦ British Foreign Office Confidential Print

F3   ❦ Central Archives of Fiji and the Western Pacific High Commission, preliminary index no. 3: Copies of despatches from the Consul-General and/or High Commissioner for the Western Pacific to the Consul, Vice-Consul and/or Deputy Commissioner, Tonga, and from the Consul, Vice-Consul and/or Deputy Commissioner, Tonga to the Consul-General and/or High Commissioner for the Western Pacific, 1860-1953.
The following series:

     F3/2 – General Correspondence – Inwards, 1878-1944;
     F3/10 – Despatches from the Consul-General to the Vice-Consul, Tonga, 1879; 1881 to 1882; 1884 to 1900; October 1913 to December 1935;
     F3/1 – Copies of Despatches from the Vice-Consul, Tonga, to the Consul, Fiji, or Consul-General, March 1864 to December 1864, November 1879 to February 1901;
     F3/19 – Copies of Despatches from the Deputy Commissioner or Agent, Tonga, to the High Commissioner 1879-1953;
     F3/43 – Miscellaneous Papers

M.O.M.C.   ❦ The Mitchell Library, Sydney, a collection of documents entitled the Methodist Overseas Mission Collection

Manuscripts and Printed Documents   ❦ The Alexander Turnbull Library, Wellington, a bound volume of papers entitled 'MSS. and Printed Documents, in connection with the Charges against Rev. S. W. Baker, Tonga 1866 and Onward'

T.G.B.B.   ❦ *Tonga Government Blue Book*

Wesleyan Mission Papers   ❦ The Turnbull Library, a collection of papers entitled Wesleyan Mission Papers

W.M.M.S.   ❦ The Wesleyan Methodist Missionary Society

W.P.H.C. Inwards Corresp. (General)   ❦ Central archives of Fiji, a collection of despatches entitled Western Pacific High Commission Inwards Correspondence (General)

NOTES

INTRODUCTION

1   Basil Thomson, *The Diversions of a Prime Minister*
2   Basil Thomson, *Savage Island: An account of a Sojourn in Niue and Tonga*
3   Sir Basil Thomson, *The Scene Changes*
4   The Samoa Agreement in Plain English, vol. 166, December 1899; A
Statesman-Adventurer of the Pacific, vol. 175, February 1904
5   Louis B. Wright and Mary Isabel Fry, *Puritans in the South Seas*, pp. 262-8
6   Aarne A. Koskinen, *Missionary Influence as a Political Factor in the Pacific
Islands*, p. 78
7   K. L. P. Martin, *Missionaries and Annexation in the Pacific*, p. 99
8   Douglas L. Oliver, *The Pacific Islands*, revised edn, p. 184
9   W. P. Morrell, *Britain in the Pacific Islands*
10   James Colwell (ed.), *A Century in the Pacific*, p. 431
11   Lillian and Beatrice Shirley Baker, *Memoirs of the Reverend Dr. Shirley
Waldemar Baker, D.M Ll.D., Missionary and Prime Minister*
12   Morrell, p. 317

CHAPTER I

1   James Calvert, Journal, Personal Papers Collection, Records of the
Methodist Missionary Society, London
2   Thomson, *The Scene Changes*, p. 143
3   Sir Arthur Gordon to the Secretary of State for Foreign Affairs, 15
July 1882, F.O. 58/177
4   J. B. Thurston to Colonel Stanley, 21 January 1886. F.O.C.P. 5310,
no. 120, enc. 1
5   Thomson, *The Scene Changes*, p. 52
6   Worthington Chauncey Ford (ed.), *Letters of Henry Adams 1858-1891*,
p. 455
7   Alfred St Johnston, *Camping Among Cannibals*, p. 2
8   *Report of the Australasian Wesleyan-Methodist Missionary Society for the
Year ending April 1871, with an Account of the Contributions for the Year 1870*
(Report A.W.M.M.S., 1870-71), p. 98

9   The Reverend Stephen Rabone to the Reverend George Baker, 31 March 1866, M.O.M.C., set 35

10   S.C. Roberts, *Tamai, The Life Story of John Hartley Roberts of Tonga*, p. 12

11   *Shipping Records*, Archives Division of the State Library of Victoria, Melbourne

12   A.W. Mackay, *Account of the Sojourn in Tonga of Shirley Waldemar Baker and the Consequences of his Tyranny*, p. iv

13   Roberts, p. 12

14   The *Castlemaine Advertiser*, 19 May 1859

15   Roberts, pp. 13 ff.

16   Baker to the Reverend John Eggleston, 18 August 1860, M.O.M.C., Uncat. MSS., set 197, item 2

17   H.N. Moseley, *Notes by a Naturalist on the 'Challenger' being an Account of Various Observations made during the Voyage of H.M.S. 'Challenger' around the World in the Years 1872-1876*, pp. 283, 287

18   J.L. Brenchley, *Jottings During the Cruise of H.M.S. 'Curacoa' among the South Sea Islands in 1865,* pp. 106, 108

19   Primary sources on this period include: G. Vason, *An Authentic Narrative of Four Years Residence at Tongataboo, One of the Friendly Islands in the South Seas* ed. S. Piggott (London, 1810); William Mariner, *An Account of the Natives of the Tonga Islands with a Grammar and Vocabulary of their Language compiled from the Communications of W. Mariner by John Martin* (2 vols), *Tongan Society,* Bernice P. Bishop Museum Bulletin no. 61 (Honolulu, 1929); A.H. Wood, *A History and Geography of Tonga* (Nuku'alofa, 1932); Monseigneur Bishop Blanc, *A History of Tonga or Friendly Islands* (California, n.d.)

20   This period has been considered in detail in the following: S. Lātūkefu, The Influence of the Wesleyan Methodist Missionaries on the Political Development of Tonga (unpublished Ph.D. thesis, Australian National University, 1967); G.E. Hammer, The Early Years of the Wesleyan Methodist Mission in Tonga (unpublished M.A. thesis, University of Otago, 1951); 'Abide' (K.M. Bates), The Foundations of Modern Tonga (unpublished M.A. thesis, University of New Zealand, 1933). Other important sources are: Reverend Walter Lawry, *Friendly and Feejee Islands, A Missionary Visit to Various Stations in the South Seas in the Year MDCCCXLVIII* (2nd edn, London, 1850); Sarah S. Farmer, *Tonga and the Friendly Islands; with a Sketch of their Mission History, Written for Young People* (London, 1855); Reverend Thomas West, *Ten Years in South Central Polynesia, Being Reminiscences of a Personal Mission to the Friendly Islands and their Dependencies* (London, 1865)

CHAPTER II

1 Captain Elphinstone Erskine, *Journal of a Cruise among the Islands of the Central Pacific, including the Feegees and Others inhabited by the Polynesians and Negro Races, in H.M.S. 'Havannah'* p. 131

2 Lieut. Herbert Meade, *A Ride through the Disturbed Districts of New Zealand, together with some Account of the South Sea Islands,* p. 306

3 Baker to Eggleston, 18 August 1860, M.O.M.C., Uncat. MSS., set 197, item 2

4 Report A.W.M.M.S. 1860-61, p. 20

5 Reverend George Lee (to Eggleston?), 6 August 1857, M.O.M.C., set 166

6 *Missionary Notices,* April 1871, p. 255, letter from Minns dated 4 November 1870

7 Calvert, *Journal,* May 1861

8 Lawry, p. 24

9 St Julian to Tupou, 25 June 1855; St Julian to Tupou. 15 October 1855; both from Foreign Office and External Papers, Archives of Hawaii, Honolulu

10 Davis to Eggleston, 18 March 1862, M.O.M.C., set 170

11 *Missionary Notices,* January 1862, p. 293; Report A.W.M.M.S. 1861-62

12 Davis to Eggleston, 18 March 1862. M.O.M.C. set 170

13 Eggleston to Davis, n.d., M.O.M.C., set 169

14 Baker to Eggleston, 21 April 1863, M.O.M.C., set iv, item 169

15 *Missionary Notices,* January 1863, p. 343

16 *T.G.B.B., Containing a List of Charges brought by the Premier of Tonga (Rev. S. W. Baker), on behalf of the Tonga Government, against the Rev. J. E. Moulton, Wesleyan Missionary, together with the reply of the Rev. J. E. Moulton made before the District Meeting of the Wesleyan Church, at Lifuka, Ha'apai, October 24 1883,* p. 16

17 *Missionary Notices,* January 1863, pp. 439-50, letter from Baker dated 11 August 1862

18 Acting Consul General Maudslay to the Marquis of Salisbury, no. 1 Consular, 23 January 1879, F.O.C.P. 4285, no. 44

19 Davis to Eggleston, 7 July 1862; Whewell to Eggleston, 23 June 1862; both from M.O.M.C., set 170

20 Baker to the Rev. Benjamin Chapman, 3 May 1876, M.O.M.C., set iv, item 101

21 Eggleston to Davis, n.d., M.O.M.C., set 169

22 Consul E. L. Layard to the Earl of Derby, 8 March 1876, F.O.C.P. 4285, no. 1

23 Baker to Chapman, 13 November 1876, Wesleyan Mission Papers, set 13

24 Baker, Memoirs, p. 10

25 Baker to Eggleston, 21 April 1863, M.O.M.C. set iv, item 101

26 Baker to Eggleston, 19 December 1863, set iv, item 101

27 *Missionary Notices*, October 1866, letter from Baker dated 24 September, 1866

28 Rabone to the Rev. George Baker, 31 March 1866, M.O.M.C., set 35; Rabone to the Rev. George Baker, 20 February 1866, Rabone to Mrs J. W. Powell, 20 February 1866; both from Letter Book of the Rev. Stephen Rabone, M.O.M.C., set 35

CHAPTER III

1 Rabone to Baker, 31 July 1868, M.O.M.C., set 35

2 *Missionary Notices*, July and October 1869, p. 148; Report A.W.M.M.S. 1869-70, p. 22

3 J. Egan Moulton and W. Fiddian Moulton, *Moulton of Tonga*, pp. 13-34

4 Layard to Derby, 8 March 1876, F.O.C.P. 4285 no. 1

5 Layard to Derby, 19 November 1877, F.O.C.P. 4285, no. 19

6 Thomson, *The Diversions of a Prime Minister*, p. 367

7 Ibid., p. 213

8 Ibid., pp. 185 ff.

9 Ibid., pp. 187-91

10 Memorandum by Alfred Maudslay, 2 November 1878, F.O.C.P. 4285, no. 45, enc. 2.

11 Friendly Islands District Meeting Minute Book, 'Minutes of a Special District Meeting held 23 August 1870', Archives of the Free Wesleyan Church of Tonga, Nuku'alofa

12 The Earl and the Doctor (The Earl of Pembroke and Doctor G. H. Kingsley), *South Sea Bubbles*, pp. 251 ff.

13 Thomson, *The Diversions of a Prime Minister*, p. 147

14 Friendly Islands District Meeting Minute Book, 'Minutes of a District Meeting held at Lifuka. Ha'apai, 23 August 1870'

15 'Natives and Chiefs in the Wesleyan Church in Tonga to the Wesleyan Ministers in their Great Assembly', 26 December 1871; Rabone to Baker, 27 December 1871; both from Manuscripts and Printed Documents. See also Moulton to Rabone, 21 May 1872, M.O.M.C., set iv, item 99; the Rev. H. Greenwood to Rabone, 10 August

1872, M.O.M.C., set 170

16 Baker to Rabone, 5 July 1872, M.O.M.C., set iv, item 101

17 *Missionary Notices*, July 1867, p. 29, letter from Moulton dated 29 March 1867

18 Affidavit of Philip Payne, 22 December 1878, *Minutes of an Enquiry by Deputation appointed by the Board of Management of the Australian Wesleyan Methodist Mssionary Society in Sydney to inquire into the Charges against Rev. S.W. Baker held at Nuku'alofa, Tongatabu 8th October 1879*, p. 21

19 Baker to Rabone, 27 December 1871

20 Moulton to Rabone, 10 September 1877, M.O.M.C., set iv, item 99

21 Greenwood to Rabone, 5 July 1872, M.O.M.C., set iv, item 101

22 Baker to Rabone, 5 July 1872, M.O.M.C., set iv, item 101

23 Ibid.

Chapter IV

1   Baker to Rabone, 5 July 1872, M.O.M.C., set iv, item 101

2   Baker to Rabone, 5 July 1872; Baker to Rabone, 18 July 1872; Baker to Chapman, 30 December 1873; all from M.O.M.C., set iv, item 101; Baker to Chapman, 23 June 1876, M.O.M.C., Uncat. MSS., set 197, item 2

3   Baker to Chapman, 30 December 1873, M.O.M.C., set iv, item 101

4   Baker to Chapman, 17 March 1875 M.O.M.C., set iv, item 101

5   Baker to Rabone, 16 December 1872, M.O.M.C., set iv, item 101

6   *Christian Advocate and Wesleyan Record* (Sydney), 6 February 1873

7   *Christian Advocate and Wesleyan Record*, 1 August 1873

8   Rev. H. Greenwood, 'Memorandum', n.d., Wesleyan Mission Papers

9   Baker to Chapman, 30 December 1873, M.O.M.C., set iv, item 101

10 King of Tonga to the Church in Sydney, 24 March 1874, F.O.C.P. 5527, no. 300, enc. 11

11 Baker to Chapman, 14 May 1874, M.O.M.C., set iv, item 101

12 Baker to Chapman, 27 February 1874, M.O.M.C., set iv, item 101

13 *Christian Advocate and Wesleyan Record*, 3 February 1875

14 *Koe Boobooi*, vol. ii, no. 6, September and October 1875

15 Baker to Chapman, 4 September 1875 M.O.M.C., set iv, item 101

16 *Minutes of an Enquiry by Deputation…* October 1879, p. 64

17 Layard to Derby, 8 March 1875, F.O.C.P. 4285, no. 1

Chapter V

1   Friendly Islands District Meeting Minute Book, 'Minutes of a Special District Meeting, 23 August 1870'

2 The *Fiji Times*, 22 October 1870

3 *Tonga Court Records*, 'In re Philip Payne', 7 September 1870 F3 /2 file 1880, item 9

4 Robert Hanslip and eighteen others to the Earl of Belmore, February 1871, F3/2, file 1880, item 9

5 Baker to Rabone, 18 July 1872, M.O.M.C., set iv, item 101

6 Baker to Chapman, 30 December 1873, M.O.M.C., set iv, item 101

7 Friendly Islands District Meeting Minute Book, 'Minutes of District Meeting, 11 December 1876'

8 Cocker to Young *et al.,* 25 November 1873, F3/43 item 12 enc. 2

9 Ibid.

10 Baker to Chapman, 3 May 1876, M.O.M.C., set iv, item 101

11 Maudslay to the Earl of Salisbury, 24 January 1879, F.O.C.P. 4285 no. 46 enc. 2

12 David Wilkinson to Gordon 5 July 1878, contained in A.P. Maudslay, *Correspondence* (a printed document containing private and semi-official correspondence between Maudslay and Sir Arthur Gordon during 1878 and 1879), p. 6

13 *Koe Boobooi*, vol. ii no. 1

14 *Koe Boobooi*, vol. ii no. 6

15 The Sydney *Evening News*, 21 October 1897

16 Maudslay to Salisbury, 23 January 1879, F.O.C.P. 4285, no. 44

17 Thomson, *The Scene Changes,* p. 143

18 *Koe Boobooi*, vol. ii no. 6 'The King's speech at the Opening, of Parliament'

19 Thomson, *The Diversions of a Prime Minister,* p. 365

20 Thomson, *The Scene Changes,* p. 143

21 Maudslay to Salisbury, 23 January 1879, F.O.C.P. 4285, no. 44

22 Ibid.

23 Layard to Derby, 8 March 1876, F.O.C.P. 4285, no. 1

24 C.F. Gordon-Cummings, *A Lady's Cruise in a French Man-of-War*, p. 19

25 Lord George Campbell, *Log Letters from the 'Challenger'* p. 130; Baker to Chapman, 15 November 1876, Wesleyan Mission Papers, set 15

26 *The Christian Advocate and Wesleyan Record*, 3 January 1877

CHAPTER VI

1 Douglas L. Oliver, *The Pacific Islands,* p. 179

2 The *Tonga Times,* vol ii, no. 1, 22 January 1876

3 The original of this paper is lost. This fragment was offered in evidence

by Maudslay: *Minutes of an Enquiry by Deputation... October 1879,* p. 88

4   Commodore Hoskins to the Secretary to the Admiralty, 19 May 1876, F.O.C.P. 4285, no. 6, enc.

5   R. G. W. Herbert (Colonial Office) to T. V. Lister (Foreign Office), 8 February 1877, F.O.C.P. 4285, no. 13

6   Gordon to Derby, 27 April 1878, F.O.C.P. 4285, no. 25

7   Moulton to Chapman, 17 March 1875, M.O.M.C., set iv, item 99

8   Moulton to Chapman, 31 August 1875, M.O.M.C., set iv, item 99

9   *Minutes of an Enquiry by Deputation... October 1879,* p. 50; Diary letter of D. Wilkinson, 15 July 1878, Maudslay, *Correspondence,* p. 24 Baker to Chapman, 17 March 1875, M.O.M.C., set iv, item 101

10   Baker to (?), 16 January 1876, Wesleyan Mission Papers, set 15

11   Maudslay to Gordon, 25 January 1879, Maudslay, *Correspondence* p. 24

12   The *Tonga Times,* vol i no. 1 22 January 1876

13   Cocker to Layard, 27 March 1876, F3/43, set 2

14   Foreign Residents in Tonga to Layard, 16 February 1876, W.P.H.C. Inwards Corresp.(General), 148/1883

15   Layard to Derby, 8 March 1876, F.O.C.P. 4285 no. 1

16   'Consul Layard's Dispatch and the Rev. S. W. Baker's Reply to the Same', 21 October 1876, Wesleyan Mission Papers, set 14, enc.

17   Statement of Sione Fetokai, 6 October 1876, Wesleyan Mission Papers, set 14

18   Weber to Baker, 29 February 1876, Wesleyan Mission Papers, set 14

19   Baker to Chapman, 3 May 1876, M.O.M.C., set iv, item 101

20   Baker to Chapman, 23 June 1876, M.O.M.C., Uncat. MSS., set 197, item 2

21   Ibid.

22   Baker to Chapman, 14 September 1876, M.O.M.C., Uncat MSS., set 197, item 2

23   'Consul Layard's Dispatch and the Rev. S. W. Baker's Reply to the Same'

24   Chapman to the Secretary, Wesleyan Missionary Society, 17 March 1877, F.O.C.P. 4285, no. 15, enc. 2

25   Baker to Chapman, 7 January 1876, M.O.M.C., Uncat. MSS., set 197, item 22

26   Friendly Islands District Meeting Minute Book, 'Minutes of District Meeting', 11 December 1876; 'Unga to Chapman, 4 January 1877, M.O.M.C., set I69

27   'Unga to Chapman, 4 January 1877; Baker to Chapman 16 January 1877, Wesleyan Mission Papers, set 15; Ebenezer Fox to Baker, n.d., M.O.M.C., set iv, item 101; Baker to Chapman, 23 May 1877, M.O.M.C.,

Uncat. MSS., set 197, item 2

   28 Maudslay to Gordon, 8 August 1878, Maudslay, *Correspondence*, p.1
   29 Baker to Chapman 3 July 1878, M.O.M.C., Uncat. MSS., set 197,
item 2
   30 Sir Julian Pauncefote to Gordon, 4 July 1879, F.O.C.P. 4285, no.78
   31 Lord Stanmore (Sir Arthur Gordon), *Fiji–Records of Private and Public
Life*, vol.iii, p.315, Salisbury to Gordon 13 June 1879
   32 Gordon to Derby, 27 April 1878, Stanmore, *Fiji Records*, vol.iii, p.100
   33 J.D. Legge, *Britain in Fiji*, 1858–1880, p.204, quoting Gordon, 'Native
Councils in Fiji 1875-80', in *Contemporary Review*, 1883, vol. xliii, p.711
   34 Gordon to Derby, 29 April 1878, Stanmore, *Fiji Records*, vol.iii, p.113
   35 Baker to Gordon, 26 June 1878, Wesleyan Mission Papers, set 15
   36 Langham to Chapman, 6 June 1878, Correspondence of Rev. F.
Langham, Dixson Library, Sydney
   37 Stanmore, *Fiji Records*, vol.iii, p.153, extract from Gordon's diary
dated July 1878
   38 The *Fiji Times*, 7 October 1882., 'Tonga No. III', one of a series of
articles (I-VII) written between September and November 1882 by a
European in Tonga, probably Robert Hanslip
   39 Langham to Baker, 30 August 1878, Correspondence of Rev. F.
Langham
   40 Baker to Chapman, 8 October 1878, Wesleyan Mission Papers, set 15
   41 Maudslay to Gordon, Maudslay, *Correspondence*, p.1
   42 Davis to Eggleston, 18 March 1862, M.O.M.C., set 170
   43 Stanmore, *Fiji Records*, vol. iii, p.109
   44 Wilkinson to Gordon, 15 July 1878, Maudslay, *Correspondence,* p.2
   45 A.P. Maudslay, *Life in the Pacific Fifty Years Ago*, p.221
   46 Maudslay to Gordon, 8 August 1878, Maudslay, *Correspondence*, p.8
   47 Baker to Chapman, 8 October 1878, Wesleyan Mission Papers, set 15
   48 Maudslay to Gordon, 8 August 1878, Maudslay, *Correspondence*, p.8
   49 Maudslay to Gordon, 30 September 1878, Maudslay, *Correspondence*, p.16
   50 Affidavit of P.S. Bloomfield, 2 November 1878, F.O.C.P. 4285,
no.45, enc.10
   51 Maudslay to the Secretary, Wesleyan Methodist Missionary Society,
Sydney, 5 September 1878, F.O.C.P. 4285, no.45, enc.6
   52 Baker to Chapman, 7 January 1876, M.O.M.C., Uncat. MSS., set
197, item 2
   53 Langham to Chapman 17 August 1878, Correspondence of Rev. F.
Langham
   54 Chapman to the Rev. M.C. Osborne, 13 September 1879, M.O.M.C., set 33

55 Langham to Chapman 3 October 1878, Correspondence of Rev. F. Langham

56 Friendly Islands District Meeting Minute Book, 'Minutes of District Meeting 12 December 1878'

57 Maudslay to Salisbury, no. 1 Consular, 23 January 1879; no. 2 Consular, 23 January 1879; no. 3 Consular, 14 January 1879; F.O.C.P. 4285, nos 44, 45 and 46 respectively

58 Wesleyan Missionary Society, London to Chapman 27 May 1879, Stanmore, *Fiji Records*, vol. iii, p. 316

59 The *Fiji Times*, 18 October 1882, 'Tonga No. IV'

60 *Minutes of an Enquiry by Deputation... October 1879*, p. 75

61 Ibid., p. 77

62 Gordon to Chapman, 22 April 1879, Stanmore, *Fiji Records*, vol. iii, p. 285

63 Maudslay to Salisbury, 24 January 1879, no. 3 Consular, F.O.C.P. 4285, no. 46

64 'Unga, on behalf of Tupou, to the Rev. B. Chapman and the Rev. W. Clarke, 17 October 1879, *Letters and Correspondence in re Tongan Affairs and the Request of H. M. King George for Tonga to be Made an Independent District*, Sydney, October 1879, p. 4

65 Ilaisi Lagi and 2981 other signatories to Chapman and Clarke 28 October 1879, *Letters and Correspondence in re Tongan Affairs...*, p. 8

66 Baker to Chapman and Clarke, 7 October 1879, *Letters and Correspondence in re Tongan Affairs...*, p. 5

CHAPTER VII

1 Blyth to Gordon, 19 June 1880, F3/12, file 1880, no. 90

2 *Tonga Government Gazette,* vol. ii, no. 6, 10 November 1880, p. 2

3 Blyth to Gordon, 3 July 1880, Stanmore, *Fiji Records,* vol. iv, p. 368

4 Blyth to Gordon, diary letter dated 20 July 1880, entry for Friday, 23 July, Stanmore, *Fiji Records*, vol. iv, p. 380

5 *Tonga Government Gazette,* vol. ii, no. 6, p. 2

6 Blyth to Gordon, diary letter dated 20 July 1880, entry for Saturday, 31 July

7 McGregor to Gordon, 14 February 1880, F.O.C.P. 4285, no. 98; Blyth to Gordon, 20 July 1880, Stanmore, *Fiji Records*, vol. iv, p. 378

8 J. B. Waterhouse, *The Secession and Persecution in Tonga*, p. 6

9 Miller to the church in Sydney, 24 March 1874, F.O.C.P. 5527, no. 300 enc. 11

10 W. G. Tubou Malohi to Symonds, 15 September 1881, *T.G.B.B. in re Eua Sheep*

11 Gordon to the Secretary of State for Foreign Affairs, 31 July 1880, Stanmore, *Fiji Records,* vol.iv, p.385

12 Tupou to Gordon, 30 September 1880, F.O. 58/168

13 Thurston to Gordon, 11 November 1880, F.O. 58/168

14 Thurston to Gordon, 17 May 1881, F.O. 58/177

Chapter VIII

1 Symonds to Gordon, 10 April 1881, F3/12, file 1881, no.7

2 Symonds to Gordon, 15 September 1881, F3/12, file 1881, no.17

3 The *Fiji Times,* 14 December 1881, letter from R. S. Swanston, n.d.

4 *Koe Boobooi,* vol.iii, no.1

5 'Second Letter, being an answer to the "Boobooi" that was Brought', n.d., F3/43, no.22

6 *Niu Vakai,* no. 1, October 1881

7 Leka and Tupouto'a to Hanslip, 7 November 1881, F3/2, file 1882, no.2, enc.1

8 Topui to Hanslip, n.d. (received by Hanslip 12 December 1881), F3/2, file 1882, no.2, enc.4

9 Baker, *Memoirs,* p.41

10 *Niu Vakai,* no.5, February 1882

11 Baker to Gordon, 15 February 1882, F3/10, file 1882, no. 3, enc.

12 Gordon to the Secretary of State for Foreign Affairs, 15 July 1882, F.O. 58/177

13 Ibid.

14 Symonds to Des Voeux, 7 December 1882, F3/12, file 1882, no.14

15 Symonds to Des Voeux, 6 November 1883, F3/12, file 1883, no.12

16 Affidavit to S. Fifita, 4 August 1884, *T.G.B.B. Correspondence between the Tonga Government and the British Government in re the Action of H.F. Symonds, Esq., H.B.M. Vice Consul Tonga, and of the Captain of H.M.S. 'Espiegle',* n.d., p.7

17 F.O.C.P. 5310, no.129, enc.19, 'Tongan Hymn'

18 T.G.B.B., *Containing a List of Charges ... Against the Rev. J. E. Moulton,* p.9

Chapter IX

1 Baker to H.B.M.'s Principal Secretary of State for the Colonies, 27 August 1874, *T.G.B.B., Correspondence between the Tonga Government and the*

British Government in re the Action of H. F. Symonds... pp. 1-9

2 Baker, Memoirs, p. 23

3 The *New Zealand Herald*, 16 March 1887, letter from the Rev. Lorimer Fison, n.d.

4 'Examination of the King of Tonga' (by Sir Charles Mitchell), 29 March 1887, F.O.C.P. 5527, no. 300, enc. 6

5 Waterhouse, *Secession and Persecution*, p. 21, letters from Moulton dated 10 February 1885, 28 March 1885

6 Ibid., p. 19, letter from Crosby dated 3 February 1885

7 'Notes of the Chief Judicial Commissioner', F.O.C.P. 5557, no. 300, enc. 10, item 4a

8 Ibid., item 4

9 Waterhouse, *Secession and Persecution*, pp. 25 ff, letter from Moulton dated 28 March 1885; the *Fiji Times*, 16 May 1885, letter from 'Our Own Correspondent' dated 4 April 1885

10 Statement by Lese Hake, 6 April 1885, F3/2, file 1885 no. 1, enc.

11 'Notes of the Chief Judicial Commissioner', item 7

12 Ibid., item 37

13 Ibid., item 16

14 Ibid., item 57

15 Moulton to Tuʻuhetoka, 17 April 1885, F3/2, file 1885, no. 1, enc.

16 Thurston to Salisbury, 30 September 1885, F.O.C.P. 5159, no. 117

17 Moulton to *Ki He Jiaji 'Uesiliana o Toga*, printed open letter dated 31 March 1885

18 Statement of Lei, 2 April 1885, F3/2, file 1885, no. 1, enc.

19 Waterhouse, *Secession and Persecution*, p. 52, letter from Moulton dated 1 August 1885

20 Crosby to Symonds, 6 January 1886, F3/2, file 1886, no. 1

CHAPTER X

1 Evidence of Penisiō Hau, F.O.C.P. 5527, no. 300, enc. 10, item 140

2 Affidavit of Soni Muli, 5 March 1887, F.O.C.P. 5527, no. 110, enc. 40

3 Evidence of Latuvaivai, F.O.C.P. 5527, no. 300, enc. 10, item 145

4 'Official Report of the Rev. S. W. Baker in regard to the Assault on Himself and Family on Thursday 13 January 1887', 15 January 1887, F.O.C.P. 5527, no. -73, enc. 7

5 Baker, *Memoirs*, p. 24

6 'Official Report of the Rev. S. W. Baker...', 13 January 1887'

7 Diary of Pro-Consul Giles, entry for 13 January 1887, F.O.C.P. 5527, no. 110, enc. 29

8   Ibid., entry for 26 January 1887

9   The *Fiji Times*, 23 March 1887, 'The Malinoa Massacre'

10 This quotation from a copy of the original which was sent to Giles who filed it in his consular records (F3/2, file 1887, no. 108). The version published in the *New Zealand Herald* on 9 February 1887 was somewhat watered down.

11 Diary of Pro-Consul Giles, entry for 20 January 1887

12 Moulton to Sir Charles Mitchell, 23 January 1887, F.O.C.P. 5527, no. 73, enc. 8

13 Leefe to Thurston, 7 February 1887, F.O.C.P. 5527, no. 73, enc. 6

14 Affidavit of Robert Hanslip, 3 March 1887, F3/2, file 1887, no. 248

15 Leefe to Mitchell, 23 February 1887, F.O.C.P. 5527, no. 110, enc. 9

16 Affidavit of E. W. Parker, 21 February 1887, F3/2, file 1887, no. 245

17 Affidavit of Robert Hanslip, 3 March 1887

18 Baker to Tupou, n.d., F.O.C.P. 5527, no. 300, enc. 21

19 Leefe to Mitchell, 15 March 1887, F3/19, file 1887, no. 18

20 Mitchell to Sir H. Holland, 6 May 1887, F.O.C.P. 5527, no. 300, enc. 2. This letter was later printed under the title 'Report by Sir C. Mitchell in connection with the Recent Disturbances in, and the Affairs of Tonga', but in this version Mitchell's comments on Baker were omitted.

21 Mitchell to Holland, 2 May 1887, F.O.C.P. 5527, no. 300, enc. 1

Chapter XI

1   Mitchell to Holland, 25 November 1887, F.O.C.P. 5783, no. 22, enc. 1

2   Mitchell to Holland, 1 September 1887, F.O.C.P. 5611, no. 89, enc. 1

3   The Auckland *Evening Bell*, 6 October 1887, letter from 'Our Own Correspondent', n.d.

4   Baker to Leefe, 30 January 1888, F3/2, file 1888, no. 29

5   The *Evening Bell*, 26 January 1888

6   Thurston to Lord Knutsford, F.O.C.P. 5784, no. 80, enc. 1

7   Mitchell, 'Memo to Sir J. Thurston's Dispatch to Lord Knutsford of August 28, 1888', 3 October 1888, F.O.C.P. 5784, no. 11 enc. 16

8   The Adelaide *Advertiser*, 29 March 1889

9   The Melbourne *Daily Telegraph*, 4 April 1889

10 Baker to Brown, 11 May 1889, Archives of the Free Wesleyan Church of Tonga, Nuku'alofa

11 Brown to Tupou, 6 June 1889, *T.G.B.B. No. 89/2, Wesleyan Church Affairs*

12 Tupou to Brown, 27 June 1889, *T.G.B.B. No. 89/2...*

13 Thurston to Tupou, 11 April 1889, F.O.C.P. 5838, no. 134, enc. 4

14 Tupou to Thurston, 15 July 1889, F.O.C.P. 5932, no. 89, enc. 6

15 Baker to Collet, 8 October 1889, F.O.C.P. 6041, no. 19, enc. 4

16 Mrs H. Symonds to Moulton, diary letter covering the period 25 June to 17 July, 1890, Archives of the Free Wesleyan Church of Tonga

17 Ibid.

18 Ibid. In the original the speeches of the king and chiefs are in Tongan.

19 Thurston to Knutsford, 31 July 1890, F.O.C.P. 6057, no. 67, enc. 1

Chapter XII

1 'Resolutions passed at a Public Meeting of the Citizens of Sydney held under the auspices of the Wesleyan Methodist Church of New South Wales, in the Centenary Hall, Sydney, August 6, 1890', F.O.C.P. 6059, no. 49, enc. 2

2 Thomson, *The Scene Changes*, p. 22

3 Thomson, *Savage Island*, pp. 181 ff.

Epilogue

1 Thomas Trood, *Island Reminiscences – a Graphic Detailed Romance of a Life spent in the South Sea Islands,* p. 74

2 J. W. Davidson, Survey of the Government of Western Samoa, Confidential Survey at the Request of the New Zealand External Affairs Department, n.d. p. 6: 'Report on speech of Tamasese at the Fono of All Samoa, November 1946'

BIBLIOGRAPHY

The following is a bibliography limited to those sources which have actually been cited or quoted in the text. Several bibliographies of Pacific historical and anthropological material are available, and the reader should have recourse to them in the event of their wishing to pursue aspects of this study in detail.

PACIFIC BIBLIOGRAPHIES LISTING MATERIAL RELEVANT TO TONGA AND THE PACIFIC IN THE NINETEENTH CENTURY

Leeson, I., *A Bibliography of Bibliographies of the South Pacific*, Melbourne, 1954

Lewin, E., *The Pacific Region: a Bibliography of the Pacific and East Indian Islands, exclusive of Japan*, Royal Empire Society, London, 1944

Martin, K. L. P., *Missionaries and Annexation in the Pacific*, O.U.P., 1924

Petherick, E. A., A Bibliography of the Pacific Islands, a manuscript bibliography in the Australian National Library, Canberra

Taylor, C. R. H., *A Pacific Bibliography; Printed Matter relating to the Native Peoples of Polynesia, Melanesia and Micronesia*, The Polynesian Society, Wellington, 1951

BIBLIOGRAPHY OF SOURCES CITED

(A) ARCHIVAL SOURCES

1. Tonga
    (a) Collection of the Rev. Dr S. Lātūkefu:
        Constitution of Tonga 1875 (original document)
    (b) Archives of the Free Wesleyan Church of Tonga, Nukuʻalofa:
        Friendly Islands District Meeting Minute Book

Moulton, J. E., *Ki He Jiaji Uesiliana o Toga*, 31 March 1885 (pamphlet)

Koe Fanoganogo Fakabulega, 21 May 1887 (pamphlet)

Symonds, Mrs H., Diary Letter to Rev. W. Moulton, 25 June–17 July 1890

Baker, Rev. S. W. to Rev. G. Brown, letter dated 11 May 1889

2. New Zealand

(a) House of Representatives, Wellington:

Printed Appendix to the Journals of the House of Representatives, New Zealand

1874, vol. i , A-3 ('Papers relating to the South Sea Islands')

1885, vol. i, A-9 ('German Interests in the South Seas: A Collection of Documents presented to the German Reichstag in December 1884')

1888, vol. i, A-3 ('Report of Sir C. Mitchell, High Commissioner for the Western Pacific in Connection with the Recent Disturbances in, and the Affairs of Tonga, 6 May 1887')

(b) Hocken Library, Dunedin:

Brown, Rev. George, *First Report* , Sydney, 1888 (pamphlet)

Report of Rev. G. Brown and Mr P. Fletcher, Commissioners to Tonga, Melbourne, 1888

(c) Alexander Turnbull Library, Wellington:

Letters and Correspondence in re Tongan Affairs and the request of H.M. King George for Tonga to be Made an Independent District, Sydney, 1879 (pamphlet)

MSS. and Printed Documents in Connection with the Charges against Rev. S. W. Baker, Tonga 1866 and onwards (a collection)

Résumé of an Enquiry in re Tongan Mission Affairs, October 1879, Auckland, 1879 (a pamphlet)

Wesleyan Mission Papers, a manuscript collection. The following files: set 6, set 8, set 9, set 10, set 12, set 13, set 14, set 15, set 16

3. Fiji
  (a) Central Archives of Fiji and the Western Pacific High
       Commission:
       Copies of despatches from the Consul-General and/or
          High Commissioner for the Western Pacific, to the
          Consul, Vice-Consul and/or Deputy Commissioner,
          Tonga, and from the Consul, Vice-Consul and/or
          Deputy Commissioner, Tonga to the Consul-General
          and/or High Commissioner for the Western Pacific,
          1860-1953 (preliminary Index No. 3) the following
          series:
       F3/2 – General Correspondence – Inwards, 1878-1944
       F3/10 – Despatches from the Consul-General to the
          Vice-Consul, Tonga 1879; 1881 to 1882; 1884 to
          1900; October 1913 to December 1935
       F3/12 – Copies of despatches from the Vice-Consul,
          Tonga, to the Consul, Fiji, or Consul-General,'
          March 1864-December 1864
       F3/18 – Despatches from the High Commissioner to
          the Deputy Commissioner or Agent, Tonga, 1879-
          1937
       F3/19 – Copies of Despatches from the Deputy
          Commissioner, or Agent, Tonga, to the High
          Commissioner, 1879-1953
       F3/43 – Miscellaneous Papers
       F-Separate, a dispatch from Consul T. Pritchard to the
          Secretary of State for Foreign Affairs dated 15 May
          1862
       Miscellaneous Papers of Fiji-Tongan Relations 1862-1869,
          Folder (g)
       Western Pacific High Commission Inwards
          Correspondence (General), (a Collection of
          Despatches), the following files: 1877, 1881, 1882,
          1883, 1884, 1887, 1889, 1891
       *Report of the Committee appointed by the Wesleyan
          Conference to consider Tongan Affairs*, February 1884,
          privately circulated pamphlet, a copy in Inwards
          Correspondence (General), file for 1884
       H.M.S. Espiègle visit to Samoa and Tonga, No. 1 May-

August 1884, Capt. Bridge R.N., Admiralty Paper in
W.P.H.C. Inwards Correspondence (General), file
for 1884

(b) Archives of the Diocese of Polynesia, Suva:
Episcopal Superintendence of the Eastern Pacific, (a
pamphlet)

4. Hawaii
Archives of Hawaii, Honolulu:
Foreign Office and External Papers of the Government
of Hawaii

5. Sydney
(a) Mitchell Library:
Papers of Rev. E. E. V. Collacott, Minutes of Local
Preachers' Meetings for the Haabai Circuit 1861–
1874
Mackay, A. W., *Account of the Sojourn in Tonga of S. W.
Baker and the Consequences of his Tyranny*, Sydney,
1897 (pamphlet)
The Methodist Overseas Mission Collection
(a manuscript collection).The following files:
Sets 33, 34, 35, 166, 169, 170
Set iv, item 99
Set iv, item 101
Uncatalogued MSS., set 197, item 7
Uncatalogued MSS., set 207
*Report of a Deputation Appointed by the General Conference
of 1884 to visit the Friendly Islands*, Sydney, [n.d.]
(a pamphlet)
(b) Dixson Library:
Langham, Rev. F., Letter Book

6. Melbourne:
State Library of Victoria, Archives:
Shipping Records
Victorian Denominational School Board Statistics, 'Abstract
of Teachers' for year ending 31 Dec. 1885';
No. 59/1469

7. Great Britain, London:
    (a) Foreign Office
        British Foreign Office Confidential Prints:
            No. 4285, 'Correspondence Relating to Tongan Affairs
              1876-1880'
            No. 5150, 'Further Correspondence Respecting the
              Pacific Islands, April to June 1885'
            No. 5159, Part V 'Further Correspondence Respecting
              the Pacific Islands, July to September 1885'
            No. 5199, 'Further Correspondence Respecting the
              Pacific Islands, October to December 1885'
            No. 5310, 'Further Correspondence Respecting the
              Pacific Islands, April to June 1886'
            No. 5350, 'Further Correspondence Respecting Affairs
              in the Navigator's Islands 1881-1884'
            No. 5341, 'Further Correspondence Respecting the
              Pacific Islands, July to September 1886'
            No. 5421 'Further Correspondence Respecting the
              Pacific Islands, October to December 1886'
            No. 5454, 'Further Correspondence Respecting the
              Pacific Islands, January to March 1887'
            No. 5527, 'Further Correspondence Respecting the
              Pacific Islands, April to June 1887'
            No. 5607, 'Secret Correspondence Respecting Samoa
              and Tonga, 1886-1887
            No. 5611 'Further Correspondence Respecting the
              Pacific Islands'
            No. 5735 'Confidential Memorandum, Samoa: View of
              Her Majesty's Government'
            No. 5783, 'Further Correspondence Respecting the
              Pacific Islands, January to June 1888'
            No. 5784, 'Further Correspondence Respecting the
              Pacific Islands, July to December 1888'
            No. 5838, 'Further Correspondence Respecting the
              Pacific Islands, January to June 1889'
            No. 5932, 'Further Correspondence Respecting the
              Pacific Islands, January to June 1889'
            No. 6041 'Further Correspondence Respecting the
              Pacific Islands, January to June, 1890'
            No. 6059, 'Further Correspondence Respecting the
              Pacific Islands, July to December 1890'

No. 6170, 'Further Correspondence Respecting the
Pacific Islands, 1891'
No. 6493, 'Further Correspondence Respecting the
Pacific Islands January to June 1894'
British Foreign Office Records Relating to the Pacific Islands,
1822-1905 (F.O./58), volume nos 150, 168, 172, 176, 177,
182, 185, 188 (microfilm in Australian National Library,
Canberra)
(b) Public Records Office:
Public Records Office, LC/3/22, 'Lord Chamberlain's
Department Physicians and Surgeons List 1846-1868'
(c) Methodist Missionary Society, Records:
Calvert, Rev. James, Journal, in Personal Papers
Collection (microfilm in Australian National Library,
Canberra)
Thomas, Rev. John, Journal, in Personal Papers
Collection (microfilm in Australian National Library,
Canberra)

(B) PUBLISHED MISSIONARY REPORTS
*Report of the Australasian Wesleyan-Methodist Missionary Society and
Account of Contributions Received*, Sydney, issues between 1860
and 1878
Report of the Wesleyan Methodist Missionary Society, London, 1840

(C) BLUE BOOKS, GAZETTES AND WHITE BOOKS
*Tonga Government Blue Book: Containing a list of charges Brought by the
Premier of Tonga (Rev. S. W. Baker), on behalf of the Tongan
Govt. against the Rev. J. E. Moulton, Wesleyan Missionary,
together with the reply of the Rev. J. E. Moulton as made before
the District Meeting of the Wesleyan Church, at Lifuka, Ha'apai
Oct. 24 1883, and the Replication of the Rev. S. W. Baker to the
same,* 7 November 1883
*Tonga Government Blue Book: Containing Documents Read Before and
Presented by the Premier of Tonga (Rev. S. W. Baker) on Behalf of
the Tongan Government to the Conference Committee on Tongan
Affairs, Together with the Reply of the Rev. S. W. Baker to the
said Committee,* [n.d.]
Tonga Government Blue Book: Correspondence between the Tongan

Government and the British Government; in re the action of H. F.
Symonds, Esq., H.B.M. Vice Consul, Tonga, and of the Captain
of H.M.S. 'Espiègle', [n.d.]

Tonga Government Blue Book in re Eua Sheep, [n.d.]

Tonga Government Blue Book in re Tonga Wesleyan Mission Affairs, [n.d.]

Tonga Government Blue Book in re Wesleyan Secession, Containing
correspondence between the Tonga Government and H.B.M. Pro-
Consul, Dr. A. G. Buckland. Correspondence between the Tonga
Government and the Revs. J. E. Moulton and E. E. Crosby B.A.
and the translations of circulars issued by the Rev. J. E. Moulton
and the Tonga Government, [n.d.]

Tonga Government Blue Book No. 89/1: Tonga Church Troubles, [n.d.]

Tonga Government Blue Book No. 89/2: Wesleyan Church Affairs, [n.d.]

Tonga Government Blue Book: Report of the Minister of Police in re
attempted assassination, May 1887

Tonga Government Blue Book: Supplement to the Report of the Minister of
Police in re the attempted assassination, 1 August 1889

The Tonga Government Gazette:

Vol. ii no. 1, 1 September 1880
         no. 6 10 November 1880
         no. 10 5 October 1881
         no. 12 25 October 1882
         no. 14 22 November 1882
         no. 15 6 December 1882
         no. 35 2 December 1885
         no. 62 23 November 1887
         no. 79 22 February 1888

Tonga Government White Book in re Wesleyan Secession. (n.d.)

(D) NEWSPAPERS, JOURNALS, PERIODICALS AND MAGAZINES

Adelaide *Advertiser*, 29 March 1889

Auckland *Evening Bell*, March 1887 to January 1888

Castlemaine *Advertiser*, 14 July 1860-3 January 1887

Christian Advocate and Wesleyan Record, 14 July 1860-3 January 1887

Contemporary Review, 1883, vol. XLIII, 'Native Councils in Fiji
1875-1880'

Fiji Times, 22 October 1870 to 2 December 1903

Koe Boobooi, vol. ii, no. 1, March 1875 to vol. iii, no. 2,
September 1881

Koe Taimi O Toga, vol. i, no. 1, March 1882, vol. i, no 2,
     April 1882

Melbourne *Daily Telegraph* , 4 April 1889

New Zealand Herald, 9 February 1887 to 11 December 1887

Niu Vakai, no. 1, October 1881 to no. 5, February 1882

Sydney *Evening News*, 18 April 1887, 21 October 1897

The Times, 30 December 1903

Tonga Times, vol. 1, no. 1, 22 January 1876

Wesleyan Methodist Magazine, July 1863

*Wesleyan Missionary Notices, Relating to Missions under the Direction of
     the Australasian Wesleyan Conference*, May 1851 to April 1871

(E) UNPUBLISHED THESES AND MANUSCRIPTS

    'Abide' (K. M. Bates), The Foundations of Modern Tonga, M.A.
        thesis, University of New Zealand, Auckland, 1933

    Davidson, J. W.,'Survey of the Government of Western Samoa,
        Confidential Survey at the request of the New Zealand
        External Affairs Dept', [n.d.], typescript, Davidson Papers,
        Australian National University.

    Fitzgerald, N. R., New Zealand Public Opinion and the Attempted
        Assassination of the Rev. S. W. Baker and His Eventual
        Removal from Tonga – A Study of New Zealand Opinion
        1887 to 1890, M.A. thesis, University of Otago, 1962

    Gunson, W. N., Evangelical Missionaries in the South Seas, 1797-
        1860, Ph.D. thesis, Australian National University, 1959

    Hammer, G. E., The Early Years of the Wesleyan Methodist Mission
        in Tonga, M.A. thesis, University of Otago, 1951

    Horne, Jason, Primacy of the Pacific under the Hawaiian Kingdom,
        M.A. thesis, University of Hawaii, 1951

    Koch, Gerd, Die fruhen Europaischen Einflusse auf die Kultur der
        Bewohner der Tonga-Inseln, Ph.D. thesis, George-August
        Universitat, Gottingen, 1949

    Lātūkefu, Rev. Sione, The Influence of the Wesleyan Methodist
        Missionaries on the Political Development of Tonga, Ph.D.
        thesis, Australian National University, 1966

    Maude, A. M., Population, Land and Livelihood in Tonga, Ph.D.
        thesis, Australian National University, 1965

    Poulsen, J., A Contribution to the Pre-History of Tonga, Ph.D.
        thesis, Australian National University, 1966

Rutherford, Noel, Shirley Baker and the Kingdom of Tonga, Ph.D. thesis, Australian National University, 1966

Scarr, Deryck, Policy and Practice in the Western Pacific, Ph.D. thesis, Australian National University, 1965

(F) CONTEMPORARY PUBLISHED WORKS AND WORKS BASED ON
     CONTEMPORARY OBSERVATIONS

Baker, Lillian & Beatrice Shirley Baker, Memoirs of the Reverend Dr. Shirley Waldemar Baker, D.M., Ll.D., Missionary and Prime Minister, London, 1951

Blamires, Rev. W. L. & Rev. John B. Smith, The Early Story of the Wesleyan Methodist Church in Victoria, Melbourne, 1886

Brenchley, Julius, Jottings during the Cruise of H.M.S. 'Curacoa' among the South Sea Islands in 1865, London, 1873

Campbell, Lord George, Log Letters from the 'Challenger', London, 1876

Crosby, E. E. (ed.), The Persecutions in Tonga as Narrated by Onlookers and Now Taking Place, London, 1886

Earl, The, and the Doctor (The Earl of Pembroke and Dr J. H. Kingsley), South Sea Bubbles, Melbourne, 1872

Erskine, Capt. Elphinstone, Journal of a Cruise Among the Islands of the Western Pacific, including the Feegees and others inhabited by the Polynesians and Negro Races, in H.M.S. 'Havannah', London 1853

Farmer, Sarah S., Tonga and the Friendly Islands, with a Sketches of their Mission History; Written for Young People, London, 1855

Foljambe, C. G. S., Three Years on the Australian Station, London, 1868

Ford, Worthington Chauncey (ed.), Letters of Henry Adams 1858-1891, London, 1930

Gordon-Cummings, C. F., A Lady's Cruise in a French Man-of-War, Edinburgh, 1882

H.B.M. High Commission for the Western Pacific. Copies of Correspondence between His Excellency, Sir John Thurston, H.B.M. High Commissioner and Consul-General for the Western Pacific, and the Hon. S. W. Baker, Premier of the Government of Tonga With reference to certain libels printed and published by him in the Australian colonies and elsewhere, Auckland, 15 March 1890

Lawry, Rev. Walter, Friendly and Feejee Islands, A Missionary visit to various Stations in the South Seas in the Year MDCCCXLVIII, (2nd ed.), London, 1850

London Medical Directory, 1847

Mariner, William, *An Account of the Natives of the Tonga Islands, With a Grammar and Vocabulary of their language, compiled from the Communications of W. Mariner by John Martin*, 2 vols, London, 1817

Maudslay, Alfred P., *Life in the Pacific Fifty Years Ago*, London, 1934
Private Correspondence between Mr. Maudslay and Sir A. Gordon. July 1878 January 1879

Meade, Herbert, *A Ride Through the Disturbed Districts of New Zealand together With some Account of the South Sea Islands*, (2nd ed.), London, 1871

Minutes of an Enquiry by deputation appointed by the Board of Management of the Australian Wesleyan Methodist Missionary Society in Sydney, to enquire into the charges against Rev. S. W. Baker held at Nuku'alofa, Tongatabu, 8th Oct. 1879

Missionary Transactions, volume 1, 'Tongataboo in the Friendly Islands, Journal of the missionaries 1797-1800', London, [n.d.]

Monfat, Le P. A., *Les Tonga ou Archipel des Amis et le R. P. Joseph Chevron – Étude historique et réligieuse*, Lyon, 1893

Moseley, H. M., *Notes by a Naturalist on the 'Challenger'*, London, 1879

Partington, James Edge, *Random Rot. A Journal of Three Years Wanderings about the World*, Altrincham, 1883

St Johnston, Alfred, *Camping Among Cannibals*, London, 1883

Stanmore, Lord (Sir A. Gordon), *Fiji – Records of Private and Public Life 1875-1880*, 4 vols, Edinburgh, 1904

Thomson Basil, *The Diversions of a Prime Minister*, Edinburgh and London, 1894
'The Samoa Agreement in Plain English', *Blackwood's Magazine*, vol. 166, December 1889
'A Statesman-Adventurer of the Pacific', *Blackwood's Magazine*, vol. 175, February 1904
Savage Island: An Account of a Sojourn in Niue and Tonga, London, 1902
The Scene Changes, New York, 1937

Trood, Thomas, *Island Reminiscences – A graphic detailed romance of a life spent in the South Sea Islands*, Sydney, 1912

(Thomas, Julian) The Vagabond, *Holy Tonga*, Melbourne, [n.d.]

(Vason, G.), *An Authentic Narrative of Four Years residence at Tongataboo, one of the Friendly Islands in the South Seas*, ed. S. Piggott, London, 1810

Waterhouse, J. B., *The Secession and Persecution in Tonga*, Sydney, 1886

West, Rev. Thomas, *Ten Years in South Central Polynesia Being Reminiscences of a Personal Mission to the Friendly Islands and their Dependencies*, London, 1865

Young, Rev. Robert, *The Southern World: Journal of a Deputation from the Wesleyan Conference to New Zealand and Polynesia*, (4th edn), London, 1858

(G) MODERN PUBLISHED WORKS

Beaglehole, Ernest and Pearl, *Pangai, Village in Tonga*, Polynesian Society Memoirs, vol. XVIII, Wellington, 1941

Benson, C. Irving, *A Century of Victorian Methodism*, Melbourne, 1935

Blanc, Monseigneur J. F., *A History of Tonga or Friendly Islands* trans. from the Tongan by C. S. Ramsay, California, [n.d.]

Chappell, N. M., *New Zealand Bankers' Hundred – A History of the Bank of New Zealand: 1861-1961*, Wellington, 1961

Colwell, James (ed.), *A Century in the Pacific*, Sydney, 1914

Davidson, J. W., *Samoa mo Samoa. The Emergence of the Independent State of Western Samoa*, Melbourne, 1967

Fletcher, C. Brunsdon, *The Black Night of the Pacific*, Sydney, 1944

Gifford, E. W., *Tongan Society*, Bernice P. Bishop Museum Bulletin no. 61, 1929

Koskinen, Aarne A., *Missionary Influence as a Political Factor in the Pacific Islands*, Helsinki, 1953

Legge, J. D., *Britain in Fiji: 1858-1880*, London, 1958

Malia, P. S. (Monseigneur J. F. Blanc), *Chez les Méridionaux du Pacifique*, Lyon and Paris, 1910

Martin, K. L. P., *Missionaries and Annexation in the Pacific*, London, 1924

Masterman, S., *The Origins of International Rivalry In Samoa: 1845-1884*, London, 1934

Morrell, W. P., *Britain in the Pacific Islands*, Oxford, 1960

Moulton, J. Egan & W. Fiddian, *Moulton of Tonga*, London, 1921

Oliver, Douglas L., *The Pacific Islands*, (rev. edn), New York, 1961

Pacific Islands, vol.iii, British Naval Intelligence Division, Geographical Handbook Series, B. R. 5195B (1944)

Roberts, S. C., *Tamai: The Life Story of John Hartley Roberts of Tonga*, Sydney, 1924

Ryden, George Herbert, *The Foreign Policy of the United States in Relation to Samoa*, New Haven, 1933

Scarr, Deryck, 'John Bates Thurston, Commodore J. G. Goodenough and Rampant Anglo-Saxons in Fiji', *Historical Studies, Australia and New Zealand*, November, 1964

    Fragments of Empire: A History of the Western Pacific High Commission 1817-1914, Canberra, 1967

Scholefield, Guy H., *The Pacific: Its Past and Future*, London, 1919

Williamson, Robert W., *The Social and Political Systems of Central Polynesia*, 2 vols, Cambridge, 1914

Wood, A. H., *A History and Geography of Tonga*, Nuku'alofa, 1932

Wright, Louis B. and Fry, Mary Isabel, *Puritans in the South Seas*, New York, 1936

INDEX

Aboriginal Protection Society: 197

Act to Regulate Hereditary Lands (1883): 132

Act Relative to Newspapers (1882): 157-58, 164

Act Relative to Sedition (1882): 157-58, 164-65

Adams, Henry: 10

'Afu, Taniela: 112-13

agriculture (Tongan): 34, 75, 131, 229

Ahome'e (Tongan Chief Justice): 146, 188, 197, 243-44

Ale'amotu'a: see Tupou, Josiah

Alexander, Czar of Russia: 31

Allen, Sir Wigram: 165

Arms Act: 205

assassination attempt on S.B.: 180, 182-86, 205-206

Ata (chief of Kolovai): 172-73, 216-17

Australian Wesleyan-Methodist Missionary Society: 11, 14-15, 42, 228

Baker, Charles: 113

Baker, Reverend and Honorable Shirley Waldemar ('S.B.'): origins and early life, 9-14, 230-37; marriage, 15; becomes a missionary, 14-16; meets Tupou, 17-18, 22; early mission work, 16, 23-26; and reforms of 1862, 31-38; as chairman of Tonga mission, 40, 102; and mission finances, 42-47, 51-54, 56-59, 64, 94-95, 97, 112-14, 119; charged with indecency, 47-49; and the 1875 Constitution, 76; his financial dealings, 35-36, 56, 90, 94, 112; and the Germany-Tonga treaty, 87-88; and the Britain-Tonga treaty, 88-89, 110, 138-42; independent Tonga Mission, 56-66, 70, 133; Layard criticises, 92-100; recalled, 101-102, 118-122; becomes Premier, 127-28; and land legislation, 131-33; and Tongan finances, 129-31, 141-42; nationalises schools, 135-36; opposition of minor chiefs, 133, 144-45; opposition of European traders, 91-99, 152-61, 164; inaugurates Free Church, 62, 133, 166-68; attempted assassination, 183-86; deportation, 215-219; last years, 223-26.

opinions of (Gordon's), 156-57; opinions of (Mitchell's), 198-99; opinions of (Thomson's), 227; opinions of (Layard's), 41; opinions of (Trood's), 227-28; for relations with individuals see entries under their names.

Baker, Family of Shirley Waldemar: Reverend George Baker (father), 9, 11-38, 230-234; Jane Gray Baker (mother), 9, 12, 237; Caroline Sarah Mallam (George Baker's second

wife), 231; Elizabeth Baker, nee
Powell (wife), 15-17, 25, 37, 40,
186, 224.
  Children of S.W. & E. Baker: Alice,
  25, 204, 217; Beatrice, 37, 185-86,
  203-204, 210; Fetu'u (son of Laura
  Baker), 226; Laura, 40, 226; Lillian,
  185-86; Shirley Jnr., 37, 90,
  185-86, 203-204, 217
Bank of Tonga: 75-76, 90, 112
beachcombers: *see* Europeans
Bindeman, George: 189
Bismarck, German emperor: 201
Bloomfield, P.S.: 45, 64, 113-14, 173,
  193
Blyth, James (H.B.M. Vice-Consul to
  Tonga): 126-27, 129, 131
Brenchly, Lieutenant Julius: 17-18
Bridge, Captain Sir Cyprian: 163-65
Britain: *see* foreign policy of
Brown, Reverend George: 115, 203,
  206, 207, 210-13, 235, 241-42
Buckland, Dr A.G.: 159
Buzacott, Reverend Aaron: 14

Cakobau, King of Fiji: 69, 71, 207
Calvert, Reverend James: 10, 26, 231
Carnarvon, Fourth Earl of (Secretary
  of State for the Colonies): 87, 100,
  196, 198, 200, 203-204, 208
Castle, Captain (HMS *Rapid*): 216
catholicism: 21, 27, 167, 226
Chapman, Reverend Benjamin
  (Secretary of the Missionary
  Committee): 59, 61-62, 74, 90,
  97-100, 102, 107, 111, 114-16, 118,
  123, 211
chiefs: their independence, 20-21; and
  the Wesleyan Mission, 58-60; and
  the 1862 code, 33-34; and the 1883
  Constitutional Revision, 132-33;
  and S.B., 143-46, 170, 187;
  persecution of Wesleyans, 170-77,
  187-88, 190-95; *see also fakataha*;
  nobility
Chile (coinage): 51, 129-30, 205

Church of England: 224-26
civil war: 18-19
Clarke (trader) *see* Von Hagen
Clarke (Chief Justice of Fiji and Chief
  Judicial Commissioner of the High
  Commission): 197-98
Clarke, Reverend William: 118, 123
Cocker, Joseph: 73, 92
coconut oil: 35, 45-47, 51
Codes of Law: Vava'u code (1839),
  21, 81; 1850 code, 20-21, 81-82,
  108; 1862 code, 31-38, 80-81; 1875
  code, 81-83, 105, 108
Collett, Wilfred (Secretary to the
  British High Commission): 213-14,
  216
Colonial Office, Britain: 99-100, 103,
  196; Secretaries of State for the
  Colonies: 28, 155, 165, 204, 209,
  218; *see also* Carnarvon, Fourth Earl of
commoners: power of chiefs over, 79;
  effects of 1875 Constitution on, 79,
  131-32; effects of revised
  Constitution on, 133
conferences of the Methodist Church:
  New South Wales and Queensland
  (1869), 40, 42; New South Wales and
  Queensland (1870), 49; New South
  Wales and Queensland (1871), 50;
  New South Wales and Queensland
  (1873), 57-58, 72; New South Wales
  and Queensland (1874), 59-60; New
  South Wales and Queensland (1875),
  62, 65; New South Wales and
  Queensland (1877), 107; New South
  Wales and Queensland (1878), 102,
  104, 106, 109, 121; New South
  Wales and Queensland (1880), 120-1,
  125-26; New South Wales and
  Queensland (1881), 134; Australasian
  (1881), 134-36, 238; New South
  Wales and Queensland (1884), 162,
  242; Australasian (1884), 166-67, 242;
  New South Wales and Queensland
  (1887), 206; Australasian (1888), 206,
  210

constitutions: 1875 Constitution,
76-77, 79, 105, 131-32, 238;
1883 Constitution, 170
copra: 45-47, 51-53, 75, 91-92,
95-96, 108, 112-114, 152, 178, 214
Council of Chiefs: 216
courts: 69-70; and Europeans, 69-70,
75, 92, 137; 1875 Constitution, 77,
137; S.B. and, 188; Gordon and,
105-106; Layard and, 92-94; Tupou
and, 152
Coventry, Frederick: 159-60
Cricket Law: 152
Crosby, Reverend E.E.: 171, 178-79,
203, 235
Cummins, Dr Geoffrey: 231
currency: 21, 129-130, 205, 208

Davis, Reverend Walter: 27, 29-30,
35, 108
Derby, Fifteenth Earl of, (Secretary of
State for Foreign Affairs): 87-88,
100, 163, 165-66
Des Voeux, Sir William (H.B.M. High
Commissioner for the Western
Pacific): 157-59, 163-66
'The Doctor': see 'The Earl and the
Doctor'

'The Earl and the Doctor' (The Earl
of Pembroke and Dr G.H.
Kingsley): 46-47, 53
education: see schools; Industrial
school; Ladies' college; Tupou
College; Tonga Government
College; Queen Salote College.
Eggleston, Reverend John (Secretary
of the Missionary Committee): 30,
35, 41
Ellis, Mrs Joan: 231
Ellis, Joseph: 12-14
Emancipation Edict: 31-32, 80; see also
Codes of Law: 1862 code
epidemics: 25, 74, 222
Erskine, Captain Elphinstone: 23-24
Erskine, Commodore James: 154

Europeans (in Tonga): S.B. secretary
of association, 36; influx after 1862
reforms, 38; and Missionary
meetings, 64; oppose Tongan law
and administration, 72-73, 91,
137-41, 160; S.B. rebukes, 98; S.B.
legislates against, 205; and the Mu'a
Parliament, 152-56, 159, 164;
triumph over S.B., 218-219
exile of Wesleyans from Tonga: 195-96
extraterritoriality provisions in treaties:
110, 138, 140

fahu: 29, 31-32, 34
Fairfax, Admiral: 209
fakamisinale: see mission finances
fakataha: 28-31, 37
Fale, Nefoto: 235
fatongia: 28-34
Fehia, Lūpeni: 172
Fehoko (judge): 156, 158
Fehoko (outlaw): 181, 184-89, 244
Fekau: 184, 188, 190, 244
Ferguson, Sir John: 234, 238, 240, 242
Fetokai, Sione: 96
Fetu'u: see Baker, Family of...
Fifita: 159
Fiji: 49, 68-69, 74, 78, 83, 93, 99,
103, 105-106, 123, 140, 194-96
Finau, Sitiveni: 188
Finau, Reverend Tēvita: 161, 184,
188, 243
Fisher, H.M.: 193
Fison, Reverend Lorimer: 168
Fletcher, P.P.: 203, 206
Fohe (chief): 187
Fonu'a, Heamasi: 173
Foreign Office (Britain): 196
Foreign Affairs, Secretary of State for:
see Derby, Fifteenth Earl of;
Salisbury, Third Marquis of
foreign policy (France): 27
foreign policy (Germany): German
interests in Samoa, 85, 201-202,
222; treaty with Tonga, 85-88;
influence in Tongan affairs,

103-104, 126, 141; accord with Britain, 140, 196; surrenders treaty rights to Britain, 201-202, 222

foreign policy (Great Britain): 85; Tonga appeals to, 27; pressure to annex Tonga, 101, 103; Sir Arthur Gordon instructs, 88-89, 235; treaty with Tonga (1879), 89, 138, 165, 170; makes Tonga a protectorate: 196, 200, 201-223, 235

foreign policy (the United States of America): 179, 208, 222-223

Foster, W.L.: 193

foto tehina: *see* minor chiefs

France: *see* foreign policy

Franco-Prussian War: 68

Free Church of Tonga: 226; establishment of, 56, 62, 167-69; Moulton against, 168-71; persecution of those who refuse to join, 169-77; seizure of Wesleyan churches, 173-74, 177-78; negotiations with Wesleyans, 175, 200, 202-203, 207-212; S.B. seeks superannuation, 224; evaluation of, 197-99

Fry, Mary Isobel: 3

Fusipala: 221

Germany: see foreign policy

Giles, William E. (H.B.M. Pro-Consul to Tonga): 186, 188, 190-92

Godeffroy, J.C. and Son: 51-53, 56, 64, 68, 82, 91-96, 104, 108, 113, 116, 118-19, 129-30, 144

Gordon, Sir Arthur (later First Baron Stanmore): as H.B.M. High Commissioner for the Western Pacific, Consul General and Governor of Fiji, 88-89, 99-100, 105, 166, 211; seeks treaty with Tonga, 88, 110; opinion of S.B., 10, 234; opposed to S.B., 104-106, 109, 138, 230, 237; has S.B. removed from Tonga, 83, 103, 106-107, 114-17, 121-23; S.B.

defies, 138-40; comes to terms with S.B., 140-42, 156; and the Mu'a Parliament, 108, 151-52, 155, 163

Gordon-Cummings, Miss: 82

Gorrie (Chief Justice, Fiji): 211

Greenwood, Reverend Henry: 40, 53, 58, 64

Grey, Sir George: 103

Ha'a Havea: 153

Haloholo (chief of 'Eua): 173, 193

Hanslip, Robert: 154, 157, 159-61, 193-94, 197-98, 213; testifies against S.B. (1879), 92, 95; leads 'beach' faction against S.B., 118-19, 131; advises Tungī and Tōpui, edits *Niu Vakai*, 147, 149-50, 153; role in assassination attempt, 183-84

Hau, Penisiō: 182-83, 188

Hawai'i: 27

High Commissioner for the Western Pacific (Britain): office created, 87; Sir A. Gordon, *passim*; Sir W. Des Voeux, 157-66; Dr W. McGregor (acting), 166; Sir C. Mitchell, *passim*; Sir J.B. Thurston, *passim*; powers of deportation of, 175, 177-78, 213-19; S.B.'s enemies seek protection, 175, 192-96

High Commissioner's Court: 89

Hoskins, Commodore A.H.: 87, 99

Hutchinson, Reverend John: 19

Industrial school: 62

Ita, Semisi: 193

Jubilee, Tongan Wesleyan Mission: 63-64, 83, 89, 108, 149

Kalaniuvalu: 21

Kaufo'ou, 'Akanesi: 172

Kaufo'ou, Elizabeth: 48

Kaumoto, 'Aisea: 182, 188-89, 244

Koskinen, Aarne A.: 3

Kingsley, Dr G.H.: see 'The Earl and the Doctor'

Kupu (chief in Tongatapu): 217-18, 224

Ladies' College: 62
Laifone, Crown Prince: 182, 189-91, 200
Laisiki (chief of 'Ahau): 174
land legislation: leases, 65, 78, 123, 132-33; rents, 130; conditions of tenure, 78-80, 131-33, 142
Langdale, Frederick: 193
Langham, Reverend Frederick: 106-107, 115, 246
Latu (outlaw): 181-89, 206, 244
Lātūkefu, Tēvita: 170
Latuvaivai, Sione: 184, 188
Laufilitonga (the last Tu'i Tonga): 19, 21
Lavaka (chief of Pea and Folaha): 173, 187
Lavinia (daughter of Kupu): 224
Lavuso: 145, 183-84, 188-89, 244
Law Relative to Treason: see Act Relative to Sedition
Law of Six and of Thirty: 178-79, 200
Layard, E.L. (H.B.M. Consul for Fiji and Tonga): 36, 41, 66, 82, 86-87, 92-99, 101, 121
Lee, Reverend George: 25, 29
Leefe, R.B. (H.B.M. Vice-Consul to Tonga): 192-93, 195-96, 203-206, 208, 213-14, 222, 245
Lehauli, Tēvita: 76
Leinstein (Assistant Premier): 214
Leka, Eliasa: 76, 144-45, 147, 150, 169, 182, 187
licences: 130-31
Lobase: 48
Lolohea, Reverend Jiosiua: 174
London Missionary Society: 47
lotu: 57, 73

Ma'afu o' Tu'itonga, Heneli: 78, 94, 109, 116, 146
Mackay, A.W.: 13, 80, 244-46
Maealiuaki: 235

Maka (magistrate at Nuku'alofa): 149
Malieto'a Laupepa (King of Samoa): 201-202
Malinoa, executions at: 181-84, 187, 243-46
Martin, K.L.P.: 3
matāpule: see minor chiefs
Matekitonga (Governor of Vava'u): 76
Mau, Josepha: 172
Maudslay, Alfred (H.B.M. Vice-Consul to Tonga): 34, 80-81, 89, 107, 109-19, 121-23, 206
McGregor, Dr William: 129, 166
Meade, Lieutenant Herbert: 24, 108
measles epidemic: 74, 222
Miller, J.P.: 73, 112, 128-29
Minns, Reverend George: 25
minor chiefs: 133, 142, 143-46, 153
Missionary Committee (Wesleyan): 15
mission finances (Wesleyan): collections, 42-46, 51, 56-57, 62; income, 112-14, 119; Missionary Meetings, 43-45, 51-53, 61, 64, 113-14, 118-19, 210; missionaries' stipends, 35, 56, 122
Mitchell, Sir Charles (H.B.M. High Commissioner for the Western Pacific): 197, 200, 202-204, 206, 209-10, 213, 243, 245
Model Deed (Wesleyan): 61, 65
Morrell, W.P.: 3
Moseley, H.M.: 17
Moss, David (Tupou Ha'apai): 70, 216
Moss, George: 216
'most favoured nation' clauses in treaties: 88-89
Moulton, Emma: 41
Moulton, Reverend James Egan: 38, 213, 235-36, 244; early life and background, 41; and Tongan literature, 90; and S.B., 41-42, 240-43, criticizes S.B., 49, 51, 72; attempts reconciliation with S.B., 90; chairman of Tonga Mission, 134; and Mu'a Parliament, 154, 159-61, 241; S.B. seeks removal of,

161-62, 166, 175, 203, 241; rallies Wesleyans against the Free Church, 168-71, 173, 176-78; blamed for the attempt on S.B.'s life, 190; recalled from Tonga, 203, 206-207
Moulton, Richard Green: 41
Moulton, William Fiddian (Lord Moulton of Bank): 41
Muʻa Parliament: origins, 109-12, 133, 144; activities of, 144-51; leaders imprisoned, 151-56; effects of activities, 153-63; aftermath of, 169, 182
Muli, Soni: 183, 188

Naisa (outlaw): 181-89, 244
Nares, Captain: 83
Nau, Joel: 101, 235
Nauhaʻamea, Samuela: 48
New Britain: 155, 211 213
New Zealand: 68, 125-26
Ngū, Wellington (Crown Prince): 79, 112, 138, 146, 151, 153, 158, 160, 166, 171, 173
nobility (Tongan): 132-33
Nuku: 184, 188

O'Dwyer, Father (Catholic missionary): 246
Oliver, Douglas L.: 85
Order of Prohibition: 217
Osbourne, Reverend M.C. (Secretary of the Wesleyan Missionary Society): 115
ʻOtuhouma, Kēlepi: 170

Palu (outlaw): 181-88, 190, 244
Parker, Edward Stone: 9, 13-14, 230
Parker, E.W.: 99, 137-38, 147-48, 154, 157, 159, 161, 193-94, 202, 205
Parkes, Sir Henry: 76
parliament (Tongan): 62, 77-78, 111, 127, 132-34, 139, 145, 148, 155, 157, 164; see also fakataha
Parsons, Thomas: 193
Payne, Francis: 113

Payne, Phillip: 69-70, 113, 137, 193
Payne, Thomas: 193
Pembroke, Earl of: see 'Earl and the Doctor'
Percival: 159
Peru: coinage, 51; slave trade, 97
Picton, Henry George: 13
Poll Tax Act (1881): 205
Powell, Elizabeth: see Baker, S.W., family of...
Press: freedom, 77, 157-58, 165; *Advertiser* (Adelaide), 211; *Advocate*, 58; *Blackwood's Magazine*, 2-3; *Castlemaine Advertiser*, 14; *Christian Advocate and Wesleyan Record*, 15; *Daily Telegraph* (Melbourne), 211; *Daily Telegraph* (Sydney), 179-80; *Evening Bell* (Auckland), 204, 205-206, 221; *Evening News* (Sydney), 13; *Fiji Times*, 69, 106-107, 148, 157, 159; *Koe Boobooi*, 62, 74, 76, 118, 128, 148, 150; *Koe Taimi ʻo Toga*, 153, 155; *Local Preachers' Paper*, 154; *Missionary Notices*, 32, 39, 42, 45, 65; *New Zealand Herald*, 190, 221; *Niu Vakai*, 149, 153, 159, 161; *Sydney Morning Herald*, 245; *Tupou College Magazine*, 161; *Star* (Auckland), 220; *The Times* (London), 10, 231; *Tonga Government Gazette*, 141; *Tonga Times*, 86, 92; *Wesleyan Missionary Magazine/Report*, 46
Privy Council of Tonga: 141, 146
prohibition: 217

quarantine regulations: 222
quarterly meetings (Wesleyan missionary): 63, 111, 116, 121, 162, 235
Queen Salote College: 191-92

Rabone, Reverend Stephen: 40, 47
Ratuivuna: 206
Raturanga: 206
Reeve, Edward: 76

Roberts, J.H.: 136
Roberts, Reverend S.C.: 12-13, 15
Royal Palace: 38, 75

Sahl, Ludwig (German Consul in Sydney): 104
Salisbury, Third Marquis of (Secretary of State for Foreign Affairs): 104, 116, 123
Salote, Queen (wife of Tupou I): 19, 30
Samoa: 68, 83, 93, 222
Schleinitz, Baron von: 86-87
schools: 38, 40-41, 62, 135, 142; see also Industrial school; Ladies' college; Tupou College; Tonga Government College; Queen Salote College; Industrial School
Schools Act: 161-62
secession (Free Church of Tonga): see Free Church of Tonga
Semisi (Vava'u magistrate): 109
Ships (visiting Tonga):
  British warships: HMS Alert, 139-40; HMS Challenger, 83; HMS Curacoa, 17, 24, 33; HMS Danae, 139-40; HMS Diamond, 197; HMS Dido, 74; HMS Egeria, 219; HMS Espiegle, 163-66; HMS Havannah, 23; HMS Miranda, 158, 161; HMS Opal, 202, 204; HMS Porpoise, 222; HMS Rapid, 216.
  German warships: SMS Adler, 202; SMS Ariadne, 112; SMS Gazelle, 86; SMS Hertha, 68, 86; SMS Nautilus, 126
  Trading vessels: Cardinal, 244; Jennie Dove, 16-17; John Wesley, 40, 52-53, 114; Lubeck, 219; Malakula, 196; Myrtle, 236; Samoa, 96; Sandfly, 159, 182, 234; Statesman, 13; Wainui, 218-19
Siasi Tau'atāina: 62-63
Siasi a Vikia (Queen Victoria's Church): 224

Simpson, Washington: 113
sivi: 51, 95
Six and Thirty, Law of: see Law of...
Smith, Dr: 107
South Sea Bubbles: see 'The Earl and the Doctor'
sovereignty (Tongan): 2, 27, 66, 69-74, 85-86, 89, 122, 142, 221-22
St Johnston, Alfred: 10-11
St Julian, Charles: 27-29, 31, 76, 85
Steinberger, A.A.: 92
Stephinson, Reverend W.G.R.: 26-27, 29-30, 40, 47-40, 59, 203
sugar plantations: 72, 117
sumptuary legislation: 81-83, 94, 96, 108, 112
Sunia (Tongan chief): 217
Swanston, R.S.: 148
Symonds, H.F. (H.B.M. Vice-Consul to Tonga): 162-63, 213-15, 244; clerk to Alfred Maudslay, 147; made Vice-Consul, 139, 143-44; and the Mu'a Parliament, 146-48, 150-54, 158-60, 182; and Basil Thomson, 182; and S.B., 164-65; removed to Samoa, 165-66

Tamasese, 201-202
Tamasese Mea'ole, 229
tapa: 82-3, 94, 96, 109, 111-12, 141
Tāufa, Asaeli: 76, 144-45
Tafa, Filipi: 183, 235
Tāufa'āhau: see Topou I or Tupou II
Tavake (son of Tōpui): 181, 184-88, 190, 244
taxation: 152, 214; land tax, 32-34; on Europeans, 160; collection of, 129; S.B. and, 129-31; resentment at, 215
Thomas, Reverend James: 89, 100-102, 104, 121
Thomas, Reverend John: 19, 28, 81
Thomson, Sir Basil: as an authority, 2-4, 227; on S.B., 10, 42, 225, 227-29, 234; on missionary collections, 43-44; on Tongan sexual

mores, 48; on the Constitution, 80-81; and Symonds and Tungī, 182; deputy Premier of Tonga, 221-22; declares Tonga a British Protectorate, 222-23

Thorley (savings bank manager): 76

Thurston, Sir John B.: 10, 166, 234; visits Tonga (1880), 139-141; visits Tonga (1885), 175, 177-78; orders to Leefe, 192; negotiates with Germany, 196; High Commissioner, 207; deports S.B., 208-10, 213-19, 220; death, 223

Tonga, Makisi: 76

Tonga, Rachel: 210-11

Tonga, Reverend Tēvita: 145, 154, 210-11

Tonga Government College: 136

Tōpui, 'Usaia: leads the Mu'a Parliament, 144-45, 147, 150-52; refuses to join the Free Church, 169; involvement in the assassination attempt on S.B., 181-84, 187; arrest, 187; trial and execution, 188-89, 215, 243-44

traders: see Europeans

Travers (Imperial German Commissioner to the Pacific): 196

Treason Law: see Act Relative to Sedition

Treasury: 75, 127-30, 214, 223

Treaty of Protection: 222-23

treaty relations between Tonga and the Great Powers: see foreign relations

Treskow (Godeffroy agent): 113

Trood, Thomas: 95-96, 112, 227-28

Tryon, Rear-Admiral Sir George: 197

Tuhoko, Lutoviko: 182, 188

Tu'i Ha'atakalaua: 18-19, 21, 26, 109, 146, 153

Tu'i Kanokupolu: 18-20, 25, 78, 109, 146, 153

Tu'ilupou: 176

Tu'ipelehake: 182, 191, 216-18, 221

Tuitavake: 183-84, 188, 190, 244

Tu'i Tonga: 18-19, 21, 26

Tuku'aho: 182, 187, 216, 218, 221-22

tukuofo: 27, 29

Tungī, 'Uiliame (heir to the Tu'i Ha'atakalaua title): 21, 26, 29, 88, 109, 116, 221, 224; and Tupou, 110-12, 187; leads conservative chiefs, 109-11, 216-18; at Mu'a, 112, 145-47, 153; involvement in assassination attempt on S.B., 182-84

Tupou I (George Tāufa'āhau): 16, 50; early life, 18-22; disputes with Wesleyan missionaries, 26-28, 123-33; his own church, 60-62, 167-77; fears of foreign encroachments, 27-30, 33, 78; 1862 Code, 31-35; 1875 Constitution, 76, 83, 85; appoints S.B. Premier, 127-28; and S.B., 68, 70-71, 83, 104, 109-10, 122, 187, 212-13, 243-44, 246-47; death, 221.
His Tongan subjects, 150-51, 216-18; and Moulton, 154, 162; and Tungī, 146-47; and Gordon, 104-106; and Mitchell, 197-200; and Brown, 212-13; and Thurston, 216-18

Tupou II (George Tāufa'āhau): 221-22, 224

Tupou, Josiah (Ale'amotu'a): 18-20, 27, 78

Tupou College: 40-41, 49-52, 58, 134, 136, 161, 190, 191-92

Tupou Ha'apai: see Moss, David

Tupouto'a (father of Tupou I): 18

Tupouto'a, Sione: 144, 150, 169

Tu'uhetoka (Minister of Police): 146, 150-51, 154, 174, 186-92, 197, 207, 214, 243, 246-47

Ulukālala, Finau Tuapasi: 20

'Unga, David (Crown Prince): 72, 79, 94, 109, 112, 116, 119, 125-26, 221

Vaea: 155

Vaka Tonga Party: 108-109

Valu, Tēvita: 145, 154
Valu, 'Uiliame: 173
Vason, George: 47
Vi, Reverend Paula: 167
Vi, Reverend Pita: 19
Victoria (Queen of Great Britain): 68,
    88, 150, 156, 192-93
Von Hagen, H. (also known as
    Clarke): 137, 152-53, 189, 217, 245
Vuna (Crown Prince): 26
Vuni: 184, 188

Watkin, Reverend E.J.: 239
Watkin, Reverend Jabez B.: 59, 89,
    100, 116, 135, 167, 186, 218; and
    S.B., 122, 234, 238-40; and
    Moulton, 100-101, 175, 224, 241;
    demotion, 100, 134, 162, 238-40;
    President of Free Church of Tonga,
    168, 170, 203, 213
Watkin, Reverend James: 40, 47-48,
    235
Weber, Thomas (Apia manager of J.C.
    Godeffroy and Son; Imperial
    German Consul-General in the
    South Seas): 64, 68, 86, 92, 95-99,
    112
Wesleyan Mission in Tonga:
    beginnings, 19; Tupou's conversion,
    19-21; attitude to Tongans, 23-24;
    rebukes Tupou over tukuofo, 26-27;
    Tupou suspects, 27; 1862 Code, 35;
    S.B. chairs, 40, 102; 'The Earl and
    the Doctor' criticise, 46-47; opposes
    independent Tupou College, 49-51;
    S.B. seeks independence for, 56-66,
    133, 142; jubilee, 63-64, 89;
    opposed to S.B., 160-61, 164-65;
    investigates S.B., 112-114; Moulton
    chairs, 134; S.B. nationalises schools
    of, 135-136; and Mu'a Parliament,
    160-61; secession of Free Church,
    166-71; persecution of Tongan
    congregations, 169-77, 190;
    churches seized, 173-74, 177-78;
    involvement in assassination attempt

on S.B., 190; resettled in Fiji,
    194-96; George Brown chairs, 207,
    210; negotiates with Free Church,
    200, 202-203, 207-12; refuses to
    bury S.B., 226; finances, 35, 42;
    see also under missionaries' names
Wesleyan Missionary Society, London:
    19, 67, 72, 97, 106, 117, 121-22
Western Samoa: see Samoa
Whewell, Reverend John: 16-17,
    24-25, 35
Whitaker, Sir Frederick: 165
Wilkinson, David: 110; 112-13
Willis, Right Reverend Alfred: 224-25
Woolmer, J.B.: 12
Woolmer, Samuel: 9
Woolmer, Reverend Theophilus:
    11-12, 231
Woolnough, Reverend G.: 239, 240
Wright, Louis B.: 3
Wylie, Reverend D.: 40, 47-49

Young, George: 193
Young W.C.: 72-73, 96

Zembsch, Captain J. (Imperial German
    Consul-General for the South Sea
    Islands): 155
Zion Church: 16, 38, 50, 53, 169, 179